ON BEING IN THE WORLD

ON BEING IN THE WORLD

Wittgenstein and Heidegger on Seeing Aspects

STEPHEN MULHALL

London and New York

First published 1990
by Routledge
First published in paperback 1993
by Routledge
11 New Fetter Lane, London EC4P 4EE

Simultaneously published in the USA and Canada
by Routledge
29 West 35th Street, New York, NY 10001

© 1990, 1993 Stephen Mulhall

Data converted to 10/12pt Baskerville
by Columns of Reading
Printed in Great Britain by
TJ Press (Padstow) Ltd, Padstow, Cornwall

Printed on acid-free paper

All rights reserved. No part of this book may be reprinted or reproduced or utilized in any form or by any electronic, mechanical, or other means, now known or hereafter invented, including photocopying and recording, or in any information storage or retrieval system, without permission in writing from the publishers.

British Library Cataloguing in Publication Data
Mulhall, Stephen
On being in the world: Wittgenstein and heidegger on seeing aspects
1. Man. Perception. Human perception. Theories of Wittgenstein, Ludwig (1889–1951) and Heidegger, Martin (1889–1976)
I. Title
121'.3

Library of Congress Cataloging in Publication Data
Mulhall, Stephen,
On being in the world: Wittgenstein and Heidegger on seeing aspects/
Stephen Mulhall.
p. cm.
Includes bibliographical references.
1. Visual perception. 2. Wittgenstein, Ludwig (1889–1951).
3. Heidegger, Martin (1889–1976). 4. Davidson, Donald, (1917–).
5. Languages – Philosophy. 6. Psychology – Philosophy. I. Title.
BF241.M85 1990
121'.3—dc20
89-35985
ISBN 0-415-10345-2

FOR MY MOTHER AND FATHER

CONTENTS

Introduction	1
1 DEFINING TERMS	6
Aspect-dawning and a picture of vision	6
Picture-objects and continuous aspect perception	15
Pictures and regarding-as	21
Aspects, aspect-blindness, and the paradox of aspect-dawning	28
2 ASPECTS AND LANGUAGE	35
The experience of meaning	35
The physiognomy of words	40
Primary and secondary meaning	45
3 ASPECTS OF THE PHILOSOPHY OF PSYCHOLOGY	53
Myths of the inner	53
Concepts of the inner	60
Aspects and the inner	71
Blind to the inner	78
4 OPPOSING TRADITIONS	91
Davidson's philosophy of language	91
The metaphysical foundations	99
A continental perspective	106
Preliminary findings	120
5 GRAMMAR, METAPHYSICS, AND CONCEPT-MASTERY	123
The universality of aspect perception	126

Grammar and metaphysics — 137
A transitional diagnosis — 152

6 ICONS, GESTURES, AND AESTHETICS — 156
Icons — 160
Gestures — 177

Conclusion — 196

Bibliography — 203

Index — 205

ABBREVIATIONS

BT M. Heidegger, *Being and Time*
BW M. Heidegger, *Basic Writings*
CR S. Cavell, *The Claim of Reason*
CV L. Wittgenstein, *Culture and Value*
GSR G. Steiner, *George Steiner: A Reader*
ITI D. Davidson, *Inquiries into Truth and Interpretation*
LC L. Wittgenstein, *Lectures and Conversations on Aesthetics, Psychology and Religious Belief*
LW L. Wittgenstein, *Last Writings on the Philosophy of Psychology*
PI L. Wittgenstein, *Philosophical Investigations*
RPP L. Wittgenstein, *Remarks on the Philosophy of Psychology*

INTRODUCTION

This book began as an attempt to provide an exegetical account of Wittgenstein's writings on aspect perception; but I found that it could only be brought to a close by relating those writings to his general philosophy of psychology, and then putting his conclusions into a dialogue with the fundamental assumptions of two other philosophers, each working in traditions very different from Wittgenstein's own. I could make sense of Wittgenstein's abiding interest in dual-aspect pictures only when it became clear that the seemingly bizarre visual experiences associated with such pictures provided a way of highlighting what is distinctively *human* about human behaviour in relation to things in the world. Moreover, it seemed that both the *transition* from the duck-rabbit to a conception of what distinguishes human practical activity from that of automata, and the precise *character* of the resulting conception, could best be illuminated by contrast and comparison with related conceptions in the writings of Davidson and Heidegger. In this Introduction, I want to outline the route taken in the chapters that follow in order to reach the conclusions just summarized.

Of all the topics which seem to have dominated Wittgenstein's thought and writings, his treatment of aspect perception is one of the least explored and least understood. The secondary literature on the topic is scarce, and typically limited to reporting some of his more obvious conclusions whilst failing to furnish a wider interpretative framework within which the force and point of those conclusions might emerge. In particular, such literature typically fails to address the more obscure and difficult features of these remarks. For example, the experience of the dawning of an aspect is often taken to be the sole focus of Wittgenstein's attention; but

INTRODUCTION

his discussion of this experience takes place against a background which embodies a large number of other concepts. The notions of picture-objects, of continuous aspect perception and of regarding-as (to take just a handful of the technical terms employed in these passages) are clearly pivotal in Wittgenstein's conception of what he is doing, and they do not carry their significance on their faces; but their precise content and the specific nature of their pivotal role is typically left completely opaque. It is to these matters in particular that this book is initially addressed.

Chapters 1 and 2 are the essential exegetical underpinning of my enterprise; they provide a detailed account of Section xi of the *Philosophical Investigations*, in which Wittgenstein's work on aspect perception reached its most polished form. In so doing a great deal of reliance is placed upon the three volumes of remarks on the philosophy of psychology recently published:[1] Wittgenstein composed the sections which go to make up Part Two of the *Investigations* by selecting remarks from his writings in the period 1946–9, and the volumes just cited cover precisely that period. They are therefore an indispensable reference point for the clarification of remarks in Section xi, but must always be regarded as preliminary, less polished and ultimately less reliable than those of Section xi itself.

Within this overall concern for exegetical clarity, however, the first two chapters play different roles. Chapter 1 is primarily designed to elicit the meaning of the obscure labels and categories mentioned above – to define the terms of the investigation. In so doing, it becomes clear that those labels and categories are in fact essential to what is taken to be Wittgenstein's central concern in that investigation – the demolition of an incoherent theory of vision. However, it also becomes clear that this concern is not as central to Wittgenstein's purposes as has been thought; the theory is indeed demolished, but Wittgenstein explicitly asserts (and the categories he employed in that demolition imply) that the significance of aspect perception lies elsewhere – in the domain of language rather than that of pictures and drawings. Chapter 2

[1] *Remarks on the Philosophy of Psychology* (hereafter abbreviated *RPP*), vols I and II, and *Last Writings on the Philosophy of Psychology* (hereafter abbreviated *LW*), vol. I. In the following pages occasional references are also made to Wittgenstein's unpublished writings; these cite the manuscript number and the relevant page within the manuscript.

INTRODUCTION

follows up this assertion and clarifies its significance.

In so doing, however, other important avenues of investigation open up. In particular, the conclusions Wittgenstein reaches in his study of aspect perception in relation to pictures and language are seen to apply to the field of psychological concepts as well; and the function of Chapter 3 of this book is to assess the nature and scope of this extension, thus beginning the task of demonstrating the connection between Wittgenstein's work in Section xi and his more general concerns.

Chapter 4 broadens the scope of the book yet further by relating Wittgenstein's writings to those of representative figures in the traditions of Anglo-American and Continental philosophy – namely, Davidson and Heidegger. Davidson's philosophy of language and action is shown to exemplify precisely the confusions against which Wittgenstein's remarks are directed, whereas Heidegger's system of thought can be seen to be grounded upon an acknowledgement of just those features of experience highlighted by Wittgenstein.

The comparison with Heidegger raises a further issue, however, since his analysis suggests that the phenomenon of aspect perception has a general application beyond even that of psychological concepts, and that it justifies the erection of a baroque metaphysical system. Chapter 5 assesses these implications, and finds that such a general application of Wittgenstein's conclusions can be justified – but only by regarding Heidegger's metaphysical insights as distorted reflections of grammatical points concerning the relations between human beings and the world of their experience.

Chapter 6 rounds off the original interpretative task of the book by examining an as-yet unclear feature of Wittgenstein's remarks on aspect perception – their relation to aesthetics – and comparing them with lectures on related material given by Heidegger. It thereby becomes clear that Wittgenstein's conclusions in this area point in precisely the directions traced out in Chapters 2 and 5, thus confirming the exegetical claims laid out there. And in addition, the assumption that Heidegger's writings might again be regarded as metaphysical distortions of grammatical points relevant in this area is shown to bear fruit, since it provides an exegetical framework within which his lectures can be successfully interpreted and yet at the same time philosophically defused.

INTRODUCTION

In effect, my limited exegetical task turns out to lead in at least two philosophically significant directions. First, it shows that Wittgenstein's investigation of aspect perception is designed to illuminate much more than a bizarre type of visual experience: in reality, it highlights what is distinctively *human* about human behaviour in relation to things in the world, what it is that distinguishes human practical activity from that of automata. Second, this investigation suggests a fruitful way of regarding the metaphysical systems of Continental philosophy – a perspective from which the significance of those systems can be appreciated without any commitment to the self-understanding of the system-builders; in this respect, the treatment of Heidegger's concept of readiness-to-hand set forth in this book is intended to stand as a paradigm for all attempts to make sense of the procedures and product of Continental philosophy. The result of this investigation therefore has consequences not simply for our comprehension of a specific domain of Wittgenstein's writings, but also for the relationship between a Wittgensteinian methodology and other philosophical traditions.

This would, accordingly, seem to be an appropriate point at which to make a general introductory remark about the philosophical methodology of my own enterprise. It will be clear to the reader that these chapters work very much within the tradition of philosophizing established by Wittgenstein; and the absence of a detailed defence of the validity of such an approach to philosophical problems and texts is in no way intended to be an evasion of that responsibility. It is rather dictated by the constraints of space, and by a conviction that this approach can best be justified by a demonstration of its fruitfulness in dissolving specific problems and revealing, through careful and attentive readings of texts, the incoherencies embedded in alternative philosophical aproaches to those problems. Unless otherwise stated (in footnotes or the main text), therefore, it should be assumed that the views presented as Wittgenstein's are those which I endorse and wish to defend.

Several people have read and commented on this book, or parts of it, at a prior stage in its life, that is, when it formed a thesis submitted for the degree of Doctor of Philosophy at the University of Oxford. I would like to thank Dr A. Kenny, Mr A. Montefiore, Mr J. Hyman and Mr S. Blacklocks for their help in this respect.

INTRODUCTION

My greatest debts are to Paul Johnston, whose friendship and philosophical acuity were of great importance during the writing of these chapters; and to Dr Peter Hacker, my supervisor, for his encouragement and example.

1
DEFINING TERMS

ASPECT-DAWNING AND A PICTURE OF VISION

At first sight, Wittgenstein's interest in the phenomenon of aspect-dawning seems strictly circumscribed: meditation upon this specific sort of visual experience is seen as likely to incline people towards a particular picture or theory of vision – indeed, it may even seem that only such a theory could account for precisely what is puzzling about that type of experience; and Wittgenstein is concerned to dispel this illusory appearance. It is the premise of this book that such a conception of Wittgenstein's purposes is radically incomplete; but in order to demonstrate this I must make use of material which emerges in the account Wittgenstein gives of this particular philosophical puzzle about vision, so this investigation will begin within those boundaries.

> I contemplate a face, and then suddenly notice its likeness to another. I *see* that it has not changed; and yet I see it differently. I call this experience 'noticing an aspect'. (*PI*, 193c)[1]

This is Wittgenstein's initial characterization of the experience he calls noticing an aspect, or (more generally) aspect-dawning; when he goes on to discuss it in detail, he prefers to use examples relating to schematic drawings or puzzle-pictures, but in all these cases the central features of the phenomenon are unchanged. In particular, the examples share the air of *paradox* which characterizes aspect-

---

1 All references to Section xi of *Philosophical Investigations* (abbreviated *PI*) will be given in the text in the form of a page number followed by a letter to indicate the position of the relevant remark on that page.

dawning as an experience; for when we notice the change of aspect, we see the figure (or face) differently and yet we also see that it has not changed. We feel that the figure is altogether different after the change of aspect – as if it had altered before our very eyes; and this is manifest in the particular way in which we are then inclined to *describe* the figure. Sentences such as 'Now it's a duck' or 'Now I am seeing a duck' are typically used in contexts where genuine perceptual changes have been observed (e.g. when a picture of a duck replaces a picture of a rabbit on a slide-show screen); and yet we are inclined to use just such a form of words in a context in which we know that there has been no such change (e.g. when the duck-aspect of a duck-rabbit drawing dawns on us). How are we to account for this?

We might feel inclined to look for an explanation in the domain of physiology (*PI*, 212c), on the assumption that the meaning of any visual concept can be reduced to reference to a specific physiological process and that the limits of what it makes sense to call a visual experience are set by physiological constraints. We might imagine, for example, that a particular pattern of eyeball movements is correlated with the perception of a given aspect, and that it is possible for such movements to jump from one pattern to another, and sometimes to alternate – thus producing the sense of paradox outlined above. The very fact that such explanations must be *imagined*, however, shows that they can reveal nothing about the concept under examination: we have an existing practice of using the relevant concept and this practice makes *no* use of knowledge of whatever physiological phenomena may be correlated with the experience our concept picks out. If those phenomena are not the grounds upon which the concept is applied, their introduction as a revelation of the 'real' meaning of aspect-dawning in fact constitutes a redefinition of that concept rather than an elucidation of it as it stands; so they cannot account for the paradox which is central to the *present* structure of that concept. The philosophical difficulty we are faced with is generated by the concept as it is; any physiological 'explanation', by redefining the relevant terms, can at best screen those difficulties from view and obscure the facts about our present linguistic practice which alone might solve our problem.

Leaving the domain of physiology, then, we might feel tempted to account for our inclination to describe our experience of aspect-dawning in this paradoxical way by assuming that there has indeed been a change, but in what we *subjectively* see – a change in our visual impression rather than in the figure itself. And since in such cases there is clearly no change in our impression of shape or colour, we might conclude that the relevant alteration must have occurred in the *organization* of our visual impression (*PI*, 196b). Such a conclusion would, however, make sense only on the assumption that visual impressions should be conceived of as inner entities of some sort, i.e. as internal phenomena that resembled all other material objects in having properties of spatial organization as well as colour and shape. We therefore find ourselves driven to adopt the picture of visual perception which Wittgenstein identifies as his general target in this stretch of Section xi;[2] and before considering how successfully such a picture might be employed in accounting for aspect-dawning, we should note its main features.

According to Wittgenstein, this picture has several key elements (*PI*, 199g): first, it presumes that our relationship with the external world is necessarily mediated by a set of inner copies of what we see, copies generated within us by the causal influence of the objects we are perceiving – it is only because objects produce such copies within us that we can describe our perceptions of the external world at all. Second, this inner copy is conceived of as a materialization, as an inner object rather like a picture; it is an entity which stands before our 'inner eye' and so can be described like any other object, but – since it is a private object – only the perceiver has access to it. Third, if this inner object with its specific properties is 'what is really seen', then a description of what is seen which goes beyond reference to colour, shape, and spatial organization can at best be an indirect result of interpreting what is really seen; it makes sense to say that we see a round face in a puzzle-picture, for example, but it would be nonsensical to say that we see its friendly smile.

Wittgenstein's primary way of undermining this picture is to show that it cannot in fact account for the phenomenon of aspect-dawning: on this view of perceptual experience, aspect-dawning

---

2 And in *Last Writings*, Wittgenstein comments: 'What is the philosophical importance of this phenomenon? Is it really so much odder than everyday visual experiences? Does it cast an unexpected light on them? – In the description of it, the problems about the concept of seeing come to a head' (*LW*,I, 172).

8

must involve either a genuine change in one's inner materialization, or a change in one's interpretation of that materialization, but neither possibility can be rendered coherent within the terms of the picture being invoked. Wittgenstein begins by exploring the first of his interlocutor's options (the one already introduced above), with the aid of two examples: the case of our suddenly seeing a human face in a puzzle-picture, and that of the schematic cube's changing aspects (*PI*, 196). If such experiences of aspect-dawning were explicable in terms of changes in one's visual impression (when the properties of visual impressions are understood in the manner suggested by this picture of vision), then any such changes should be manifest in the way we depict or represent what we see; for just as we can represent changes in our impression of shape and colour by altering the shape and colour of our representation of what we see (e.g. in a drawing), so we can represent changes in the organization of our visual impression by altering the organization of our representation of what we see. For example, if someone sees a row of equidistant points as a row of pairs of points whose inner distance is smaller than the outer distance, he can then say that he sees the row as organized in a certain way, for the picture he might make of the row would have a particular organization (*LW*,I, 444–5). In the case of the face in the puzzle-picture, however, Wittgenstein's interlocutor cannot make good his claim that the organization of his visual impression has changed, for the alteration he experiences is not expressible in his representation of what is seen (*PI*, 196b). In so far as it makes sense to talk of one's visual impression having a particular organization (i.e. the sense in which 'organization' is on the same level as colour and shape), it would therefore seem that one's experience of aspect-dawning is not explicable in terms of a change in that organization. To persist in so doing would entail making the visual impression (understood as an inner object) into a strangely shifting construction, since it would involve countenancing the possibility of changes in that entity which cannot be registered in those outer pictures upon which the interlocutor's hypothesized inner pictures are supposed to be modelled (*PI*, 196e).

For Wittgenstein's interlocutor, then, it cannot be the case that the forms of words we use to express our experience of aspect-dawning (e.g. in the case of the duck-rabbit, such phrases as 'Now it's a rabbit' or 'Now I'm seeing it as a rabbit' (*PI*, 195b,d,h) refer to genuine changes in our visual impression; as their invocation of attributes going beyond colour, shape, and organization would anyway suggest, they must accordingly be regarded as *indirect* descriptions of what is really seen. Wittgenstein's interlocutor is therefore moved to argue that when, for example, we say 'I see the figure as a box' we do not really see that aspect but rather an array of lines on the page which we then interpret indirectly according to habits formed by past visual experience (*PI*, 193g).

This fall-back position is, however, untenable: for, as Wittgenstein points out, to call the description of an experience 'indirect' makes sense only in circumstances where we can also give a direct description of that experience; we can intelligibly refer to the description 'That paint is the colour of blood' as an indirect one because we can also describe the colour directly, viz. 'That paint is red'. With regard to 'I see the figure as a box', on the other hand, it is Wittgenstein's claim that no such more direct way of referring to the visual experience involved is available; so it makes no sense to regard it as an indirect description. If Wittgenstein is correct, then, the interlocutor's attachment to the erroneous picture of visual perception leaves him with no coherent account of aspect-dawning at all.

But what exactly does Wittgenstein mean by his claim that no more direct way of referring to one's visual experience is available in the context of aspect-dawning? The content of this claim is spelt out in another of his examples, by means of which he further specifies the nature of the experience he is labelling 'aspect-dawning' (*PI*, 196f; *LW*,I, 492–500). In the case of a schematic cube, someone might notice the three-dimensional aspect of the figure for the first time, but he may convey this discovery in the following way: 'What I see in front of me is this [pointing to a copy of the figure]; it could also be described as a drawing of a cube [pointing to a three-dimensional model]'. Here the reference to the model is being treated as an optional extra, something which is superfluous to the task of reporting what is perceived because the copy is felt to be a complete and accurate description of the figure (*LW*,I, 500); the primary function of the reference to the model is rather to express the kind of view the observer now has of that figure. It may be necessary to express his subjective visual experience, but the fact of its superfluity as a contribution to reporting what is perceived shows that the observer has simply noticed that the figure he is observing *can* be looked at in another way (*LW*,I, 492).

In such circumstances, the interlocutor's talk of alternative ways of describing one's visual experience would make sense, for here the observer's reference to the model would indeed be an indirect way for him to describe what he sees. However, such a use of the reference to the model could *not* be a manifestation of aspect-dawning; for an experience of aspect-dawning is one in which the use of a representation of what is seen which invokes the aspect is *not* an optional addition – it is the only possible expression of our visual perception. The copy is no longer regarded as a more direct or precise report of the figure perceived; rather the reference to the model is an essential means of expressing *what we see*, as if a new copy of the figure were required, although this is not in fact the case (*LW*,I, 496). Aspect-dawning is *characterized* by the observer's felt need to employ a representation which might otherwise refer to subjective visual experience – to one way of seeing the figure – as if it were the report of a new perception. It *must* be so characterized, because it is precisely this combination of felt need *and* the implication of a perceptual change that creates the paradoxical air definitive of aspect-dawning experiences – the paradox manifest in our saying of a figure we know to be unchanged: 'Before I saw something else, but now I see a cube' (*LW*,I, 493).

For Wittgenstein, therefore, his interlocutor's account of aspect-dawning is not only an inadequate explanation of that peculiar visual experience: it distorts precisely the feature of that experience which made the use of the erroneous picture of perception tempting in the first place. It leaves no place for the crucial point that in experiences of aspect-dawning the sentence 'Now it's a rabbit!' is not being used as an ordinary perceptual report but rather as an exclamation (*PI*, 197b); it gives expression to our visual experience in the sense in which an exclamation (such as 'It hurts!') manifests pain. The analogy Wittgenstein posits here is designed to highlight two features of aspect-dawning: first, that the form of words employed therein is a spontaneous reaction to what we see, a direct expression (*Ausserung*) of our visual experience rather than the end-product of an inference we make from the nature of our visual impression – no inner entity need be hypothesized to mediate between the perceived object and our verbal response to it. And secondly, it highlights the sense in which the verbal *Ausserung characterizes* the experience it expresses; like an exclamation of pain, the utterance of such a form of words is a criterion for the nature and existence of the visual experience of aspect-dawning – we have no independent means of specifying (or individuating) that visual experience in contrast to other such experiences except by means of the felt need to use that specific piece of verbal behaviour in this particular context (*RPP*,I, 13).

With this more accurate characterization of aspect-dawning in place, we can provide an account of some of the other features of that phenomenon which will dispel their air of mystery and so eliminate the need to employ a theory or picture of visual perception in order to explain them away. One reason for adopting that picture, for example, might be a sensitivity to the fact that aspect-dawning seems to involve something more than merely registering what is perceived: when the rabbit aspect of the duck-rabbit flashes upon us, perhaps after a period of looking closely at the figure, some element of thought seems to be bound up with the experience. The hypothesis of an inner entity in the role of what is subjectively seen did appear to account for this feeling, since it presupposed an intermediary process of interpretation; but once this hypothesis is jettisoned, the specific form and role of the experience-expression can be seen to be the true source of that feeling. The point is that the verbal expression, which has the form of a description of what is perceived, is related in a particularly intimate way to the visual experience it expresses in this special context. In standard contexts of describing an object we perceive, we can normally provide a perceptual report without being particularly struck by the object concerned, but in the case of aspect-dawning the perceptual report functions as an exclamation – it manifests a spontaneous reaction to what is perceived and yet, since that reaction takes the form of a perceptual report rather than merely a start or a wordless exclamation, our observer's felt need to employ such a form of words shows that anyone experiencing the dawning of an aspect is *thinking* of what he sees (*PI*, 197c). The characteristic exclamation of aspect-dawning is both a report of what is seen and a cry of surprise or recognition (*PI*, 198a); it signals an *occupation* with the object which is the focus of the experience.

Awareness of the intimacy of the relationship between the experience of aspect-dawning and the forms of its linguistic expression implies a more *general* conclusion about the nature of visual perception, viz. that our primary evidence for the character of a person's visual experience – that facet of his behaviour which gives content to assertions concerning how he is seeing something – is his representation of what he sees (*PI*, 198b). We have thus far been concentrating upon verbal representations, but a point Wittgenstein is concerned to emphasize is that such representations can assume a wide variety of forms; and once it is recognized that these representations are the outward criteria of which any inner process or event stands in need, then we can appreciate the elasticity of the concept of 'what is seen' (*PI*, 198c). We can, for example, describe the contours of a landscape by hand-movements in space (*PI*, 198d), a facial expression by mimicking (*PI*, 198e), a drawing by pointing to a three-dimensional model (*PI*, 196f); in all such cases, differences in the representations proffered by two people (whether by employing different modes of representation or different specifications within a given mode) count as grounds for saying that they are seeing something differently. When we suddenly recognize an old friend, our seeing the familiar face in the altered one is manifest in our belief that we could now portray his face differently (*PI*, 197g).

This general point allows us to make sense of certain features of everyday visual perception which must remain opaque to any advocate of the erroneous picture of vision. Take, for example, the matter of our ordinary descriptions of people's facial expressions: according to Wittgenstein's interlocutor, when in such descriptions we employ concepts to do with facial expression, we are in fact choosing a mode of interpreting the arrangement of colours and shapes which we really see. If, however, such a hypothesis were correct it would render inexplicable the obvious fact that we cannot describe an inverted picture of a face in terms of its facial expression (*PI*, 198f) – the face's properties of colour and shape are not altered by the inversion, so why should we find it impossible to interpret those properties in our usual way? On Wittgenstein's account, on the other hand, the mystery disappears because we have no prior commitment to the idea that the visual impression be invariant across such differences in circumstance; on the contrary, the difference in the way that the given object is described in this unfamiliar context is precisely what gives us grounds for asserting that the object is being perceived differently in that new context.

This point can be pursued further. Imagine the case of someone who takes a few seconds to recognize an object (perhaps because of unusual lighting conditions) and compare him with someone who recognized that unusually-lit object immediately (*PI*, 197d). The proponent of the erroneous picture of vision must argue that both people have the same visual experience: they see the same object, and so must really have the same visual impression (since that impression is an inner materialization created by the object itself), but one of them is more quickly aware that the object falls under a certain sort of description. If that were so, however, both people should in general be capable of describing the object perceived in terms of its shape and colour (i.e. in terms of the properties the inner copy also possesses) with equal accuracy (*PI*, 197f); but such is not the case. In general, someone who immediately recognizes an animal as a rabbit will proffer a description of it which is not couched purely in terms of its shape, and he would not find it easy to provide the latter type of description; whereas the person who fails to recognize it as a rabbit will be unable to offer anything other than a description of the strange animal's shape. Within the terms of the erroneous picture, this is inexplicable; according to Wittgenstein's account, we have no a priori grounds for assuming a uniformity of visual experience independently of uniformity in proffered representations of what is seen, and so examples such as this (which in effect show that such uniformity does not exist) cannot subvert our position.

In other words, viewing the visual impression as an inner materialization creates problems rather than solves them, because it in effect presupposes that all descriptions of what is seen either are, can or should be couched in terms of arrangements of colour and shape; the reality of visual experience simply does not match up to the expectations generated by this would-be explanatory model. Of course, it is no part of Wittgenstein's purpose to deny that descriptions of what are seen are *ever* couched in colour/shape terms. It is obviously the case that *one* type of representation of what is seen is indeed an accurate copy of the shape and colour of the perceived figure – for example, a two-dimensional drawing or the corresponding form of words; philosophical confusions arise only when it is assumed that a description couched in terms of shape and colour is the sole genuine form of describing what is really seen (*PI*, 200a). Not only is it extremely unnatural – and peculiarly difficult – to proffer descriptions of the colour-shape type in many contexts, but it is also impossible to capture certain kinds of difference in our visual impressions of some objects solely by means of accurate copies (*PI*, 198g). The difference between our impressions of a schematic drawing of a tree and an inverted version of that drawing can be expressed by inverting a copy of one of them; but concepts such as neatness or ease (i.e. non-spatial concepts) are an essential part of any description which might adequately capture the differences between our impressions of a written English word and its mirror image.

When we simply return to our everyday practice with the concept of 'seeing', then, the sheer diversity of what can count as a 'description of what is seen' becomes clear. Indeed, it is precisely the interlocutor's fixation upon an exclusive and rigid paradigm for such descriptions that accounts not just for his general misconceptions about vision but also for his specific misrepresentation of the experience of aspect-dawning. We might say that the concept of seeing makes a tangled impression because it *is* tangled (*PI*, 200a); but this means only that the task of obtaining an *Ubersicht* of this domain of our linguistic practice requires careful and detailed descriptions of our use of that concept – it does not justify the imposition of a crudely simplifying model upon the recalcitrant complexities of reality.

PICTURE-OBJECTS AND CONTINUOUS ASPECT PERCEPTION

The material summarized in the previous section is often taken to be the heart of Wittgenstein's treatment of aspect perception. This is hardly a surprising presumption, since that material covers a great deal of ground: the erroneous theory of vision has been shown to be incapable of explaining what it was designed to explain, to distort the central features of aspect-dawning which seemed to demand theoretical explanation in the first place, and to render certain features of ordinary visual perception wholly mysterious. Furthermore, Wittgenstein's alternative account of the matter has shown itself to be more faithful to the features of aspect-dawning and of ordinary visual perception which the erroneous theory distorts or renders anomalous.

None the less, a central lacuna remains: for if the erroneous theory's putative explanations of the central paradox in aspect-dawning stand revealed as empty, Wittgenstein's treatment of that same visual experience has not yet been seen to engage with or account for that sense of paradox with any more success. Even after being brought to see that the relevant form of words is being used as an *Ausserung* rather than a standard perceptual report when aspect-dawning is at stake, it remains just as puzzling that we should reach for an *Ausserung* which carries the paradoxical implication of changes in the observed figure despite the fact that we are aware that no such change has taken place. In addition, our exegesis thus far has left undefined and unexamined several concepts which seem to play a significant role in Wittgenstein's consideration of these matters: for example, the notions of picture-objects, continuous aspect perception, regarding-as and aspect-blindness.

In the rest of this chapter, I will argue that these notions are essential elements in Wittgenstein's attempt to dissolve the air of paradox surrounding aspect-dawning: only against a background organized in terms of those concepts can this seemingly mysterious visual phenomenon be seen as not really mysterious at all. Accordingly, in this and the following section of the chapter, I shall argue for a particular interpretation of these key background concepts; and in the fourth section I will utilize the results of that analysis to present an interpretation of Wittgenstein's general strategy for dissolving the air of paradox surrounding the experience of aspect-dawning.

The account of Wittgenstein's interest in aspect-dawning presented thus far leaves unexplained his need to use what he calls picture-objects (*PI*, 194) as the primary means of investigating this phenomenon; and this feature of his treatment can seem particularly puzzling when we remember that his own original characterization of aspect-dawning involves the perception of a facial resemblance rather than an aspect of schematic drawings (*PI*, 193). In fact, however, the choice of picture-objects is (at least partly) dictated by Wittgenstein's concern to reveal the inapplicability of the erroneous theory of vision to more general cases of everyday perception.

Thus far he has shown that his interlocutor's picture of vision, with its emphasis upon interpreting such arrays of lines in terms of concepts which are somehow foreign to our immediate visual impression, is internally incoherent when applied to the specific experience of aspect-dawning (since it presupposes a distinction between direct and indirect descriptions which has no basis in such contexts). It would, however, seem much more plausible to adopt such an interpretative model of vision in contexts of ordinary perception of pictures and drawings; for *they* function as representative symbols, seeming to refer beyond themselves to that which they represent, and so a description of them in terms of what they represent seems obviously to be an indirect one. This impression can only be strengthened by taking *schematic* drawings as one's examples, since they achieve representative status with the bare minimum of pencil-strokes and thereby seem to flaunt their immediate material basis as much as their pictoriality. The claim that, for example, we (immediately, directly) *see* a pair of ears when we glance at the lines of a duck-rabbit sketch can seem like a bizarre misuse of language – for how can it be possible to *see* a bare figure according to such a complex interpretation (*PI*, 200d)? In dealing with this general problem by concentrating on such schematic drawings, therefore, Wittgenstein is allowing his opponent to make the best possible case for his theory; even in these circumstances, however, that theory will turn out to be erroneous.

When we look at a drawing of an animal transfixed by an arrow (*PI*, 203b), is it more correct to say that we *see* the arrow or that we merely know that the two bits sticking out at either side of the animal's silhouetted neck are supposed to represent parts of an arrow? It is important to remember that our interest in this question is conceptual: unlike the case of seeing an animal who has in reality been transfixed by an arrow, we feel a certain reluctance to say that our perception of the pictured arrow is a case of *seeing* an arrow, but also a similar unwillingness simply to refrain from applying that concept (*PI*, 203c). We need to bring to explicit attention our grounds for being inclined to apply or withhold the concept, i.e. to make clear the sense in which this is (and is not) a case of seeing (*PI*, 203d).

According to Wittgenstein, the concept of seeing is forced on us (*PI*, 204g) because our immediate response to the question 'What are you seeing?' when shown the drawing even for a moment would be to proffer a representation which involved reference to an arrow; we would describe what we saw as a picture of a transfixed beast, or draw a copy showing some sort of animal transfixed by an arrow

(*PI*, 203f). What are we to make of this claim? We noted earlier that the criterion for an observer's visual impression is the representation he offers of what he sees, so this is clearly the correct domain of evidence in which to look if we are to justify a claim to see the arrow; but of course someone who simply knows what the drawing is supposed to represent could also offer a description or copy of what he sees which would refer to an arrow. The crucial distinction between seeing and knowing must therefore lie rather in the fact that someone who *sees* the animal as transfixed by an arrow would give this type of description *immediately*, as an instantaneous reaction to a momentary view of the drawing; nor would he have regarded his response as being one among several possible interpretations of what he had seen (*PI*, 204c). If the first thing to jump to someone's eye is: there is an animal transfixed by an arrow, then although the best description he could give of what he momentarily glimpsed might be faulty in many respects, it would be a very definite *sort* of description – there would be certain mistakes he would *not* make (*PI*, 204a). Someone who knows rather than sees the arrow would not see it *at once* as an arrow, he would not be unhesitating in his recourse to the relevant description; he would rather need to read the drawing like a blueprint, inferring certain things from its particular properties of colour and spatial arrangement (*PI*, 204h).

Such seem to be the differing grounds upon which the concepts of knowing and of seeing are applied here; and it is important to note the analogy between the type of grounds which distinguish seeing from knowing and those upon which we applied the concept of aspect-dawning in the previous section of this chapter. In the two cases there is a very specific sort of relationship between the perceiver and the form of words he reaches for to represent what he sees: in both cases, the form of words is given immediately and spontaneously; in both, no alternative form of words constitutes a genuine alternative for the perceiver. It is, however, equally important to note that what is evident here is an analogy rather than an identity: otherwise, Wittgenstein would be committing himself to the claim that aspect-dawning experiences were a universal component of all visual perception, and this is something he explicitly denies (*PI*, 195a–d). What is captured in talk of seeing an arrow rather than knowing that certain lines represent an arrow is the readiness-to-hand of a certain form of description (and a corresponding absence of grounds for hypothesizing an intermediary process of interpretation); but what that claim presupposes is that the relevant form of words is still functioning in the standard way as a *description* of what is seen. To say that a particular sort of description is reached for spontaneously, and that it is not treated as one of several possibilities, is not to say that it is no longer a description but an *Ausserung*: and it is only when the description of the object in terms of the aspect is being used as an *Ausserung* of a specific experience that we can talk of aspect-dawning. As we have already seen (e.g. with the duck-rabbit) we *can* have experiences of aspect-dawning with respect to schematic drawings, but when looking at the drawing of the transfixed animal in an everyday context, the arrow-aspect does not continuously dawn on us; we are not consciously occupied with the drawing as a transfixed animal the whole time (*PI*, 204b). Nevertheless, the fact that aspect-dawning is not a universal component of visual perception does not necessitate denying the possibility of a separate justification for using the concept of seeing here; and the analogy we have just been pointing out goes some way towards making that separate use of seeing intelligible to us.

What follows from this reading of the seeing vs. knowing passages in Section xi is, accordingly, that Wittgenstein's introduction of picture-objects is designed precisely to elucidate the nature of this threefold distinction between aspect-dawning, seeing, and knowing; and that it does so by highlighting the existence of a conceptual space or category between the specific experience of aspect-dawning and the interpretative or inferential model of perception summed up under the label of 'knowing'. Even though the seeing/knowing distinction is only elaborated in those precise terms later in the text, the essence of this point is clear in embryo from the first moment at which Wittgenstein introduces his concept of a picture-object:

> I shall call the following figure, derived from Jastrow, the duck-rabbit. It can be seen as a rabbit's head or as a duck's.
>
> And I must distinguish between the 'continuous seeing' of an aspect and the 'dawning' of an aspect.
>
> The picture might have been shewn me, and I never have seen anything but a rabbit in it.

DEFINING TERMS

> Here it is useful to introduce the idea of a picture-object. For instance [bare sketch of a face] would be a picture-face.
>
> In some respects I stand towards it as I do towards a human face. I can study its expression, can react to it as to the expression of the human face. A child can talk to picture-men or picture-animals, can treat them as it treats dolls.
>
> I may, then, have seen the duck-rabbit simply as a picture-rabbit from the first. That is to say, if asked 'What's that?' or 'What do you see here?' I should have replied: 'A picture-rabbit'. If I had further been asked what that was, I should have explained by pointing to all sorts of pictures of rabbits, should perhaps have pointed to real rabbits, talked about their habits, or given an imitation of them.
>
> I should not have answered the question 'What do you see here?' by saying: 'now I am seeing it as a picture-rabbit'. I should simply have described my perception: just as if I had said 'I see a red circle over there'.
>
> (*PI*, 194–5)

What Wittgenstein here calls 'continuous aspect perception' is *not* a specific visual experience – it is not something given expression by a form of words used as an exclamation or an *Äusserung*: continuous seeing of an aspect is characterized precisely by the *refusal* to employ the relevant form of words in the manner used by Wittgenstein to define what he means by aspect-dawning. Rather, it involves an immediate, spontaneous reaching for the relevant form of description; we employ those words as a simple perceptual report, without any awareness that it is one of several available options. This preliminary characterization is enough on its own to reveal that, for Wittgenstein, 'continuous aspect perception' is just another label for what he is investigating in his later separation of seeing from knowing. Indeed, even without the later example of the transfixed animal drawing, the quoted passage is enough to imply that continuous seeing of an aspect is to be contrasted with the interpretative model of perception; for someone who has never seen anything but a rabbit in the dual-aspect picture-object is most definitely *not* inferring its picture-rabbithood from an immediate perception of an array of lines.

To summarize: picture-objects are schematic drawings one of

whose functions is to clarify Wittgenstein's category of continuous aspect perception (what he later calls seeing as opposed to knowing) by permitting him to exemplify for the reader precisely the reactions which define that category. Even though they are as far away from fully-fledged drawings and pictures as it seems possible to get whilst still being recognizable as representative figures – even though they seem to be closer to minimal scribbles than pictures (*RPP*,II, 219) – our attitude towards them is typically not that of someone who regards them as if they were blueprints which have to be interpreted before reaching a conclusion as to what they are supposed to represent. In other words, even in a context which one might be tempted to describe as a best case for the interlocutor's claim that everyday perception of drawings is a matter of the interpretation of colour/shape arrangement, the claim fails; it would be as unnatural and difficult to describe the duck-rabbit in terms of line arrangements as it would to describe a real rabbit in such terms (*PI*, 197f). The erroneous picture of vision is just as erroneous in the domain of everyday perception as it is in the specific circumstances of aspect-dawning.

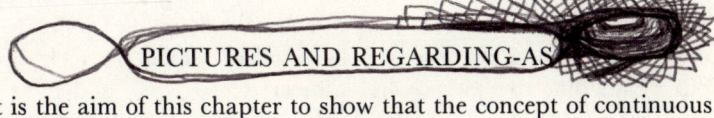

PICTURES AND REGARDING-AS

It is the aim of this chapter to show that the concept of continuous aspect perception just introduced constitutes the centre-piece of Wittgenstein's attempt to dissolve the air of paradox surrounding the experience of aspect-dawning; in order to see this, however, we must examine the nature of that concept in much more detail; and this entails expanding the focus of our investigation into the domain of pictures *per se*.

If it is indeed typical for us to see continuously the pictorial aspect of *picture-objects* (of figures that are closer to objects than pictures, as it were), then it would seem sensible to expect to find a similar conceptual category or logical space in the domain of fully-fledged pictures; and it is indeed part of Wittgenstein's purpose to emphasize just this point – as the following quotation confirms.

> How would the following account do: 'What I can see something *as*, is what it can be a picture of'?

> What this means is: the aspects in a change of aspects are those

ones which the figure might sometimes have *permanently* in a picture.

(*PI*, 201b)

Let us begin with the applicability of the notion of aspect-dawning. It might seem implausible to talk about aspect-dawning in relation to fully-fledged pictures, when the duck-rabbit has been our paradigm for such an experience: for in this new context there is typically no scope for a *change* of pictorial aspects, since most conventional pictures have no built-in ambiguity. However, according to Wittgenstein, this does not prevent us from talking about aspect-dawning altogether. Even with respect to a portrait of a friend, for example, that aspect can still sometimes dawn on us, for we are not always *concerning* ourselves with that picture as the particular portrait it is (*PI*, 205g). A picture does not always live for us when we are observing it (*PI*, 205h), we are not always thinking of or occupied by the aspect under which we see it; and it is this element of thought which characterizes the experience of aspect-dawning. In the case of conventional pictures, this element is manifest in the way we describe what we see: we say 'Her picture is smiling down at me from the wall' (*PI*, 205h), or, in a special tone of voice, 'The sphere is floating!' (*PI*, 201e); we point to a picture-rabbit and say 'See, it is looking!' (*PI*, 205i). In such cases our sense that the picture has almost *become* what it depicts is strongly analogous to our sense of a paradoxical change in the duck-rabbit when a new aspect dawns. It is of course undeniable that no *change* of aspect is at stake here – we do not express the experience by saying 'Now I see it as. . .' because that formulation alludes to a change (*PI*, 195d) and to attempts to bring about that change (i.e. to 'trying to see it as. . .'), whereas neither possibility makes sense in the case of conventional pictures. Nevertheless, the grammatical analogies we have noted ensure that it remains intelligible to talk of aspect-dawning here.

Wittgenstein begins to justify the claim that *continuous* aspect-perception is also exemplified in our relationship to fully-fledged pictures in his usual way – by contrasting it with an interpretative relationship to such things. When we look at pictures we do not proffer a description of them as if it were one of many possible interpretations, e.g. 'It may also be something that has fallen over, but what I see in front of me is *this* [colour-shape copy]'; we say rather that 'This glass has fallen over and is lying there in fragments.' (*PI*, 201c). As with picture-objects, then, one of the reasons for calling continuous aspect perception a case of seeing rather than of knowing is the *immediacy* of the description offered (*PI*, 204c); someone who treats all pictures as if they were blueprints might intelligibly be described as interpreting an array of lines and colours and inferring that the picture was intended to represent a certain sort of object, but someone who spontaneously describes a briefly glimpsed picture in terms of the object it might stand for or depict is showing that he sees the aspect rather than the precise two-dimensional array of colours and lines.

It is crucially important to note the precision of Wittgenstein's claim here. He is *not* simply saying that anyone who describes a picture in terms of the object it depicts or represents is continuously perceiving its pictorial aspect. Such a claim would not pick out one particular attitude towards pictures as opposed to others, because it constitutes a way of defining the concept of a picture *per se*: a picture just *is* the sort of thing that is correctly described by describing what it represents. The focus is rather on the *readiness-to-hand* of that correct form of description; and this readiness-to-hand is a manifestation of the perceiver's *taking for granted* the identity of what he perceives – a criterion for the fact that its being a picture, and moreover a particular picture (a picture of something in particular), is simply not at issue for him.

This is the point Wittgenstein is making when he introduces the notion of regarding-as – a notion which, to judge by the context of its introduction, is simply another label for continuous aspect perception:

> If you see the drawing as such-and-such an animal, what I expect from you will be pretty different from what I expect when you merely know what it is meant to be.
>
> Perhaps the following expression would have been better: we *regard* the photograph, picture or drawing as we do the object itself (the man, landscape, and so on) depicted there.
>
> (*PI*, 205e)

A general attitude or relation towards pictures *whose pictorial status is not in doubt* is being described here; and the idea is not that people who take up such an attitude are confusing symbol with reality, as if a mistake was being made. It is not that they think that the pictures really *are* the objects depicted, but rather that *in some respects* they stand towards pictures as they stand towards the things depicted – and thereby reveal the fact that the picture's specific identity (i.e. its being a depiction of something specific) is something they take for granted. One of those respects is the unhesitating way in which one describes the picture in terms of what it represents. But it is *the readiness-to-hand* of the relevant form of description rather than its being the form of description it is that reveals the presence of continuous aspect perception; and it does so by making manifest the perceiver's *attitude* to the picture – by showing that he unhesitatingly *treats* it as the picture it is (*PI*, 205a).

The point here is not to make hypotheses about the cause of such an absence of hesitation on the part of the viewer (*PI*, 201f); it may well be that custom and upbringing help to determine the styles of painting which have this sort of impact on any particular individual, just as two people may react differently to the individual examples of picture-objects we have discussed. The important point is to note that there *is* such an unhesitating verbal reaction, i.e. that there is such a phenomenon as continuous aspect perception (*PI*, 201d); the concept picks out a specific type of reaction to pictures in which those pictures convey something to us in an immediate way, and contrasts it with another possible type of reaction (*PI*, 205f).

The specific feature we have just noted relates only to one type of verbal reaction; as such, it forms only a part of a cluster of phenomena that are drawn together by means of the concept of regarding-as; our general attitude to such figures, the way of treating them which is under examination, is made manifest in other fine shades of both verbal *and* non-verbal behaviour (*PI*, 205a). As Wittgenstein put it when introducing the idea of picture-objects (*PI*, 194c), we can, for example, study the expression of a picture-face, react to it as to the expression of a human face, as well as unhesitatingly describe its smile as friendly or weak. It is in relation to fully-fledged pictures that he begins to spell out some of these other criteria of continuous aspect perception.

One such manifestation of this attitude is our tendency to *take for granted* the relevant object's relation to other objects, e.g. by treating it as grouped together with a particular range of objects and as distinct from certain other such ranges. Once we see an arbitrary cipher as a letter in a foreign alphabet, for example (*PI*, 210c), one manifestation of that change in attitude towards it would be our grouping it together with other letters from various alphabets rather than with other arbitrary ciphers; and our seeing it as clumsy rather than correct would come out in our treating it as we would other letters produced in a similarly deviant way rather than as we would treat other correctly written ones. People who see the same object differently show this, amongst other ways, in the differing types of contrast and comparison which make sense to them or which they take for granted in their treatment of that object: seeing a picture as an example of seventeenth-century Dutch landscape painting (cf *LW*,I, 750) involves locating it very precisely within the general domain of cultural artefacts – e.g. as being akin to tables or stools which exemplify the same Dutch milieu but unlike chairs which exemplify other cultural styles; whereas someone who does not recognize it as part of that milieu would find such comparisons and contrasts difficult to follow. The two people would, as it were, know their way around within the world of paintings in very different ways.

The type of attitude being picked out here presupposes an unhesitating awareness that the objects we encounter in the world are always objects of a certain *kind* – otherwise we would not be capable of taking it for granted that they fall into certain groupings in virtue of their similarities to and differences from other related objects. Once again, of course, what makes us say that someone is really *seeing* the pictorial aspect of a given picture involves subtleties of behaviour – his behaviour must, for example, show him to be *taking as given* the identity of the painting as the particular painting it is, rather than assuming that it belongs together with pictures rather than arbitrary ciphers and then inferring what precisely it depicts; his relation to pictorial symbols is the relation of someone for whom that realm of objects comes ready-organized, as it were. Continuous aspect perception is manifest in a certain *kind* of knowing one's way around within the world of pictures.

It can also, however, be manifest in knowing one's way around within a *particular* picture or drawing. Schematic drawings play an important role in descriptive geometry, for example, and in such contexts the difference between knowing what the drawing is supposed to represent and seeing it in that way is manifest in one's familiarity with the practice of operating with the drawing (*PI*, 203b). Someone who is seeing such a drawing three-dimensionally is distinguished by a certain *kind* of knowing his way about in the drawing, perhaps by moving his pencil around within the figure as if he were moving it around within a three-dimensional model or indicating the three-dimensional relations between the picture-elements in his gestures. It is not that someone who merely knows what the drawing represents could not learn to operate with the figure, but rather that he would exhibit a different kind of mastery of that technique; someone who is seeing the figure three-dimensionally reveals in his behaviour that he takes that three-dimensionality for granted – the specific identity of the drawing is not a hypothesis for which he feels the need to give reasons (*PI*, 198d).

In the realm of pictorial art, too, the capacity to find one's way around within a picture (and the familiarity with the picture as a *particular* painting or drawing thereby revealed) is evident. Questions of phrasing by the eye or ear appear to be prerequisites for aesthetic understanding (*PI*, 202h), in the sense that the terms in which one grasps and evaluates the purpose or significance of works of art presuppose the capacity to perceive such aesthetic objects in terms of concepts which confer a very particular overall form or organization upon it. Essential to one's grasp of a piece of music, for example, may be the ability to see certain sections as introduction and conclusion (*PI*, 202h); but a direct perception of the piece in those terms clearly involves an attitude towards it which is very different from that of treating it as a sequential assemblage of notes which must then be interpreted (*LW*,I, 677). And just as the sort of reproduction of a musical piece which manifests a correct understanding of that piece is one which possesses those fine shades of expression that convey its organization in terms of an overall purpose or such 'elements' as a conclusion and introduction (*PI*, 207a), so our gestures and verbal behaviour in relation to a landscape painting – our way of treating it – reveals whether we are *taking it for granted* that its basic elements are representations of the elements of the landscape (trees, houses and so on) rather than colour-patches on canvas (i.e. *taking it for granted* that it is a picture not merely a coloured surface).

Finally, on the most general level we can say that the regarding-as relation to pictures is made manifest in the particular role paintings and pictures play in our lives: unlike blueprints or working drawings, paintings are typically hung on the wall to be seen and admired – to give pleasure to ourselves, our friends and visitors (*PI*, 205c). The delight we take in a beautiful landscape may lead us to put a painting of that landscape on our wall; but such a mode of treating pictures would make no sense to people who found such representations to be repellent distortions of the objects represented (*PI*, 205f). In both cases, the different ways in which the paintings are treated, the different roles they play in the lives of the relevant people, manifest the degree to which those people are at home with those objects understood as the particular kind of objects they are. It is perhaps again worth emphasizing here that nothing hangs on our choice of paintings and blueprints as examples of pictures which evoke the attitudes of regarding-as and knowing respectively: it is conceivable that some people would treat our working drawings as they do the objects they depict, and it is also possible that a troublesome process of acculturation or learning might be required in order to understand paintings as the objects they depict. For our concerns, however, any such painful learning would be mere history (*RPP*,I, 1018), and the particular sort of picture towards which a given set of people stand in a relation of regarding-as a matter of indifference; the crucial point is simply that a *conceptual* distinction between this type of relation to pictorial symbols and other possible types exists, and that the distinction rests on fine shades of behaviour of the kind we have been describing above.

To summarize: I have been arguing that continuous aspect perception (regarding-as) in relation to pictures is a matter of attitude, a way of taking a picture or drawing; certain modes of awareness of its internal composition and of its precise relationship to other kinds of object are simply ways in which the degree to which we take for granted its identity as the particular picture it is become manifest in our lives. This way of taking pictures is *not* a hypothesis the perceiver makes on the basis of colours and shapes he 'really' sees, but rather an orientation which provides the framework within which he might go on to make certain hypotheses. One could say: when we regard a picture as the object it represents, we do not treat it as an object in its own right – as a material object consisting of an arrangement of lines or colour-patches.

ASPECTS, ASPECT-BLINDNESS, AND THE PARADOX OF ASPECT-DAWNING

On this interpretation, the nature of the distinction Wittgenstein is anxious to draw between aspects and colour or shape (understood as objects of perception – *PI*, 193a) becomes clearer:

> If I saw the duck-rabbit as a rabbit, then I saw: these shapes and colours (I give them in detail) – and I saw besides something like this: and here I point to a number of different pictures of rabbits. – This shews the difference between the concepts.
>
> (*PI*, 196h)

In other words, while we could in principle give an exact representation of the picture-rabbit's colour and a detailed copy of its shape, there could be no such thing as giving an exact copy of its 'picture-rabbitness' (short of a completely unhelpful reproduction of the duck-rabbit figure in its entirety); we would rather point to other pictures of rabbits (cf. *PI*, 212a). For the rabbit-aspect is not a property or feature of the drawing in the way the shape of the ears or the colour of the eye-dot are distinct material properties of the figure; describing something as a picture-rabbit relates to the perceived object considered as a whole, identifying it as a particular kind of thing (i.e. as a drawing) rather than to specifiable parts or elements of it considered as a material object (i.e. as an arrangement of marks). The distinction was marked when we looked at the case of the three-dimensional aspect of the schematic cube earlier in this chapter (*PI*, 196; *LW*,I, 500); for there the form of words we use as an *Ausserung* is one which explicitly relates to a way of seeing the figure as a whole, not to a hitherto unnoticed property of that figure. When an aspect of a picture dawns, we recognize that a new *kind* of description of the perceived figure might be given, and we *see* it in those terms; when we continuously perceive that aspect, we take the status of the figure as a particular kind of thing (viz. a picture) for granted.

The categorial difference between aspects and colour or shape is, then, to be viewed as the difference between concepts which register the *kind* of object something might be and concepts which pick out material properties of objects – but we should also note here that the properties picked out by concepts of colour and shape are distinctive in that any object must possess them in so far as it can intelligibly be described as a material object at all. For an object to be a material object at all it must be a candidate for description in terms of colour and shape, and so *a fortiori* a description in such terms must be applicable to any specific *kind* of object – but in recognizing that an object can be seen as a specific kind of thing, we simultaneously recognize that the object can also be described in terms of parts or elements applicable to that kind of object alone.

It follows that colour and shape concepts should be seen as being on the same level as the property concepts whose applicability to an object is licensed by a recognition of the kind of object it is, rather than being on the same level as aspect concepts as we have been defining them. For example, a description in terms of colour and shape is more akin to describing a picture-rabbit in terms of its long ears and teeth (i.e. in terms of the properties or parts into which that kind of object can be broken down) than to describing it simply as a picture-rabbit (i.e. in terms of what we have been calling an aspect); and the nearest equivalent in the colour-shape conceptual system to describing an object as a picture-rabbit is to describe it simply as a material object. In this sense, aspects are on a different level to colour and shape because the latter describe parts or properties of objects rather than objects considered as a whole; and also because aspect concepts determine an object as being a particular kind of object and therefore cannot be applied to all objects, whereas colour and shape concepts necessarily apply to all kinds of objects because they determine, as Kant would have said, the concept of an object in general.

For Wittgenstein, however, this exploration of the nature of aspects and of our general relation to pictures is primarily intended to cast light on the experience of a change of aspects (e.g. in the case of the duck-rabbit), and more particularly upon the paradoxical air which surrounds such experiences. It will be remembered that this paradox consists in the sense that the object perceived had changed in some way, even though none of its properties had altered; we perceive that a picture-duck might also be used as a picture-rabbit, but give expression to this perception in terms which suggest that the figure *itself* had changed. If, however, we bear in mind the point that we generally regard pictures as we do the objects they depict, then our inclination to express the experience of a change of aspect in this way becomes less surprising.

When we continuously perceive one aspect of a picture or drawing, our verbal and non-verbal behaviour towards it is already similar in certain respects to the ways in which we respond to the object the figure depicts (*PI*, 206i): the tie-up between the depiction and what it depicts (i.e. its identity as a specific picture) informs our relationship with it to such an extent that we regard a picture-duck and a picture-rabbit as being as different as are the duck and the rabbit they depict. It is therefore the very reverse of surprising to find the realization that the same figure is *both* a picture-duck *and* a picture-rabbit being given expression in terms which suggest that the figure itself has altered, i.e. that a pictured duck has been transformed into a pictured rabbit, one sort of picture-object into a very different sort. It is entirely to be *expected* that someone whose behaviour typically manifests his taking for granted the specific identity of picture-objects will be inclined to express his sudden realization that a given picture-duck *is also* a picture-rabbit in a way which would be apt for registering the perception of a picture-duck *changing into* a picture-rabbit. One could go further: if someone is incapable of such experiences of aspect-dawning, one has grounds for doubting that his general attitude to pictures is one of continuous aspect perception.

In other words, looked at from this perspective, the capacity to experience the dawning of a new aspect must be seen as simply *one* (admittedly striking) criterion for a person's general relation to pictures being one of continuous aspect perception. Indeed, it is only because the interpretative model of vision is blinding us to the true nature of our typical relation to pictures that we are inclined to find this central feature of aspect-dawning paradoxical at all. For it is only if we treat pictures as pictures and not as colour/shape arrangements (and so regard a picture of a duck as being as different from a picture of a rabbit as a real duck is from a real rabbit) that the dawning of the aspect will naturally be experienced as a bizarre fluctuation in the identity of a picture-object rather than the simple discovery of an alternative mode of interpreting this particular arrangement of lines.

This last point is confirmed by the implications of Wittgenstein's answer to the question of what an inability to see something *as* something would be like (*PI*, 213f); for his final characterization of such aspect-blindness renders salient the conceptual connection between aspect-dawning and continuous aspect perception which we have just been asserting.

His preliminary definition of aspect-blindness adverts to an inability to see a change of aspects, i.e. an inability to experience aspect-dawning; but the lack in which we are interested is not simply a failure to perceive the applicability of a new form of description, for someone could become aware of that and still not experience aspect-dawning (*LW*,I, 492–3). The aspect-blind person is capable of noticing, for example, that the double-cross can also be described as a black cross on a white ground, but he is not supposed to say 'Before, I saw a white cross, but now it's a black cross!' The crucial point is that the aspect-blind could call the picture first one thing, then another, but they could not experience the change as a jump from one aspect to another (*PI*, 213g) – and this 'could' is a conceptual or logical limit, not a causal one. The concept of aspect-blindness is characterized by the lack of any verbal or non-verbal behaviour which might manifest any sense that a paradox lies at the heart of a change of aspects: such people would not feel inclined to say that the perceived figure was the same and yet not the same (*LW*,I, 174), that after every change of aspect it was as if they saw a different object (*RPP*,II, 42), that two aspects might seem to be incompatible with each other (*RPP*,I 877).

If we assume, then, that someone cannot experience a change of aspect – that he cannot, for example, see the schematic cube three-dimensionally first one way then another – then it follows that he could not *continuously* see the schematic drawing of a cube as a cube, i.e. could not stand to a picture of a three-dimensional object as he does to the three-dimensional object (*RPP*,II, 479). The conclusion that the possibility of experiencing aspect-dawning is a function of our general attitude to pictorial symbols when an aspect-change is not in question (*PI*, 214a) is once again unavoidable: for unless we were capable of continuously seeing a given aspect, the inclination to express our experience of a change of aspects in terms which suggest that the figure has altered before our eyes would be entirely alien to us.

It should be stressed that this is a conceptual rather than a causal point: as we saw earlier, one of the defining characteristics of continuous aspect-perception is behaviour which manifests the attitude of regarding a figure or picture as we do the object it depicts, i.e. treating it in certain respects as if it were the object it represents, spontaneously describing it in terms which standardly apply to the depicted scene, etc.; and the inclination to express the realization that such a figure might be used to depict two different sorts of object in terms which imply that the *figure* has assumed a very different form is simply a further manifestation of this general attitude. Since – as we know – the felt need to employ such a particular form of words in the verbal *Ausserung* of one's experience of aspect-dawning is what defines the content and nature of that experience, the aspect-blind person's failure so to express his awareness of an aspect-change must be seen as having a double function: it manifests his incapacity to have a specific visual experience and thereby reveals that his general relation to pictorial symbols is not that of continuous aspect perception (*PI*, 214a).

So how *are* we to imagine his attitude towards pictures? A crucial point to note is that aspect-blindness does not exclude the possibility of learning the relevant technique of pictorial representation; an aspect-blind person could recognize the schematic cube as a representation of a cube (*PI*, 213g), it is rather that he treats all pictorial symbols as we would treat blueprints or working drawings. In effect, therefore, the concept of aspect-blindness picks out the attitude towards pictures which we have been tracing out in some detail earlier, one which contrasts with continuous aspect perception: aspect-blindness involves interpreting what is directly seen, reading the relevant information off the figure or picture as if it were a blueprint, knowing what a given symbol is supposed to represent rather than seeing it in that way. The aspect-blind person would be able to work according to a pictorial representation but it would never be possible for him to take a picture for a three-dimensional object (as – analogously – we sometimes do with *trompe-l'œil* architecture)[3] (*RPP*,II, 479); he would at most see a

---

3 Wittgenstein's phrase 'take a picture for a three-dimensional object' suggests that he is employing an example of misperception to *define* aspect-seeing – as if the latter were a perceptual defect. This implication goes against the thrust of his general remarks in this investigation, and should therefore be revised. He need only claim that the capacity to perceive *trompe l'œil* in terms of an illusory dimension of depth (i.e. to perceive it as such constructions are *supposed*

kind of diagram in a photograph, treating it as we treat a map – he could gather various things from it about the landscape but could not, for example, admire the landscape in looking at the map or exclaim 'What a glorious view!' (*RPP*,I, 170); he could learn that a picture of a runner portrays a runner, but would show no sign of appreciating that motion was as manifest in the picture as it would be in the runners in a race (*RPP*,II, 483). His behaviour fails, in other words, to manifest any of the fine shades which reveal that someone is regarding a picture as one does the object it depicts.

What, then are we to say in conclusion about this part of the tangled concept of seeing? In all three of the categories we have been examining in this chapter – those of aspect-dawning, continuous aspect perception and knowing what a figure is supposed to be – the same drawing could be under observation, so in one sense nothing different is seen in the various contexts, i.e. the object perceived does not alter. In another sense, however, we are rightly inclined to say that what is seen *is* different in the three cases, that different visual experiences and/or visual impressions are involved. The ground for this inclination is not, of course, that some hypothetical materialization produced inside us has different properties on these different occasions, but rather that we *describe* what we see differently in those contexts (*PI*, 202b): differences in the representation of what is seen are what give content to claims about variations in an observer's visual experience (*PI*, 198b). In the case of aspect-dawning with reference to the floating sphere painting, for example, we might express our sense of this difference by saying 'Surely I see something *different* when I see the sphere floating from when I merely see it lying there'; such an expression conveys no independent evidence confirming the relevant difference, but by simply repeating in one sentence the two different ways of describing the painting which an observer might be inclined to use, it exemplifies the real grounds for asserting the existence of a difference (*PI*, 201g).

That difference can be summarized in the following way. Just as aspect-dawning is distinguished from continuous aspect perception

---

to be perceived) is one which the aspect-blind lack, and that this lack renders them immune from a particular sort of perceptual error to which those who can perceive aspects are vulnerable but to which they need not succumb.

by a perceptual report becoming an *Ausserung* and being used to manifest a sense that the perceived object is somehow altering, so continuous seeing of an aspect is distinguished from merely knowing what a figure is supposed to represent by a difference in the way we describe what we see: we say of a picture of a horse, for example, that 'That horse is galloping' rather than 'It may also be a galloping animal' (*PI*, 202e). These are the ways in which Wittgenstein begins to account for our sense that we *see* aspects: he renders salient the precise sense in which aspects are indeed 'seen' (*PI*, 203c–d).

This account does, however, leave opaque the question of the *philosophical* import of aspect perception for Wittgenstein: recognizing the usefulness of such distinctions in avoiding confusions about the nature of aspect-dawning does not carry with it any clear sense of Wittgenstein's *deeper* reasons (if any) for expending so much time and energy upon this part of the tangled concept of seeing. It is the contention of this book that such deeper reasons do exist; and in the next chapter I shall attempt to plot out the avenues opened up by the labels and categories laid out in the preceding sections.

2
ASPECTS AND LANGUAGE

THE EXPERIENCE OF MEANING

The importance of this concept [of aspect-blindness] lies in the connexion between the concepts of 'seeing an aspect' and 'experiencing the meaning of a word'. For we want to ask 'What would you be missing if you did not *experience* the meaning of a word?'

(*PI*, 214d)

For Wittgenstein, the central importance of his investigation of aspect perception lies in the fact that words too can be the focus of aspect perception: as we will see, *all* the conceptual distinctions I have been highlighting in the realm of general relationships towards pictorial symbols find an analogous application in the field of attitudes towards linguistic symbols – towards language in general. Once again, the category of aspect-dawning is the one whose applicability can most easily be seen in this new domain. Wittgenstein points out that an aspect-dawning experience can be elicited by focusing on words, by attempting to *mean* them in different ways when pronounced in isolation or by perceiving a change of aspect from meaningful symbol to sound when an isolated word is pronounced many times over (*PI*, 214d); and he asks how significant the inability to experience such things might be. In this section, I shall attempt to answer his question; and to avoid confusion, I shall refer to the linguistic equivalent of aspect-blindness as 'meaning-blindness' (*RPP*,I, 189).

It should first be emphasized that, for Wittgenstein, the meaning-blind would *not* be incapable of grasping the linguistic technique of which any given word was the bearer simply because they could not experience its meaning. To think otherwise is to imagine that a particular psychological event or process which may sometimes accompany our use of a word or sentence in certain contexts in fact constitutes its meaning; whereas understanding a word or sentence is more akin to an ability – to mastery of a technique – than to a psychological act, state, or process. This can be seen simply from the fact that the relevant psychological experiences are relatively rare: the sensitive ear which shows me that I experience the word in various ways when pronouncing it in isolation would surely also show me that often I do not have any experience of it at all in the course of using it in ordinary conversation (*PI*, 215h); and even if an 'expert' in such matters were to claim that he always experienced the meaning of a word he used, it would hardly be plausible for him to go on to claim that in all the varying contexts of a given word's use precisely the same experience or feeling was present (*PI*, 215g).

Moreover, were it to be the case that the experience of meaning had the necessary ubiquity for its postulated role, it would still remain completely irrelevant to questions of linguistic understanding because no psychological event or process accompanying a word could have the consequences of meaning (*PI*, 218d); that is, such experiences have no place in our grounds for attributing linguistic understanding to any agent. If someone feels a given word pronounced in his hearing to be strange in its use, for example (*PI*, 214f), and yet goes on to explain what the sentence in which it is embedded meant, employ the sentence himself in appropriate contexts and respond appropriately to its utterance by someone else, then we would be justified in saying that he understood the partially coded sentence; experiences of understanding get covered up by the use of (or practice of using) the relevant piece of language, i.e. by behaviour which manifests a mastery of that practice (*RPP*,I, 184).

The same point can be made from the perspective of the speaker or author of a sentence rather than the hearer (*PI*, 214e). The question of how someone meant a word is clearly a question of intention, and it is answered by reference to facts about and features of the situation which bear no relation to how he experienced the relevant word. If someone tells us 'Wait for me by the bank' (*PI*, 216h) and we are uncertain whether he meant the river bank or the Bank of England, then we can ask him how he intended his utterance to be understood; in doing so we make reference to a definite time – the time at which the ambiguous word was uttered – but not to an experience which occurred at that time.

This is a general point about the concept of intention: if, for example, I see an ice-cream van approaching I may fetch my wallet and go to meet it; in such a mundane context I may not be aware of any particular psychological experience of 'intending', yet if I were stopped and asked 'Why have you left the house?' I should express my intention. No specific psychological experience is either necessary or sufficient for a person's having a given intention; the person concerned does not read off the nature of his intention from an inner experience but rather manifests it in his speech and action, and if another person wishes to discover what the first person's intentions might be he will not ask him about any accompanying psychological experiences he might have undergone. These observations hold *a fortiori* for the specific case of our intentions in using language: accompanying psychological experiences are not the meaning or intending (*PI*, 217a), they do not form part of the content of the concept – although such psychological or behavioural phenomena are the characteristic accompaniments of purposeful speech, *they* are not the intending or meaning (*PI*, 218e).

The point to be remembered here is that intention is a psychological concept of a different sort from that of the experience of meaning. Both relate to the mental life of a person, but they take up different aspects of it; and the difference is a matter not of the concepts labelling different processes – as if intention were an articulated or non-articulated process which paralleled certain modes of acting and speaking (*PI*, 217b), when it is not a *process* at all – but rather of the structures of the concepts reflecting the different *interest* we take in the two sorts of psychological phenomena (*PI*, 217d). If we want to know what someone meant by a word (*PI*, 217i) then we are interested in the purpose of his uttering the word and thus with the point of that particular piece of behaviour; although the question is couched in a way which suggests that something happening at that moment determines the meaning of the word (i.e. as if some psychological occurrence originates a symbolic convention), it is in reality aimed solely at elucidating which symbolic convention is being drawn upon – at discovering what significance his speech-act was intended to have (*PI*, 218c). In the case of the experience of meaning, by contrast, the time-reference built into the concept also refers to an occurrence at the relevant moment (*PI*, 217h). The experiences a speaker has whilst speaking may reveal hidden motives for his action (*PI*, 217d) but tell us nothing about how he meant his words; and such reactions to another person's verbal behaviour, although potentially very informative about various facets of the hearer's relation to the people and topics under discussion (*PI*, 217j), presuppose the hearer's understanding of the words being used and so cannot constitute that understanding. If we are interested in the meaning of words in a particular conversation or thought, we focus on the language of which they are a part and the context of their employment (e.g. the intentions of the speaker), and not upon accompanying experiences (*PI*, 217e).

The importance of the experience of meaning cannot therefore reside in a putative contribution to the phenomena of conferring or grasping linguistic meaning. Perhaps, then, its interest lies rather in the attitude towards language which it exemplifies. We can begin to appreciate this if we emphasize the analogy that Wittgenstein himself was concerned to press between the experience of meaning and experiences of aspect-dawning in general (*PI*, 214d). As was the case with other experiences of aspect-dawning, a form of words used in a particular way in one context is employed very differently in another: with experiences of meaning, a form of words standardly employed to report a speaker's intentions or to describe the technique of a given word's use (i.e. with reference to word-synonymy, explanations of meaning, and so on) is utilized as the expression of an experience undergone in very specific circumstances – we move from 'The word has this meaning' to 'I said the word in this meaning'. The original employment of the word 'meaning' is closely related to questions of use and purpose – words are said to have different meanings if they are employed as part of significantly different techniques of use, and a speaker's intentions with respect to the meaning of his utterance depend upon such factors as the context and purpose of his utterance as well as the nature of his audience; in the game of experiencing meaning, however, words are uttered in isolation, apart from the practice of linguistic interchange and divorced from specific purposes (*PI*, 215c) – and yet we are inclined to use the word 'meaning' here too.

This inclination to take over an expression from its standard use and employ it as a verbal *Ausserung* of an experience, thus revealing a sense that an ambiguous word encountered outside the contexts of use which determine its meaning on a given occasion can nevertheless *manifest* one meaning rather than another, is strikingly analogous to experiences of aspect-dawning in relation to picture-objects such as the duck-rabbit: such ambiguous bare figures encountered outside a determining pictorial context (as mere potential elements of fully-fledged pictures, as it were [*PI*, 201b]) nevertheless seem to *become* one sort of picture-object rather than another. Aspect-dawning experiences of the linguistic kind may, however, seem more bizarre than their pictorial analogues – particularly when the analogy is stated so starkly; but Wittgenstein regards this appearance as illusory and attempts to dispel it in several ways, one of which involves pointing out that there are other linguistic phenomena which manifest precisely the same type of inclination.

The most obvious examples are to be found in the domain of literature. Wittgenstein points out that our relationship to language when it is being employed in poems and narratives is not the same as when we are merely interested in the information that a particular form of words is imparting (*PI*, 214g). In such contexts, a sentence can strike me as like a painting in words, and an individual word as like a picture (*PI*, 215c); just like the case of a portrait or photograph living for me ('Her picture smiles down on me from the wall!' – *PI*, 205h), words can sometimes seem to be a *manifestation* of their meaning, to be a living embodiment of the sentiment or thought they express. We may be able to give an explanation of why a particular formulation of this sentiment strikes us in this way (e.g. causal associations, or the skill of a reader whose intonation can transform one's perception of the spoken words – *PI*, 214g, 215b), but this leaves untouched the fact that we are inclined to express our being struck in precisely this sort of way. It is *this* fact in which Wittgenstein is interested; and when we compare the experience of word-meaning with such examples of aesthetic experiences, we can begin to see that such phenomena are more ubiquitous than might at first be thought.

So, we can provisionally conclude that there are analogues to aspect-dawning in the domain of language which go beyond the 'game' of experiencing meaning; but comparison with aspect perception in general can also take us in the direction of suspecting an analogue of *continuous* seeing of aspects in this domain. If we recall my earlier conclusion that the capacity to experience aspect-dawning was simply one striking manifestation of a more general attitude to pictures, then we must regard the capacity to experience a word's meaning as one very clear indication of the typical human relationship towards language – a relationship in which, just as we regard pictures as we do the objects depicted, i.e. exhibit the various fine shades of behaviour which manifest continuous aspect perception, so we regard words as having a familiar physiognomy (*PI*, 218g), i.e. exhibit the various fine shades of behaviour which constitute continuous meaning perception. Wittgenstein's physiognomy metaphor is one of the most puzzling of the many opaque images at work in these writings, and its centrality to his strategy is by no means obvious. In the next section of this chapter I will argue for an interpretation of it which accords it just such a central role; for a grasp of that metaphor will turn out to be essential to a grasp of what Wittgenstein takes to be the constitutive elements of the attitude of continuous meaning perception.

THE PHYSIOGNOMY OF WORDS

First, then, we should ask ourselves what general attitude to language can be seen as manifest in the forms of words we choose to give expression to experiences of meaning; why do we find those forms of expression natural or ready-to-hand in such contexts? Wittgenstein emphasizes that the grounds for ascribing the experience of meaning to a given person include his being inclined to express his experience by saying that a word tends to lose its meaning and become a mere sound when repeated several times; but it would make no sense to describe words as *becoming* mere sounds (*PI*, 214d) if he standardly perceived or experienced them as mere sounds in the first place. It seems rather that a new aspect has dawned on that person: he suddenly notices that spoken words can also be viewed as sound-patterns, but the impact of his experience lies in his not having detached this aspect from the phenomenon of spoken language beforehand in his everyday linguistic interchanges. The verbal behaviour which characterizes aspect-dawning therefore also manifests the nature of our normal relationship with language – we directly perceive the written and spoken elements of language as meaningful words and sentences, not as sounds-or-marks-to-be-interpreted; and the meaning-blind person's failure to exhibit that same verbal behaviour thereby reveals that he continuously perceives speech as an emission of sounds which then have to be interpreted to elicit their meaning. Once more the category of continuous aspect perception finds its place between the experience of aspect-dawning and the interpretative model of perception.

A second indication of the nature of continuous meaning perception is also to be found in the forms of words employed to express the experience of meaning, particularly when an ambiguous word is the focus of attention. As we noted earlier, in ordinary contexts questions about a word's meaning relate not just to that specific word but also to its points of similarity and contrast with neighbouring words and techniques of use; we talk, for example, of a word having this one meaning or of its being used in several different ways, and also of two words only sounding the same but having no other connection with each other – and a host of related forms of expression (*RPP*,I, 354). The crucial point is that the experience of meaning follows these turns of speech exactly; talk of pronouncing a word in each of its different meanings, for example, presupposes a sense that the word does have more than one meaning and a capacity to distinguish those meanings – perhaps by reference to examples of other words whose use resembles one of those meanings.

In other words, for the experience of meaning to take the form it does – for its characteristic verbal *Ausserung* to involve that form of words – the person undergoing the experience must regard the language he has learnt as being organized in a certain way; he must treat the bearer of any given technique of use as if it had a precise location within the realm of language which is conferred upon it by relations of similarity and contrast with other words and the corresponding techniques of their use. As we saw earlier in the case of aspect perception in the context of descriptive geometry or music, so in the context of language the experience of meaning signals that capacity to know one's way around a given realm which is another of the defining characteristics of continuous aspect perception; the terms in which the realm is organized (e.g. 'introduction' and 'conclusion' vs. 'synonymy' and 'ambiguity') may differ, but the *familiarity* with which one moves around within the domain they define – and thus our familiarity with the specific identity of the given word – is the same.

This second indication, with its emphasis upon the familiarity of our relation to language, links with Wittgenstein's claim that our typical relationship to language is manifest in the way in which we generally choose and value words (*PI*, 218g) – for this too is indicative of the profound familiarity of the physiognomy which words present to our gaze. When we choose among words, for example, it is possible to say a great deal about a fine aesthetic difference; we can explicitly assess the extensive ramifications effected by each candidate word (*PI*, 219b) and that field of force is decisive in settling the correctness of our choice. At the same time, however, very often no such process of explanation and judgment takes place – at last a word comes and our dissatisfaction dissolves (*PI*, 218h). This seemingly paradoxical conjunction of features becomes perfectly comprehensible if we regard it as a manifestation of continuous meaning perception. The absence of interpretative procedures signals the fact that often we immediately perceive the rightness of the word on its face, as it were: such a direct perception would of course be unintelligible in the absence of principles of organization within the given language, but it is equally true that such perceptions are not arrived at by utilizing our grasp of that organization as if it were a map or a diagram; rather, the immediacy of those perceptions signals the depth of our assimilation of that organization. It is as if the given word's location within the linguistic field – its tie-ups of comparison and contrast – had been absorbed into (and helped constitute) its own unique physiognomy.

Sometimes, our sense of the word's identity involves tie-ups of a sort that are not directly linguistic. Such sensitivity is manifest, for example, in our inclination to predicate colours of vowels. The meaning-blind person would be perfectly capable of associating particular colours with certain vowels, perhaps as a result of certain causal psychological habituations; but even given the relevant associations, he would react uncomprehendingly to the question 'Is "e" yellow or purple?' What is of interest is not hypothetical causes of the phenomenon (*PI*, 216c) but the *form* the phenomenon takes: unlike the meaning-blind, we are inclined to treat as intelligible a question expressed in a way which implies that elements of language can be compared with reference to features which belong not to them but to phenomena with which they are associated in certain contexts. The fancy that such features might be regarded as objective properties of the linguistic symbols themselves – as if a letter's associations had been taken up into it (*PI*, 218g) – thus indicates two things: first, that an essential contribution to a word's physiognomy for us is the non-linguistic background against which its features are habitually seen; and secondly, that we find it natural to talk as if we perceive that background in the word itself – we do not read off those tie-ups but rather *see* them in the face which the word presents to us (*RPP*,I, 322).

People are also sometimes inclined to say that a name fits its bearer, e.g. that the name 'Schubert' fits Schubert's works and Schubert's face (*PI*, 215f); despite being well aware that the name does not stand in a relationship of fitting to its bearer and his works, they still find themselves needing to use the word 'fitting' in order to give adequate expression to their feelings about the name (*LW*,I, 69). Clearly the eight-letter ink-mark 'Schubert' has no similarity by sound or appearance with a particular human being or set of musical compositions, and the internal grammatical relation between that name and its bearer which is set up by the practice of using the ink-mark as that man's name is not one of 'fitting'. On the other hand, the techniques of a word's use ensure that it will habitually be encountered against a reasonably specific and reoccurring background of objects, persons, and circumstances: and if our assimilation of the word *as the bearer of a specific technique* is a deep one, then our sense of the non-linguistic background against which the word's technique of use locates it will tend to be assimilated in its turn, and so will naturally help to define our sense of that word's particular physiognomy.

We might say, then, that the name 'Schubert' seems to fit its bearer just because familiarity with the use of that name hangs together with familiarity with the non-linguistic context into which that particular word fits with the smoothness of habituation; we might explain the habituation causally, but the way in which we are inclined to give expression to that sense of smoothness – in terms of the word's being a *portrait* of its bearer (*LW*,I, 70) – manifests an attitude to language which is not explicable solely in such terms. For we react to such associative and linguistic tie-ups as if they had been *absorbed* by the word: we are capable of responding to that word as if it carried such tie-ups on its face, as if it were a manifestation of every aspect of its meaning. Mere *awareness* of all those tie-ups would not entail the adoption of such an attitude, for one could admit their existence and find the idea of the word's *absorbing* them incomprehensible: someone who had to read off such tie-ups from the word and simply hypothesized that a given association was being invoked in this particular context rather than reacting directly to that invocation – someone who had to *interpret* words in terms of their meaning – would not be manifesting the attitude of continuous meaning perception. Someone who *did* manifest that attitude – who did treat words as if they manifested every aspect of their significance – would thereby be revealing his unhesitating awareness of that word's specific identity.

This attitude towards letters and individual words is matched at other linguistic levels (as it were); the specific form of attachment to our words that is manifest in the way we choose and value words (*PI*, 218g) is also evident in the aesthetic role certain texts can play in our lives. This attachment comes out not just in those specific contexts when a word or a sentence strikes us as being a living embodiment of its meaning; it is also evident in many of our everyday practices of using language when experiences of meaning are not at stake. For example, we have a practice of hanging texts on the wall (*PI*, 205c), as if a certain form of words were an embodiment of their meaning: that is, we treat them with the respect we have for the sentiment they express (i.e. manifest the linguistic equivalent of regarding pictorial symbols as we do the objects they depict), and we find them to be a fully apt expression of their meaning. We might not accord such honorific status to another form of words which attempted to convey the same sentiment: to understand that text fully, we might feel, is to appreciate that it could not be replaced by any other – only those words in that order will do (*PI*, 531).

Once again, whatever the causal mechanisms which bring about such attitudes in relation to one text rather than any other may turn out to be, the interest of this phenomenon for our investigation is simply that such attitudes do exist. They show that we do not treat all language as if its meaning required deciphering in the way a blueprint or a working drawing may have to be interpreted before the information it conveys is elicited; for if we did, then it would seem as appealing and natural to hang texts on the wall as it would to display an engineer's blueprint of a cathedral in order to be able to appreciate the spiritual magnificence of that edifice. If we regarded all language as we do the disposable prose of telegrams, prose designed purely to convey information (*RPP*,I, 325) – if we could not see the meaning of forms of words manifest in their faces just as we see emotions manifest in the faces of old friends, or sense the absolute specificity of those respective physiognomies – then it would make no sense for us to employ texts in the ways we do.

Let us step back for a moment from the detail of Wittgenstein's examples and remind ourselves of their general import. The ways in which we choose and value our words manifest the sense in which we think of them as having familiar physiognomies: these physiognomies consist in the highly specific identity conferred upon them by their place in the structure of the language as a whole *and* by the system of associations and circumstances within which the specific techniques of their use locate them. In effect, then, our inclination to regard *words* as having assimilated these tie-ups is a reflection of the degree to which *we* have assimilated those words; our attachment to them indicates our familiarity with and mastery of them. It therefore indicates in addition the inappropriateness of the interpretative model of our relationship to language: the words of a natural language are too close to us to require that their meaning be read off or hypothesized. Continuous meaning perception is designed to highlight the sense in which words are ready-to-hand for us.

PRIMARY AND SECONDARY MEANING

Of all the examples of our typical human tendency to regard words as having assimilated their meanings, however, the most glaring one in this context is the phenomenon of experiencing meaning itself; as we noted in the case of pictures and picture-objects, the capacity to experience aspect-dawning is a striking criterion of the corresponding attitude of continuous aspect perception. The point becomes obvious if we recall the question to which the meaning-blind are defined as being incapable of responding: 'Say the word "bank" and mean the bank of a river.' For such an instruction to make sense, one must be inclined to regard a word as something which carries its meaning on its face; to find talk of pronouncing a word in one or other of its meanings intelligible, when the situation in which one is pronouncing it lacks any contextual features which might determine which technique of using that word was being employed – indeed, when that situation is designed to highlight the fact that the ambiguous word retains the very same appearance and sound in all of its uses – is to exhibit in one's behaviour the feeling that beyond its visual and aural properties a word has a physiognomy which manifests its meaning and which can be emphasized and experienced (*PI*, 218g).

The point which is of most interest about such cases, however, is that they manifest a sense of words as having physiognomies in a *second* way. The experience of meaning is characterized by a willingness to employ the word 'meaning' as the *Ausserung* of an experience undergone in very specific circumstances – to talk of saying a word in one meaning rather than another; but as we saw earlier in this chapter, the standard use of the word 'meaning' is to report a speaker's intentions or to describe the technique of a given word's use (e.g. with reference to word-synonymy, explanations of meaning, and so on). In the context of the experience of meaning, none of these questions of use and purpose has any obvious application, for the given words are uttered in isolation, apart from the practice of linguistic interchange and divorced from contexts which would determine which of their meanings was dominant (*PI*, 215c) – and yet we are inclined to use the word 'meaning' here too.

This highly specific use of 'meaning' therefore differs significantly from its standard one (i.e. its use in questions of understanding word-meaning), but it would be wrong to suppose that we could use another word entirely for the new context (*RPP*,I, 685): we could not express what we want to say about pronouncing a word in isolation except through using the word 'meaning', with all the implications it carries as a result of its familiar use (*PI*, 216c). In other words, it is the term 'meaning' as the bearer of a specific technique (rather than as a mark with a particular appearance or sound) which we employ in this new context – we reach for the word as if it carries its original implications on its face, as if we can preserve those implications despite the alteration in circumstances which puts this in question. The 'game' of experiencing meanings thus exemplifies the general attitude of treating words as if they can take up their meaning into themselves, can absorb or assimilate the technique of their use (*PI*,

218g) in two ways. It is the word 'meaning' *as well as* whatever word is being said in one of *its* meanings that is being treated as if it had taken up its meaning into itself.

Of course, the inclination to take over an expression from its standard technique of use and employ it as a verbal *Ausserung* of an experience is precisely what characterizes *any* experience of aspect-dawning, whatever the object of that experience may be; to that degree, *any* experience of aspect-dawning reveals on the part of the perceiver that attitude towards language that we have been calling continuous meaning perception. In such contexts, the relevant word becomes an essential part of the expression of one's visual experience rather than simply an element of a perceptual report, and so its employment in that context is significantly different; but at the same time, it is as a word with a given meaning rather than as a meaningless sound that the word is felt to be an apt expression of that visual experience, so its use in this new context makes manifest the fact that one regards it as the specific word it is rather than a symbol whose meaning can be elicited only by interpretation. In this sense every experience of aspect-dawning reveals as much about one's relationship with language as it does with pictures or picture-objects.

To appreciate the full significance of this point, we need to explore it in more detail; for it then becomes clear that this sort of parasitic extension and transformation of language is present on two levels in any aspect-dawning experience. We can begin to explore the first level by noting that, for any aspect-dawning experience, if we are to be capable of regarding the relevant *Ausserungen* as bearers of specific techniques, we must – tautologically – be acquainted with those original techniques of use; in other words, the new mode of employing such words is parasitic upon the old. On this level, the parasitism is exemplified in two ways: the first has to do with the way we define the *kind* of aspect which dawns on us, and the second with the way we specify which *particular* aspect we have suddenly noticed. In certain situations (for example when we perceive a human face in a puzzle-picture) we find ourselves inclined to describe the kind of change involved as one relating to a change in the picture's organization – as if parts went together which before did not (*PI*, 208d); even though we know that no actual rearrangement of the picture's constituent parts has taken place, and so must be using the notion of 'organization' or 'going together' in a non-standard way (*PI*, 208c), it is the implications carried by the terms as bearers of those standard techniques of use which characterize the kind of change we have experienced. In a parallel way, the particular word we reach for to express our experience of aspect-dawning makes it clear which *particular* aspect has dawned; but someone capable of feeling it necessary to employ the words 'base' and 'apex' as part of his verbal *Ausserung* – rather than, for example, the term 'wedge' or 'mountain' – must be familiar with the different original meanings of those words (*PI*, 208e).

There remains, however, a *second* level at which this parasitic relationship between linguistic techniques is exemplified in any experience of aspect-dawning. This derives from the fact that the person experiencing the dawning of a pictorial aspect does not simply reach for the appropriate concept; he employs it in a particular form of words, as part of a behavioural syndrome, which implies that the perceived figure has altered its properties. In the case of the triangle, for example, such a person expresses himself as if the figure had changed its orientation on the paper (e.g. in response to the question 'Where is the apex of the triangle?' he says 'First I saw it up there, but now it's down here') rather than simply noticing that the same figure could represent differently oriented objects. For the form of words 'Now I'm *seeing* this as the apex' to make sense – to seem appropriate – to a given person, he must not only grasp the concept of an apex and be inclined to use it in this modified way, he must also be inclined to use the concept of 'seeing' in a similarly modified way. In effect, the concept of 'seeing' plays a role in the experience of aspect-dawning which is precisely analogous to that of the concept of 'meaning' in the experience of meaning.

This parasitic relationship between linguistic techniques is an instantiation of what Wittgenstein means by primary and secondary meaning (*PI*, 216c):

> Here one might speak of a 'primary' and 'secondary' sense of a word. It is only if the word has the primary sense for you that you use it in the secondary one.

> The secondary sense is not a 'metaphorical' sense. If I say 'For me the vowel *e* is yellow' I do not mean: 'yellow' in a metaphorical sense,– for I could not express what I want to say

in any other way than by means of the idea 'yellow'.

(*PI*, 216e,g)

As Wittgenstein's illustrative example of finding Wednesday fat or lean makes clear (*PI*, 216c,d), there are three key aspects to this notion of primary and secondary meaning. The first is that secondary uses of a given word do not illustrate but rather presuppose (and simultaneously go beyond) its primary use: even if I am inclined to regard Wednesday as fat rather than lean, I could not explain the meanings of 'fat' (or of 'lean') by pointing to the examples of Tuesday and Wednesday; I could only explain it in the usual way, employing verbal definitions or paradigmatic examples relating to the primary use of the word. Second, no other word would do to express my inclinations in these contexts: it is the word 'fat' with its familiar meaning, rather than any other word, which is the apt expression of my feelings with respect to the question about Wednesday. Third, the possibility of giving causal explanations of my inclination to employ a word in a secondary sense is irrelevant to the conceptual issue at stake here: it may be that I am inclined to call Wednesday fat rather than lean because in the past I was taught by a fat teacher on Wednesdays (*LW*,I, 795), but this does not explain away the inclination; it still constitutes the basis of a very specific sort of language-game.

The specificity of its nature might be stated as follows: in secondary language-games, words understood as the bearers of specific techniques of use are reached for as the only possible way in which to give expression to one's feelings, inclinations, and experiences. As we noted in the first chapter, then, the forms of words used to express experiences of aspect-dawning – being employed in a secondary sense – must be seen as criterially related to those experiences, in the sense that we have no means of assuming the existence or specifying the nature of such experiences independently of the felt need to use that specific piece of verbal behaviour in that particular context. However, it then follows that those incapable of so employing these forms of words must be deemed incapable of having the feelings, inclinations, and experiences which are thereby given expression: in the absence of the experience-expression and its behavioural analogues, we could have no grounds for attributing those feelings or experiences to a given person – such an attribution would make no sense.

This suggestion that the aspect-blind's relationship to language effectively shuts them out from ranges of human feeling and experience is confirmed by Wittgenstein's example of the geographical illusion (*PI*, 215d). This is an experience whose content is necessarily verbal in the sense that the relevant feeling is individuated by the person's felt need to employ the word 'knowing' or 'conviction' to express it; it is not that the phrase 'knowing the direction of X' is an accurate description of an experience which might exist independently of such verbal behaviour, but rather that the form of words is a defining manifestation of the experience – a primitive reaction (*PI*, 218b).

For Wittgenstein, in other words, our attachment to words – our tendency to assimilate them – is like the acquisition of a second nature: pre-linguistic reactions which are a part of human nature form the precondition for acquiring language in the first place; but the acquisition of forms of linguistic behaviour shapes that nature and leads in its turn to a new realm of spontaneous *linguistic* reactions – ones possible only because of one's mastery of language (*RPP*,I, 131).

In so far, then, as the aspect-blind lack the general capacity to comprehend the link between primary senses of words and their secondary senses, they reveal themselves to lack a range of 'primitive' linguistically shaped reactions. This lack crucially constrains their access to certain linguistic practices, just as a child's pre-linguistic reactions determine whether he can be taught to use language in the first place; and not all of those practices are purely expressive in function. One of Wittgenstein's examples of a secondary linguistic practice is that of calculating in the head (*PI*, 216f), comprehension of which is parasitic upon a grasp of calculating on paper or in the head; and the implication would seem to be that any linguistic practice the learning of which relies upon the student's capacity to see it as a variation upon (rather than an extension of) a previously acquired concept (*LW*,I, 69–70) would not be accessible to the aspect-blind *by this means*.

In addition, of course, such primary-secondary links between language-games confer patterning upon language as a whole, providing a means of achieving an *Übersicht* of very variable and varied terrain – an *Übersicht* which can aid one's mastery of the language. The question of the degree to which the logical geography of a language is run through with and given a unity by such similarities between linguistic structures is not one which can be answered a priori; but to the degree that it is, the aspect-blind will be fated to stumble around within it – competent to employ certain techniques, unable to grasp others, and blind to the patterning which makes such an agglomeration of linguistic suburbs into a city (*PI*, 18).

In general, however, the sorts of secondary use upon which Wittgenstein focuses are expressive in nature – from the example of Schubert's name to that of the geographical illusion, they provide a speaker with the means necessary for the articulation and individuation of feelings, inclinations, and experiences. This point should not be surprising if one reminds oneself of the structure of other forms of expressive human behaviour, such as ritual practices. The movement of thought embodied in magical practices to do with locks of a person's hair or effigies of that same person (e.g. burning a lock of hair stolen from one's enemy), and manifest in twentieth-century behaviour such as prizing the portrait of a loved one, is also central to the logic of primary and secondary meaning; things related to a given person (or technique) are taken to embody the essence of that person (or technique).

In this respect, aspect-blindness locks the sufferer out of language as an expressive medium: he is incapable of manifesting the reactions and related behaviour which alone would confer sense upon the attribution of such feelings to him. In his alienation from (rather than assimilation of) language, he is condemned to an impoverished inner life; he lacks the second nature which language confers upon human beings. Little wonder that Wittgenstein describes such a person's uncomprehending query about the justification of secondary uses as 'having a different racial origin, as it were' (*LW*,I, 56) – for it is the question of someone with a very different nature: it is as if the aspect-blind are a different race of people, 'a different type of man' (MS 169, p.2).

The importance of the connection between aspect perception and language should by now be clear; but it is by no means the only avenue of philosophical significance which opens up from Wittgenstein's writings on this topic. On the general level, given my claim that the attitude of continuous aspect perception is the true focus of Wittgenstein's concern with aspects, we are left with the question of whether the importance of that attitude is exhausted by its role in the domain of language; and on a more specific level, the context in which Wittgenstein's writings on aspect perception emerge independently suggests a link between aspect perception and two other specific areas of human life. First, the closing remarks of Section xi in *Philosophical Investigations* modulate from aspect perception to such matters as the relationship of psychological concepts to human behaviour and the consequent role of fine shades of behaviour; similar issues are interwoven with remarks on aspect perception in the manuscripts and typescripts from which this section was compiled, and this strongly suggests that aspect perception is closely tied up with matters in the philosophy of psychology. Secondly, as I have already noted in these chapters, another theme which weaves through Wittgenstein's remarks on aspect perception is that of aesthetics – in particular, the evaluation of music and painting.

The remainder of this book is structured according to the following assumptions: in order to approach the general question about the import of continuous aspect perception, I must first address the specific links suggested by the above remarks about context; and before I can deal with the link to aesthetics, I require clarity concerning the area of psychological concepts. Accordingly, in the next chapter I shall explore in some detail Wittgenstein's general view of psychological concepts, in an attempt to make clear the degree to which those views can only be correctly understood if seen in the light of his investigation of aspect perception.

3
ASPECTS OF THE PHILOSOPHY OF PSYCHOLOGY

Since this chapter covers a great deal of ground, it may be useful to offer a preliminary overview of its structure. The first section shows how Wittgenstein's private-language argument undermines any attempt to regard psychological concepts as referring to a duplicate realm of events and entities hidden within the human subject; and the second section shows that acceptance of this argument does not entail that psychological concepts must be treated as a species of behavioural concepts. The third section demonstrates that Wittgenstein's attempt to steer between dualist and behaviourist misconceptions of the mental results in a view of psychological concepts which can best be summarized by characterizing them as aspect concepts. The question of what might constitute continuous aspect perception in this domain is then raised; and a provisional answer is arrived at in the fourth and final section by developing an interpretation of the concept of aspect-blindness in opposition to one proposed by Stanley Cavell.

MYTHS OF THE INNER

In our everyday dealings with other people our knowledge of – and relationship towards – their moods, states of mind, and feelings seems bound up with a perception of their inner life as being hidden behind, and hinted at by means of, their outward behaviour. We speculate, with some interest, about the deep emotions concealed by a friend's placid exterior: we sometimes find it impossible to imagine what thoughts are going through a stranger's mind; and we might be unable to judge whether a grimace of pain masks an intention to deceive. When philosophers respond to this picture of 'inner' and 'outer' without careful examination of the precise techniques of its application, or of the specific grammatical relations between concepts of the inner and the outer which this picture dramatizes and conceals, they tend to construct myths of the inner. Cartesian philosophical systems, for example, embody the central tenet that inner states – whose perception in others is a matter of induction from external behavioural evidence – are identified in ourselves by means of some species of unmediated recognition, the inner eye having no barrier of flesh and blood to penetrate. Such direct acquaintance with our private inner events and processes (i.e. with the referents of our psychological concepts) is accordingly seen as the necessary ground of our capacity to grasp the content and significance of the huge array of corresponding concepts: for within the constraints of such a myth, attaching meaning to psychological terms could only come about through a mode of private ostensive definition – a ceremony of inward attention through which each human being confers upon himself the gift of a language for the inner.

The radical incoherence of this notion of a 'ceremony' is the guiding principle of Wittgenstein's exploration of the philosophy of psychology; it is therefore crucial that I begin this chapter by delineating the soundness of that principle. As Wittgenstein puts it in his later writings (*RPP*,I, 397), there is a direct and an indirect way of gaining insight into the impossibility of a private ostensive definition; and his example of the motor-roller illustrates this (cf. *Zettel*, 248). According to a certain design for the construction of a steam-roller, the motor is located inside the hollow roller whilst the crank-shaft runs through the middle of the roller and is connected at both ends by spokes to the roller wall; the cylinder is then fixed to the inside of the roller. At first glance this construction looks like a machine but in fact it is a rigid system and the piston cannot move to and fro in the cylinder. Just as we unwittingly deprived the motor-roller of all possibility of movement, so the private linguist deprives his ostensive definition of the capacity to perform its intended function; but this can be seen directly and indirectly in both situations. We might see directly that the motor-roller cannot function, since one could roll the cylinder from outside even when the 'motor' was not running; but we can also trace out the linkages of the mechanism from motor to roller and perceive thereby that it is a rigid construction and not a machine at all. In this brief exposition of the private language argument, we shall begin with the indirect method of perceiving the impossibility.

A private language consists of words which refer to the speaker's inner experiences – his sensations, feelings, moods, and the rest; since these inner experiences are regarded as entities whose presence or absence can be known only to the person whose experiences they are (i.e. since the terms of the language refer to epistemically private entities), it follows that another person is incapable of understanding the language which gives them expression. The point is not that another person is simply incapable of telling whether the words of this language are being used accurately, i.e. are being used only when their referent is present; it is rather that these words are *defined* by means of the entities to which they refer, so that another person's lack of epistemic access to those entities entails an inability to grasp the meaning of the terms which refer to them. The private linguist, however, claims to be able to understand and utilize the words of his private language because he can confer meaning upon them. He can (he asserts) use a term 'S' to refer to (e.g.) a sensation by associating the sign with the sensation and then employing the sign (perhaps by writing it in a diary) when the same sensation recurs in the future.

For the moment, we shall ignore any difficulties concerning the private linguist's capacity to grasp the concept of a 'sensation' (as the term is standardly used) in isolation from our natural expression of sensations, and instead concentrate upon the point that the ceremony by means of which the sign and the sensation are associated is intended to be a kind of definition of the sign 'S'. This basic conferral of meaning takes the form of an ostensive definition – the private linguist says the sign to himself and at the same time concentrates his attention on the sensation, as if inwardly pointing to it. Any definition, however, must be capable of being used as a standard for distinguishing between correct and incorrect use of the sign it governs; and since the sample sensation referred to in this putative ostensive definition is in principle accessible only to the private linguist, he alone is capable of employing that sample as part of a rule governing future uses of 'S'. In other words, if it can be shown that the private linguist cannot use the sample as a standard of correctness in the future, then the original ceremony cannot intelligibly be described as a 'definition' at all, and the private linguist's claim to be able to confer meaning on the terms of his language will have been shown to be empty.

Since the sign 'S' has been defined by reference to the type of sensation involved in the original ceremony, then – in order to mean something by 'S' when he uses it in the future – the private linguist must be able to produce an accurate memory of that particular sensation. The key question for the private linguist therefore becomes: are any criteria available to him which might give content to the notion of his being able to produce an accurate memory of the original sign-sensation correlation? Note that the question is posed at the conceptual level; we need to examine whether it *makes sense* to imagine the private linguist having an accurate memory of the sample sensation, rather than whether we can offer a cast-iron guarantee of the accuracy of this individual's memory on a given occasion. It is the intelligibility rather than the truth of the private linguist's claim to have remembered the sample sensation that is at issue.

Let us imagine a concrete situation: at some time after the original ceremony, the private linguist says 'I have "S"'. In order to check whether he has remembered correctly to which sensation 'S' refers, he calls to mind his memory of the sample sensation upon which he concentrated his attention in the original ceremony. The private linguist feels that this process of appealing from one memory to another is precisely analogous to the case of someone checking his memory of a train departure-time by calling to mind how a page of the timetable looked; and since the latter procedure is of a sort which is ubiquitous and unproblematic in everyday life, the former process must also be legitimate.

In fact, however, the analogy breaks down because the private linguist is not appealing from one memory to another, independent one. In order to check whether he has correctly remembered to which sensation 'S' refers (i.e. the meaning he claims to have conferred on 'S'), he calls to mind a memory of his original sign–sensation correlation – perhaps in the form of a mental table in which the sign 'S' is placed next to a memory-sample of the relevant sensation; but since this table exists only in his mind, all he can do is *remember* which sample goes with 'S', i.e. remember what 'S' means. And, of course, it is precisely his memory of what 'S' means that he is trying to confirm. The process of looking up a mental table to justify his memory of what 'S' means is not independent of what it is to justify; it is in fact merely a repetition of the process which stands in need of justification, and so cannot count as a 'justification' of it at all. It is precisely analogous to the case of someone buying a second copy of the morning newspaper in order to confirm the correctness of its constituent reports.

At this point, the private linguist might simply decide to rely upon the correctness of his memory; using his memory twice over may not strengthen his case, but this does not in itself entail that his memory is not to be relied upon at all. After all, in everyday life it is often the case that we have no independent means of justifying our memory-claims, but this does not render senseless the question of our memory's accuracy.

Here, we reach the crux of the argument. The private linguist's original ceremony was intended to ensure that 'S' was correctly used if and only if the type of sensation picked out in that ceremony recurred, and so it follows that the private linguist's memory of the sample-sensation can only be used as a standard of correctness if it is the *right* memory, i.e. if it is a memory of the sensation he originally labelled 'S', as opposed to one of another type of sensation or indeed of any other element in his stream of consciousness. Accordingly, before he can use his memory of the sample of 'S' as a standard of correctness, he must be able to show that this memory is correctly describable as a memory *of* 'S' (rather than of anything else); but *ex hypothesi* the only standard available for distinguishing between correct and incorrect use of 'S' is the memory of the sample itself. It is *not* that the private linguist must make use of the same memory a second time to confirm itself; rather, in order to remember what 'S' means, he must be capable of accurately remembering the sample of 'S', but in order to be capable of telling that it is indeed a memory of 'S', he must know what 'S' means. Before the private linguist can intelligibly use his memory of 'S' as a standard of correctness, he must first employ it as a standard of correctness in order to check upon its suitability for that role.

No sceptical claim about memory is being invoked here: Wittgenstein is not claiming that the private linguist has no means of verifying the accuracy of his memory, but rather that the very notion of his remembering the putative sign–sensation correlation *aright* lacks any criteria that might render it intelligible. In order to identify his memory as a memory of the sample of 'S', he must know what 'S' means (i.e. what counts as correct or incorrect applications of it), despite the fact that it is precisely this knowledge (of the meaning of 'S') that he is trying to remember. The private linguist makes incoherent demands on his memory, asking that it perform a task that cannot intelligibly be formulated; he has unwittingly constructed a rigid set of conceptual linkages and thereby deprived himself of the possibility of meaningful linguistic movement – for if it can make no sense to conceive of the private linguist as correctly remembering the sample sensation used in the original ceremony, and if that ceremony cannot therefore be said to have established a rule (a standard of correctness) governing the use of 'S', then the ceremony of private ostensive definition cannot intelligibly be described as a 'rule' or 'definition' at all. The idea that a system of rules for word use might be grounded on private ostensive definitions is simply incoherent.

To return to our analogy with the motor-roller: it was also possible to perceive *directly* that such a motor-roller could not function simply by noting that one could roll the cylinder from outside even when the 'motor' was not running; and the second strand of Wittgenstein's attack on private ostensive definition can be seen as involving an equally direct approach. It is best summarized in his story about the beetle in the box (*PI*, 293). The private linguist's conception of his inner world runs parallel to the following hypothetical situation: suppose that every human being has a box with something in it which we call a 'beetle', and suppose further that no one can look into anyone else's box, whilst everyone claims to know what a beetle is only by looking at his own specimen. Here, we can easily imagine that everyone has something different in his box, or that the contents of each box are subject to constant change; but if the word 'beetle' is to have a use in these people's language, it would not be used as the name of a thing. The object in the box can have no place in the language-game at all, not even as a 'something, I know not what', for it would be consistent with our hypothesis that each box be empty.

In saying, however, that we can divide through by the thing in the box, we are not denying the existence of the inner; we are rather rejecting a particular picture of the grammar of our concepts of the inner. Although that picture seems to underwrite the reality of the inner world by mythologizing psychological events, states, and processes as entities within that realm, it has the ironic consequence of evacuating that world of all substance; for if we construe the grammar of psychological concepts on the model of 'object and name', the object drops out of consideration as irrelevant.

Our indirect approach to this issue revealed that private ostensive definition cannot suffice to confer a technique of use upon the sign 'S' because it failed to establish any standard for distinguishing correct from incorrect uses of 'S'; our direct approach asserts, in effect, that once we assume that the sign 'S' *does* have a use in the language, the hypothesis of there being a private inner entity or process which it names stands revealed as doing no work at all. We should not, however, conclude from the demonstrated incoherence of the notion of a private language that human beings are incapable of referring to or speaking about their own psychological states and feelings; the point is rather that, in coming to see that the grammar of those concepts in terms of which we *do* refer to and speak of our inner life cannot intelligibly be construed on the model of *naming* objects, we also cease to regard the corresponding facets of our hearts and minds as types of *object* – i.e. as private entities for which a procedure of naming might be appropriate. Such a mythologized view of the inner feeds on and expresses a distorted grasp of psychological concepts: to view sensations, thoughts, and emotions as inner entities which are inductively correlated with their behavioural manifestations – as if human inhabitants of the world each *contained* a world as well – is to sever an internal relation without which the technique of employing the relevant psychological expression falls into incoherence. In a crucial sense, the private linguist goes wrong from the very first moment of his fantasy; he begins by taking it for granted that sensations can be divorced from their publicly accessible manifestations, and thus the whole tenor of his thinking is constrained by a failure to realize that the everyday concept of sensation (which he is attempting to explicate) is embedded in a practice which depends for its coherence upon the existence of external expressions and manifestations of the relevant 'inner event'. The best way to undermine any continued temptation towards such mythologized views of the inner must therefore be to sketch a picture of the grammar of our psychological concepts which makes evident the essential role played by human behaviour and its contexts in the application and explanation of psychological terms in general.

CONCEPTS OF THE INNER

The structure of psychological concepts manifests a first-person/third-person asymmetry which the mythological view of the inner we have been dissecting fails to register accurately; for whilst the possibility of error exists in third-person applications of psychological terms, that same possibility is excluded in the case of first-person present-tense uses of those terms. If it were correct to view the inner as a realm of epistemically private entities to which each person has sole access, then first-person present-tense psychological utterances would have to be viewed as descriptions of those entities; on such a model, however, it would be at best a contingent fact that a given speaker did not err in such descriptions – it would be logically possible for him to misdescribe the objects of his inward observation (just as he might misdescribe objects in the external world), and yet the hypothesis that a speaker might be in *error* concerning what he was thinking (as opposed to being deceitful about it) makes no sense. Our conceptual framework provides no conceivable grounds for doubts of this sort (cf. *LW*,I, 896–8); one might say that the function 'X is in error' has no value when X = the speaker.

The philosophical damage cannot be repaired by suggesting that a speaker's reports on the entities and events of his inner world have certainty conferred upon them because of the uniquely privileged perspective from which he observes them; for the conceptual point that error is logically excluded simultaneously excludes the possibility of regarding those 'reports' as conveying certain knowledge. The truth is that such utterances should not be regarded as observations at all – unlike the case of third-person applications of such terms, first-person psychological utterances do not rest upon any evidential basis; they function not as reports concerning the speaker's inner life but rather as manifestations of it, and in the absence of an evidential base the concept of 'error' lacks any purchase. The vision of human beings as observers of their own inner world requires a notion of a contrast between inner and outer evidence for psychological states in general, the assumption being that other people must build hypotheses about a given person's inner life on the basis of outward behavioural evidence in default of access to the inner evidence with which that observed individual is acquainted. The grammar of our psychological concepts reveals that there is no such thing as inner evidence for the application of such terms; and in removing one pole of the evidential dichotomy we thereby deprive the other pole of any significance (*LW*,I, 77).

Of course, for the advocates of this distorted vision of human beings and their relation to their inner world, the collapse of this evidential dichotomy is tantamount to a collapse of the distinction between concepts of the inner and concepts of the outer; if our only grounds for applying concepts of the inner must be sought in the field of human behaviour (in third-person applications of the relevant terms), has not the private-language argument simply effected a behaviouristic reduction of concepts of the inner to concepts of the outer? Such a conclusion is too hasty: it fails to see that a recognition of the lack of observational grounds for first-person present-tense psychological utterances does not signify a denial of the role played by the form of such utterances in the overall structure of psychological concepts; and it ignores the possibility that psychological concepts and behavioural concepts relate to the complex field of human behaviour and utterances in very different ways. It is these grammatical points which must now be investigated.

If we begin by noting the different ways in which concepts of the inner and concepts of the outer relate to human behaviour, it is at once possible to see the sense in which a grasp of aspect perception can facilitate our movements within this conceptual space; for, just as we saw in Chapter 1 that aspect concepts seem to transcend immediate perceptual experience by invoking non-visual relations and references (*PI*, 209b ff), so we might express the difference between concepts of the inner and concepts of the outer in a preliminary way by suggesting that, whilst behavioural concepts avoid invoking references and relations which go beyond pure descriptions of perceived bodily movements and patterns of behaviour, psychological concepts relate to *aspects* of the human behaviour we observe (*PI*, 179a). To describe that behaviour unhesitatingly in terms of psychological rather than behavioural concepts is to manifest the adoption of a certain attitude towards it

– it is to treat that behaviour as directly expressive of an inner life.

The difference in meaning between psychological concepts and bare behavioural ones can be said to rest in part upon the fact that it is behaviour-in-context that is the bearer of psychological significance. We can begin to explore the role of 'context' here by noting that in becoming a fully-fledged member of a human community a person gains access to a complex weave of expressive behaviour, including modes of facial expression and of more general bodily movements which count as manifestations of inner states. At least part of the expressive significance of any gesture or facial arrangement, however, depends upon the field of other possible expressions and gestures which form part of the culture's repertoire; it is in contrast to these other points on a given dimension of variation that the identity of any one such point or possibility is constituted and its impact upon (or significance for) an observer derived. Take the concept of a facial expression: it could not be acquired by someone who had seen examples of only one facial expression, who had only ever seen sad faces, for that concept has its existence only within a play of the features (*LW*,I, 766); teaching the concept to him requires isolating a particular dimension of variation by pointing to samples of different points along that dimension – it involves conveying one particular way in which objects can vary, can differ from and resemble one another. This means that the significance of the dimension as a whole and of the specific points along it are intrinsically interdependent: the general dimension of variation is defined by the various points along it, and each specific point is given by its difference from the other points – to say that a face was sad would mean something very different if our concepts picked out only two different facial expressions.

It follows then, that part of what makes a joyful smile what it is (for example) is the fact that it differs from an uncertain smile or an angry grimace; but the point applies to much more general patterns of human behaviour. Grief, for instance, is an emotion manifest in certain sorts of facial expression, bodily gestures, and utterances. If, however, such grieving behaviour alternated every five seconds with a pattern of joyful behaviour, then it would not make sense to give either behavioural pattern its normal psychological designation; and if the person concerned had only two modes of behaviour open to him (e.g. anger and joy), so that his facial expression and general behaviour could not embody any other pattern, then neither available pattern could have its usual psychological significance. We can thus perceive one sense in which the psychological import of human behaviour depends upon its context – the context here being the field of expressive possibilities bequeathed to a person by his culture and by those natural reactions of his own upon which any culture builds.

Another sense of 'context' that is relevant here is the sense that our application of a specific psychological concept to a given facet of human behaviour is grammatically related to the antecedents and consequences of that behaviour – in such a way that identical behaviour, when embedded in different 'narrative' backgrounds, carries very different psychological significance. A child who is crying because she fell over and grazed her knee would thereby be manifesting pain, but the same behaviour on the part of a child who has lost her mother would be a manifestation of anxiety. In these examples, it becomes clear that treating human behaviour as a manifestation of one psychological state rather than another is equivalent to regarding it as an intelligible human response to the circumstances embodied in the relevant background.

A similar point can be made with reference to the relation between the behaviour said to manifest an inner state and the *consequent* pattern of behaviour exhibited by the person concerned. An expression of thoughtful concentration on a particular task, if followed by a series of careless or mechanical attempts to perform that task, would contribute towards depriving the original attribution of 'thoughtfulness' of any sense. In general, part of the function of ascribing psychological states to someone is to pick out certain patterns of future behaviour which it might be reasonable to expect from that person – a function whose point is obvious given the impact that the behaviour of others may have upon our own plans and way of life.

However, none of this implies the existence of a *necessary* connection between certain modes of present and future behaviour; it is simply that (in contradistinction to behavioural concepts) any given attribution of a psychological state to a given person's present behaviour makes sense only if, in general, that behaviour hangs together with a characteristic context of behaviour – in terms of both antecedents and consequents – in the absence of which the grounds for applying that concept are undercut.

The motivational antecedents made manifest in the context of the behaviour (i.e. the 'occasion' of the behaviour) assumes greater importance as the sophistication of the psychological states attributable to the subject increases. In more primitive contexts – if, for example, we see someone writhing in agony in a pool of blood – the existence of natural expressions of the sensation of pain provides a ground for ascription of pain; but there is no such thing as the natural expression of someone dissimulating pain (*LW*,I, 44). In order to justify a claim that a child, on a given occasion, is crying in order to attract attention rather than as a result of being in some pain, we cannot simply point to her crying behaviour; we must rather convince our interlocutor that the child intends to gain attention, which involves a reliance on the knowledge that the pleasure consequent upon having sympathy directed towards one provides a plausible motive for the relevant behaviour in this context.

The same point can be made for other concepts, such as that of lying, which have no associated natural expression in behaviour; in general, it is part of our understanding of lying that there be an intelligible motive for so doing, that there be something which occasions it. This does not, of course, mean that motiveless lying is a contradiction in terms: part of the horror in *Othello* is precisely due to our perception that Iago's motives for hounding his master are inadequate or non-existent – but would the evil he thereby represents be so terrifying if such an absence of motive were commonplace? If such exceptional cases became the rule, our concept of lying would lose its point (*RPP*,I, 780).

At this stage, it becomes relevant to note that the aspect of human behaviour-in-context which is perhaps most significant in grounding attributions of sophisticated psychological states is linguistic behaviour. However, in order to appreciate the full force of this remark, we should first acknowledge the way in which looking at language-use as a complex form of human behaviour clarifies the relation between linguistic and non-linguistic behaviour at a more primitive level. This relation is of course most evident in the situation of teaching and training children in the employment of first-person utterances, but an examination of such contexts is not intended to imply that questions of conceptual genesis are at issue; it is rather meant to highlight a conceptual connection between language-use and non-linguistic expressive behaviour which would obtain even if human beings entered the world with a fully-fledged linguistic capacity. To take the case of pain and pain-behaviour, for example (*PI*, 244): a child who has hurt himself cries and flinches, and an adult can then teach him first exclamations and later complete sentences to use in such circumstances in the future.

Three crucial points follow from this description of the form linguistic training typically takes. First, the possibility of teaching and training in this sphere would seem to depend upon the existence of more primitive natural expressions of the relevant inner state or event in the child's behavioural repertoire, since in their absence the notion of circumstances in which it would be appropriate to use a given linguistic utterance would lack any content. Second, the description suggests that such linguistic behaviour should be treated not as a report based on observational grounds but as a replacement for more primitive non-linguistic behaviour, and so as performing the function of a *manifestation* of the speaker's inner life. Third, whilst in one sense the linguistic behaviour substitutes for non-verbal behaviour, in another sense it constitutes an *extension* of it by giving the child access to more complex forms of human behaviour.

This last point is of central importance. If the process of teaching and learning a language is seen to involve the gradual acquisition of increasingly complex structures as an extension of the more primitive ones already mastered, it follows that teaching concepts such as 'intention' or 'hope' – which (unlike sensations) are not manifest so overtly in specific forms of primitive non-verbal behavioural reaction – can begin with the inculcation of a relatively primitive fragment of *linguistic* practice, and therefore requires only a correspondingly primitive fragment of *non*-linguistic behaviour to be a part of the pupil's repertoire. If, for example, a child who is placed inside a cot with a toy just beyond his reach outside the railings proceeds to stretch out his hand towards the object and express annoyance when he fails to grasp it, it would be appropriate to say that he was trying to reach the toy; and it would also be an appropriate context in which to begin teaching him how to express his intentions by using the word 'want'.

It may seem that the above type of account is not appropriate for all psychological concepts; for example, it is not clear what sort of primitive behaviour in a child who has not learnt to speak might constitute a natural expression of hope. Difficulties are generated here, however, primarily because of a tendency to concentrate upon non-verbal behaviour exclusively, and thus to forget that as soon as certain (admittedly primitive) forms of linguistic behaviour are mastered, the pupil thereby gains access to the sort of logical space necessary for the manifestation of certain sophisticated inner states. 'Hope' is in fact a good example of what is meant here (*PI*, 174a). If a child crawls towards the door, then turns and asks 'Daddy home?' before turning back to the door, it would make sense to say that she was hoping that her father would return, and we could then perhaps begin to teach her the relevant primitive fragment of our linguistic practices with the concept. And of course as her command of past and future tenses develops, so the child will acquire the type of linguistic behaviour necessary for the attribution of more complex modes of hope to be rendered intelligible.

The preceding description of language acquisition can thus be seen as embodying two general conceptual morals. First, it shows that the denial of the mythological vision of the inner (i.e. the refusal to treat first-person psychological utterances as reports about observed inner entities) does not leave us bereft of an account of the process of learning to employ such utterances: despite their not being employed on the basis of evidence, their correct use can be seen as a matter of employing them in appropriate circumstances (e.g. in the case of 'I'm in pain', only when the speaker is in pain), and thus of the pupil assimilating the relevant forms of words into his behavioural repertoire. Second, this description highlights the fact that the grounds for ascribing psychological states and occurrences to a given person lie in the complex field of behaviour-in-context by emphasizing that the process of teaching the relevant first-person utterance (i.e. of grafting it on to more primitive behavioural forms) is controlled by a grasp of which patterns of non-verbal behaviour can intelligibly be treated as expressive of the psychological state involved. Once the linguistic version of this behavioural pattern is correctly assimilated by the pupil, he is now capable of exhibiting modes of behaviour which might make the attribution of more sophisticated psychological states intelligible.

In other words, the point about the earlier description of the child's primitive hoping behaviour is that the precise meaning of her utterance is an essential element within it; it alone permits us to suggest that the child has something specific in mind, and to relate that specific something to the other aspects of her behaviour in that context in a way which gives point to our application of the concept of hope. There are, however, additional and equally important respects in which the precise form of words uttered by a speaker should be seen as internally related to the precise type of inner state thereby made manifest. This becomes evident in the expressive aspect of language in general.

To begin with, a central part of understanding many linguistic utterances is the capacity to see them as expressive of the particular human being who utters them. Take as an example our hearing someone say 'I am afraid': we will almost never have to ask the speaker whether he was making fun of his fear, discovering it in himself, reluctantly confessing it or expressing it like a scream, because our awareness of the tone of voice and context of the utterance is enough to provide this information. Just as human behaviour-in-context is expressive of mind, so the linguistic behaviour of human beings can give expression to the speaker's inner state when perceived in context. And just as human behaviour in general – with its flexibility and variety of facial expression and bodily movement – has the logical multiplicity necessary for the application of a complex field of psychological concepts, so such elements of verbal behaviour as intonation, inflection, and the speed and rhythms of the utterance provide a similar multiplicity within a more narrow focus for the application of those concepts.

There remains, however, a further respect in which language-use must be viewed as expressive of mind. A human being in a state of deep despair may come across Marlowe's line in *Dr Faustus* ('perpetual cloud descends') and acknowledge it as a uniquely appropriate articulation of the state of mind in which he finds himself; it may even be a means of allowing him to understand more clearly the precise nature of his own mood and feelings by permitting him to put that facet of his inner world to words for the first time. It is a commonplace of artistic criticism that the process of a widening education in poetry and literature is simultaneously a process of clarifying and extending our comprehension of the possible varieties of human suffering, exaltation, and experience; and it is undeniable that certain aspects of our appreciation of certain types of aesthetic object rest upon a capacity to respond to (and find assimilable) certain complex modes of manifesting psychological states and attitudes.

Such aesthetic understanding – that specific field of human relationships to language, the world and other people – is simply one example of a more general phenomenon, one which is evident, amongst other ways, in the case of primary and secondary meanings of terms. As we saw in Chapter 2, three related qualities characterize the primary-secondary meaning relationship: it is only if a word has a primary sense for the speaker that he can use it in the secondary one; the secondary sense is not 'metaphorical', in that no alternative word could express what the speaker wants to say; and explanations of secondary meaning can only make use of examples of the word's primary employment. As I also pointed out in that earlier chapter, a large proportion of the examples of words with primary and secondary senses that Wittgenstein offers fall across the boundary between the inner and the outer realms in the following way: primary senses tend to refer to the public, intersubjective world whilst secondary senses tend to relate to the inner world of the subject. This is true of 'calculating' and 'calculating in the head'; 'unreality' and the 'feeling of unreality'; 'fitting' and the feeling that a name 'fits' its bearer; 'word-meaning' and the 'experience of word-meaning'; knowing where a city lies and feeling as if we knew; and so on. The general way of stating the parallel primary-secondary/outer-inner relationship which we employed in that earlier context was that it only makes sense to say that someone has had certain experiences (feelings, inclinations) if he manifests linguistic behaviour of a sort which presupposes his mastery of a public, intersubjectively checkable technique (*PI*, 208).

Thus, it became clear that a large range of inner states, attitudes and experiences are made manifest in a person's behaviour by his finding a certain form of words appropriate in a given context – indeed, the relevant concepts can only intelligibly be applied to another person on the basis of his uttering the appropriate form of words. In effect, this highlights the role of linguistic behaviour as a complex field which permits fine-grained distinctions between a person's psychological states in the absence of apppropriate distinctions being manifest in non-verbal behaviour (e.g. the difference between a dull ache and a throbbing pain). Furthermore, the point that a given speaker's capacity to employ the relevant terms in their secondary sense is dependent upon his having mastered the technique of their primary employment suggests a way in which that speaker's linguistic training might plausibly lead to his assimilating such secondary senses of words and going on to use them in appropriate contexts.

Putting these two observations together, we can reinforce the conclusion that, contrary to certain mythical views of the inner, a human being's inner states are not merely inductively and externally related to the repertoire of behaviour through which he makes them manifest. Rather, the gradual acquisition of increasingly complex patterns of linguistic behaviour should be seen as being at the same time the provision of expanding access to a sophisticated field of verbal reaction which can assist in *constituting* as well as refining the form and structure of his self-expression and thereby of his inner life.

Of course, in suggesting that clarity follows from regarding first-person psychological utterances as being on the same level (as it were) as non-linguistic elements of a person's behaviour, we are in effect simply highlighting the asymmetry between first-person and third-person uses of psychological expressions from a slightly different perspective. For whilst third-person uses of such terms *are* grounded on observation of the subject's behaviour, to say that first-person uses of the same terms should be treated as linguistic behaviour which is an *expression* of the subject's psychological state is equivalent to saying that it should not be viewed as a description based on self-observation. The *subject* is certainly not basing *his* utterance on observation of his own actions or behaviour; but since that utterance is not thereby being treated as a bare noise, this view of first-person psychological expressions avoids anything which might be sensibly regarded as behaviourist reductionism. Since the private-language argument showed that such linguistic expressions are not based on observation of epistemically private entities, the conclusion would seem to follow that such utterances are not the result of *any* sort of observation.

This conclusion is itself essentially a restatement of the grammatical remark with which this section of the chapter began: namely that the concepts of doubt and error (i.e. of the subject's making a mistake) have no application to first-person present-tense psychological utterances. This can easily be made explicit. If a person's relation to his own behaviour *did* parallel that of his relation to another person's behaviour with respect to the ascription of psychological states, i.e. if he had to make both types of ascription by observing the relevant person's behaviour, then the types of doubts and errors which can occur in the case of ascribing such states to others could also occur in the case of ascribing them to himself. Yet it is precisely this type of error which is excluded in the case of first-person psychological utterances, and which is another of the logical distinguishing marks of psychological concepts. If, for example, all uses of the form of words 'I was lying' were the result of inferences made from the speaker's observation of his own behaviour, then that utterance could never be used as a *confession* (*RPP*,I, 703), i.e. it would lose its characteristic role, one in which the issue of whether the speaker has made a mistake cannot intelligibly be raised.

A further way of expressing this asymmetrical immunity from error would be to say that, in a situation where we are attempting to discover someone's psychological state, the truth of that person's own expression of his inner state is guaranteed if he is sincere, whereas the sincerity of our ascription of a given state to him is not enough to guarantee its truth (*PI*, 224f). The special role of first-person utterances in the grammar of psychological concepts is thus that special applications can be made of (special consequences drawn from) confessions whose truth is guaranteed by their truthfulness. The fact that doubts can be raised concerning third-person ascriptions which make no sense in the case of the corresponding first-person form means, for example, that if a person's future behaviour fails to hang together with the nature of the psychological state to which he earlier gave linguistic expression we can exclude the hypothesis that the subject misidentified his inner state from consideration as an explanation of the discrepancy.

We might therefore summarize the conclusions of this section as follows: psychological concepts retain their distinctiveness from behavioural ones despite the absence of epistemically private entities as referents of those concepts. In treating human behaviour as expressive of an inner life, we are applying to it concepts which relate essentially to behaviour-in-context and which embody a first-person/third-person asymmetry: and these are elements which logically distinguish psychological from behavioural concepts.

What must now be made more explicit is the sense in which we can legitimately treat psychological concepts as aspect concepts.

ASPECTS AND THE INNER

In the first section of this chapter, we saw that psychological concepts cannot be dismissed as candidates for the category of aspect concepts on the ground that they refer not to facets of human behaviour but to a realm of entities and processes which is entirely distinct from that of the behavioural: to regard these concepts in that way is to fall victim to an ultimately incoherent mythology of the inner. The second section of the chapter blocked off the other obvious way of denying that psychological concepts relate to facets of human behaviour, viz. that of claiming that such concepts relate *purely* to behaviour, that they are in fact behavioural concepts. To make such a claim is to fall victim to the obverse or underside of the first mythology we identified, by assuming that a denial of that particular fiction of the inner is equivalent to the denial of the inner itself. I had already noted an initial similarity between aspect concepts as they were described in the previous two chapters and the psychological concepts we have been examining here: namely that concepts of the inner invoke references and relations which go beyond the bare behaviour exhibited by human beings in just the way that aspect concepts applied to visual symbols invoke references and relations which are not purely visual. Having now advocated a perspective on psychological concepts in which linguistic expressions are treated as sophisticated refinements and extensions of non-verbal behaviour, we are in a position to see that there are further respects in which concepts of the inner resemble our paradigmatic aspect concepts.

We saw earlier, for example, that the capacity to perceive a particular aspect of a given object (of a cipher, or a painting) presupposed a grasp of a general dimension of variation in terms of which the object could be located by comparison and contrast with other objects (*PI*, 209b, 210b), and that this dimension was articulated in the relevant conceptual technique. It has been one of my central aims in this chapter to show that precisely the same points can be made about facets of human expressive behaviour, and to reveal thereby the role of our linguistic practice in the provision of this particular frame of reference. The expressive significance of (e.g.) a facial expression is partly *constituted* by contrast with the other facial expressions which our system of psychological concepts picks out as such. In other words, what we *mean* by a specific psychological term is partly constituted by its relations of contrast with other such concept-terms in the system; and the usefulness (as well as the possibility) of applying that system of concepts to human behaviour rests upon the fact that human linguistic and non-linguistic behaviour-in-context exhibits a corresponding variability and multiplicity – indeed it is this logical multiplicity in human behaviour that is often projected upon a hypothetical inner world of subtly differentiated entities and processes by those attached to mythical views of the inner. We thus have no reason to regard psychological concepts as significantly different in nature from the pictorial and linguistic aspects we examined earlier: they do not pick out a separate realm of entities hidden behind human behaviour, but rather constitute a system which applies to the behaviour itself, but in ways which differ significantly from purely material (i.e. behavioural) concepts. They take up *aspects* of such behaviour.

If this assertion is correct, then we should be able to find analogues of the key conceptual categories Wittgenstein identifies in other areas of aspect perception in the realm of psychological concepts. As is often the case in this investigation, examples of aspect-dawning are by far the easiest to come by; and, again as one might expect, the examples which predominate are of aspect-dawning without a change of aspect – analogues to living pictures rather than to duck-rabbits. There are many occasions in which one is profoundly struck by the particular shade of consciousness manifest in someone's expression or behaviour; on such occasions, it is not just that we see *that* the person is fearful or joyful – we *see* the fear in his stance, the joy in her face. Similar experiences might be cited in relation to language as well as to facial expression or behaviour; for in certain contexts, we can *experience* the expressive meaning of a form of words, *hear* the emotion in an utterance.

For the purposes of this book, however, the most important consequence of regarding psychological concepts as aspect concepts is the implication that *continuous* aspect perception might be the appropriate way of categorizing our ordinary attitude towards the behaviour of others. As in earlier chapters, the central way of elucidating the nature of that attitude must be in contrast with that of aspect-blindness: we must ask ourselves what the difference might be between *seeing* in terms of the relevant aspects and merely *knowing* that such aspects are there to be seen. Since, however, the notion of aspect-blindness was not specifically defined by Wittgenstein with respect to the sphere of other minds, we can only apply it within that sphere by imagining what a consistent extension of it from the analogous situation with respect to pictures and words might be.

Aspect-blindness in relation to pictures involved the need to interpret what the picture might be intended to represent from a direct perception of its arrangement of colours and shapes, i.e. from its properties as a material object in its own right; and the forms of verbal and non-verbal behaviour which characterize such blindness were seen to be manifestations of a certain general attitude towards pictures – a mode of treating them which revealed an orientation towards them as *material* objects rather than as representative symbols or *meaningful* objects. This was my interpretation of Wittgenstein's remark that the aspect-blind regard pictures as we do blueprints – they could not immediately see the pictured scene or object in the picture.

If this is a correct reading of how the aforementioned relation of knowing is to be understood, then the analogous application of the concept of aspect-blindness in the sphere of psychological concepts must be one in which the aspect-blind need to infer or hypothesize the psychological significance of a piece of behaviour from an immediate perception of its constituent behavioural elements: rather than seeing the friendliness of a glance, they infer from the shape, colour, and movement of the perceived glance that it must have been friendly (*RPP*,I, 1102). The aspect-blind thus manifest an orientation towards human behaviour in which it is treated as *behaviour* rather than as *human* behaviour – they do not treat it as behaviour expressive of mind.

It follows by contrast that continuous aspect perception is characterized by modes of verbal and non-verbal behaviour which reveal that one is treating the other's behaviour as *human* behaviour – as behaviour which *is* expressive of mind. The most prominent manifestation of this attitude – as always – has to do with the immediacy or readiness-to-hand of the relevant forms of description: someone who spontaneously and unhesitatingly describes the behaviour of others in terms of psychological concepts, who would find it unnatural and difficult to describe what he sees in terms of purely behavioural concepts, who does not regard his description in terms of psychological concepts as one option among many – such a person thereby makes manifest the fact that he regards the behaviour of others as human behaviour, as precisely the sort of behaviour it is.

This emphasis on the immediacy of forms of description does not, however, exhaust our means of characterizing continuous aspect perception in the domain of psychological concepts. Further points suggest themselves, once again upon the model of points employed in other domains to characterize the analogous attitude. We might begin by mentioning an element of the general *Gestalt* built up in psychological concepts which has been left in abeyance thus far, viz. the relation that those ascribing the given psychological state have towards its manifestation in another person. We noted earlier that if someone's 'smiling' expression were merely one of three which he or she was able to adopt, it would not be what we call a smile; and part of the reason for that is not just the truncated field of expressive contrasts in which it is embedded but also our own consequent inability to respond towards it as we do towards a smiling face (cf. *LW*,II, 111). The response of others to a certain psychological state in another partly characterizes that inner state: pain is something we respond to in others by sympathizing or failing to do so, love and hatred in another person are not phenomena to which we are indifferent, being certain that someone else is glad to see me involves feeling secure in my own pleasure (*LW*,II, 58). The same point holds for concepts not so closely linked to the emotions; a certain society might consist of people who regarded lying behaviour by others as a sign of madness, and who therefore responded to its manifestation by locking up those who were caught acting in that way. Would this be our concept of lying?

In other words, a crucial aspect of understanding a psychological concept involves grasping the role of the relevant technique in the form of life concerned. It picks out a mode of human behaviour towards which we are very likely to have a certain attitude, since the behaviour of others affects us and since the mode of behaviour concerned is accessible to us in our own life – it is an option we can adopt or shun. As in the examples of continuous aspect perception examined in earlier chapters, therefore, this reaction to human behaviour as the specific human behaviour it is manifests a particular orientation or attitude towards what one is perceiving: unless one were taking its status as a particular form of *human* behaviour for granted, one could hardly be so immediately and unhesitatingly sensitive to its more fine-grained features or to its general value in human intercourse.

A related point – one which is also dependent upon the particular grammar of psychological concepts – is even more pertinent. If the significance of a given segment of human behaviour as a manifestation of the inner is dependent upon the characteristic antecedents and consequents which hang together with a given psychological state, as well as upon the field of contrasting modes of behaviour available within the relevant culture, then a familiarity with the culture itself must be crucial for the capacity to apply the relevant concepts in an intelligible way. This sort of information is not likely to be given to us merely by asking the inhabitants of that culture, since, although they learn the relevant concepts against the background of these available contrasts and patterns, they do not thereby learn to describe that background: a familiarity generated through experience would therefore seem to be required.

Of course, a similar point holds at the level of individuals as well as of individual cultures. The multi-faceted array of facial expressions, gestures, and behaviour syndromes acquired by one individual will not be identical to that of any other, nor to that of a hypothetical set of Platonic ideal types stored in their shared culture – and minor deviations from expected paradigms might therefore carry great psychological significance. Only extended acquaintance with the individual concerned can generate the familiarity with his own repertoire of expressive behaviour which is essential for psychological concepts to be applied to him with any subtlety or fine shading.

These points are not, of course, intended as empirical hypotheses concerning the amount of experience necessary to master the application of psychological concepts. They are rather intended to highlight the fact that our typical mastery of those concepts is not so much a question of learning universal rules as a matter of knowing one's way around within a cultural or personal world – a world in which specific co-ordinates are defined by relations of similarity and contrast with other co-ordinates, and make sense only against a background or frame of reference which is taken for granted. Another way of putting this would be to say that a capacity to respond to the specificity of the given cultural or personal world presupposes or manifests an unhesitating recognition of that world *as the world of a person*: unless one regarded his or her behaviour as behaviour expressive of mind, one could hardly respond to it as giving expression to a particular mind in a particular way. We saw earlier that such knowing one's way around in a particular realm characterizes continuous aspect perception; now we can also see that this familiarity is related to one's familiarity with the relevant conceptual technique in the specific and varied contexts of its application.

We can now perhaps appreciate more fully the aptness of Wittgenstein's 'physiognomy' metaphor in capturing our sense of the readiness-to-hand of words. The familiar physiognomy of a friend's face, and the familiar physiognomy of a word's face: both forms of expression make manifest our sensitivity to the unique identity of that which we are observing, to our sense that they each make up a world that we have assimilated and in which we are at home. Thus, our knowing someone well comes out in the unhesitating way we take for granted the genuineness or insincerity of his expressive behaviour: our familiarity with the fine shades of his behaviour sensitizes us to the precise shade of consciousness to be seen in his face and gestures, and so we come to know our way around with him – his habits, tastes, enthusiasms, and typical modes of expressing or concealing his thoughts and feelings. A crucial part of this understanding is thus a matter of being able to make the right connections – to see a particular expression as a manifestation of a precise state of mind, to link that inner state with something in the situation to which that person is likely to have responded, to foresee just how his future behaviour will reveal or repress that response and what the consequences of such revelation or repression might be.

As we saw in Chapter 2, a precisely analogous capacity for moving around within tie-ups is part of linguistic understanding – the full significance of a given utterance may depend upon its precise nature as a form of words (what sort of person from what sort of background would choose to express himself that way?) and upon the precise choice of words within the phrase, a choice which takes account of the field of force of a given word and the tie-ups of similarity and contrast with related words. In all these ways, linguistic understanding can be seen to involve a sensitivity to the specificity of the utterance, an awareness of the specific physiognomy it turns to our gaze. Indeed, we might regard this linguistic application of the word 'physiognomy' to be not so much a metaphorical as a *secondary* use of the word – for what other word has the implications that this one amasses from its primary use in relation to facial expressions, implications which we need to express the similarities in conceptual structure and attitude which we can now see in the domains of language and of people?

With this analogy between words and people in mind, we should note in conclusion a further feature of our typical attitude to human behaviour that has emerged in this chapter. My delineation of psychological concepts and their grammar revealed the application of such concepts to involve reference to certain characteristic surroundings of human behaviour – not just to a given type of behavioural pattern but also a relation of that pattern to the occasion of the behaviour and to certain types of consequent reactions and behaviour. These concepts, in effect, draw together a certain *Gestalt* of behaviour (including future actions), utterance, and occasion; but even though the relation between the elements in the general pattern helps to constitute the meaning of the relevant psychological expression, their interconnections are not *necessary* ones. Human behaviour exhibits little of the identity of circumstances, of reactions to given circumstances, or of the exact similarity of future behaviour manifest by those in a given state which might give point to a conceptual structure in which such elements were necessarily yoked together. On the other hand, human behaviour *does* involve the sort of rough and approximate regularities which render useful the application of a set of concepts which treat it as falling into a variety of loose patterns that reappear.

If, however, our psychological concepts are such that a looseness of fit between the elements of certain behavioural *Gestalts* is postulated, then our capacity to apply them must involve an ability to perceive human life as 'the same occurring again – but with variations', i.e. a capacity to respond to new combinations of behaviour, utterance, and circumstance as a variation on one of the loose patterns. This point applies not only to the variety of human circumstances encountered by adults in their day-to-day existence;

it applies also to the learning process whereby a child's grasp of very simple, rudimentary psychological states is transformed (refined, extended) through time and experience into the grasp of an adult upon larger types of variety and complexity. He, too, must be capable of treating the latter type of pattern as a more complex variant of the former; and since in this respect he resembles someone capable of seeing bare schematic drawings as pictures of rabbits, i.e. since both such capacities involve drawing relations of comparison with other examples of things falling under a certain conceptual dimension or system (whether that of rabbit pictures and rabbits or of psychological states), we can provide a further ground for regarding the perception of psychological states as a type of continuous aspect perception.

The above preliminary points should be sufficient to allay any fears that the notion of aspect perception is being extended illicitly to the psychological realm; what we must now do is to explore the philosophical significance of that extension by examining in more detail the consequences that aspect-blindness might have in this domain.

BLIND TO THE INNER

> Imagination is called for faced with the other, when I have to take the facts in, realize the significance of what is going on, make the behaviour real for myself, make a connection. 'Take the facts in' means something like 'see his behaviour in a certain way', for example, see his blink as a wince, and connect the wince with something in the world that there is to be winced at (perhaps a remark which you yourself would not wince at), or, if it is not that, then connect the wince with something in him, a thought, or a nerve. 'Seeing something as something'... is the principal topic of the chief section of what appears as Part II of the *Investigations*.
>
> (*CR*, 354)

The above quotation from Stanley Cavell's *The Claim of Reason*[1] can stand as an appropriate way of summarizing the main conclusion to be derived from the previous sections of this chapter; it might

---

1 S. Cavell, *The Claim of Reason* (Oxford: Oxford University Press, 1979) – hereafter known as *CR*.

also be useful to follow the avenues of exploration Cavell takes as leading off from this basic connection between psychological concepts and aspect perception, since it seems at least arguable both that he manages to raise the correct issues and also that the errors he makes in delineating them can help to refine our understanding of Wittgenstein's detailed treatment of aspect perception.

Cavell begins to explore this terrain with the following statement:

> The idea...is that human expressions, the human figure, to be grasped, must be *read*. To know another mind is to interpret a physiognomy, and the message of this region of the *Investigations* is that this is not a matter of 'mere knowing'. I have to read the physiognomy, and see the creature according to my reading, and treat it according to my seeing. The human body is the best picture of the human soul – not, I feel like adding, primarily because it represents the soul but because it expresses it. The body is the field of expression of the soul.
>
> (*CR*, 356)

The best way of characterizing this formulation, I would suggest, is to describe it as holding error and insight in a tension which threatens to collapse them together at any moment. The error involved is stated more explicitly elsewhere when Cavell says: '"Seeing something as something" is what Wittgenstein calls "interpretation"' (*CR*, 354); for it is one of the fundamental aims of Wittgenstein's treatment of aspect perception to show that aspect-dawning and continuous aspect perception are a matter of seeing *rather than* of interpretation (cf. *PI*, 212d). For Wittgenstein, the notion of interpretation carries connotations of making inferences, forming hypotheses or drawing conclusions – as if when someone sees a friendly glance in another's eye, what really happens is the direct perception of shapes, colours, and movement which are then interpreted to mean that the glance is a friendly one (*RPP*,I, 1102). A crucial motivation for stressing the aptness of the concept of seeing in these contexts is precisely to underline the sense in which the friendliness of the glance is as directly, as immediately perceived as the colour of the eyes might be thought to be.

In employing the notion of interpretation to characterize our relation to other people Cavell is therefore using a concept which, as defined by Wittgenstein in this context, can only help to draw the reader away from one of the key insights which emerges from Wittgenstein's treatment of this issue; and the misleading connotations ramify beyond this initial stage. As we noted in the previous chapters, part of the force of employing the concept of seeing with respect to aspect perception is that it characterizes the perceiver's general orientation towards the object of his perception – seeing behaviour as expressive of mind involves treating that behaviour in a certain way, taking its status as the field of expression of a mind for granted. As we just saw, Cavell preserves these ideas of 'attitude' and 'mode of treatment' in the way he characterizes his notion of interpreting a physiognomy; but, because he links them together with 'interpretation', he makes it easy for any reader of Wittgenstein to misinterpret the nature of the relation between those three ideas. Given the connotation of making inferences which is carried by 'interpretation' in these stretches of Wittgenstein's writings, it would be natural to think that Cavell is positing a three-stage inferential process at the basis of our relationship to other people: first we interpret the physiognomy, then we must let that interpretation mould our perception of the person, and then we must treat that person in a way which accords with the way we see him. In reality, Wittgenstein is positing internal relations between these concepts: for him, to say that we see the behaviour as expressive of mind is to say that we treat it in an appropriate way; describing oneself as seeing emotion in another's face is a manifestation of a certain general attitude towards the person; and accordingly, someone who needs to interpret the perceived physiognomy cannot intelligibly be said to have the attitude towards that behaviour (the capacity to treat it appropriately) which is grammatically bound up with calling the relation one of seeing.

What makes Cavell's use of the term 'interpretation' seem so perverse is that it is clear in other parts of his text that he is concerned to emphasize the very insights that his terminological predilection encourages his readers to cancel. He says in the passage quoted earlier, for example, that interpreting a physiognomy is not a matter of 'mere knowing'; and in another passage he states: 'Wittgenstein's expression "The human body is the best picture of the human soul" is an attempt to. . .express the idea that the soul is there to be seen, that my relation to the other's soul is as immediate as to an object of sight' (*CR*, 368). The accuracy of these insights does not, however, excuse or justify Cavell's use of 'interpretation'; it rather highlights its inexplicability, and does nothing to lessen the importance of recognizing just how much of a potential for misinterpretation is created by his decision to employ the term in this way.

A second issue Cavell takes as leading off from the observation that our relation to the inner states of others involves aspect perception can best be approached by registering those facets of the grammatical structure of psychological concepts which lead people to say that we can never be certain of someone else's inner state. Although it is important to note that this conclusion lacks the general scope often claimed for it – there are countless situations in which the criteria for the application of the relevant concept are fulfilled and intelligible grounds for doubt are clearly lacking: we know that a tennis-player in the Wimbledon final intends to win, that a woman who picks up an umbrella before leaving the house believes that it might rain – it is also important to acknowledge that there are many situations in which grounds for claiming to know with certainty that a person is manifesting a given inner state are not available. The crucial question then becomes: how are we to account for this lack of certainty?

The answer cannot simply be that the evidence provided by an individual's behaviour and its surroundings is merely an indirect symptom of the inner reality to which our psychological concepts refer. Our examination of first-person utterances showed that they were not grounded upon evidence uniquely accessible to the subject; and if no such direct, inner evidence actually exists, it could make no sense to talk of behavioural evidence as being indirect merely because it is external – just as the dichotomy between inner evidence and outer evidence breaks down when one pole of the contrast is removed, so the direct/indirect dichotomy must collapse if it makes no sense to talk of inner evidence. In the only situations where it makes sense to talk of 'evidence for the inner' at all, that evidence takes the form of behaviour (verbal and non-verbal) in a certain context. It must therefore be the case that the uncertainty we feel about ascribing psychological states on the basis of such evidence lies, not in any putative contrast with other types of evidence which *can* provide certainty, but rather in the nature of the evidence itself.

We might say that the relevant grammar embodies indeterminacy: that is, that the conceptual structures involved are founded upon modes of evidence which are not capable of providing certainty in every case. Even when we have a person's utterances to go on, in certain situations we are unable to point to grounds which might justify our being certain that the speaker is being sincere or truthful – the criteria of truthfulness (the fine shades of present behaviour which lead us to trust or doubt someone's sincerity) cannot in themselves guarantee veridical knowledge in *all* cases. The characteristic of our psychological concepts which is relevant here is that they unify disparate elements – occasion, utterance, and behaviour – into a *Gestalt* which fits together only loosely. There is no necessary connection between the elements such that the presence of one guarantees the presence of the others; and yet the concept can only be said to be correctly applied if the person involved exhibits reactions and behaviour which, in his circumstances, can be seen as an instantiation of this general pattern or as a variation of it. In principle, moreover, one key element of that pattern is never available when one looks at a person's facial expression or present behaviour and attempts to assess his state of mind, viz. the pattern of his future behaviour and reactions which it is part of the function of psychological concepts to predict. Even in the case of first-person utterances, questions of their truthfulness will in the end often be settled by looking at how the individual's future actions hang together with his professed inner states.

Of course, long experience with a particular culture and a specific individual can lead to increased sensitivity concerning the fine shades of that person's behaviour and the relation of those fine shades to the more coarse-grained reactions and behaviour with which they are drawn together by our psychological concept. But this observation about the connection between experience and understanding in this area (cf. *PI*, 227h) carries as its obverse a reminder of the role played by *imponderable* evidence in ascribing psychological states (*PI*, 228b–d). The point here is that even in those situations in which no evidence is available by means of which we might convince others of the validity of our judgements, we feel absolutely certain that, e.g. this person whom we know so well is genuinely unhappy rather than merely seeking attention. If such certainty cannot be cashed in terms of intersubjectively valid

grounds for a knowledge claim, how are we to understand it?
Wittgenstein suggests that we regard it as a matter of taking up a
position in relation to the person concerned (cf. MS 174, p. 115);
our certainty that he is unhappy is manifest in our attitude of
sympathy towards him, our attempts to discover the source of his
unhappiness and alleviate it – in short, in a variety of modes of
behaviour which reveal our taking the genuineness of his
expressions of unhappiness for granted.

We can thus see once more the importance of that element in the
general *Gestalt* built up in psychological concepts which concerns
the relation those ascribing the given psychological state have
towards its manifestation in another person. It is this facet of such
concepts and their use which Cavell treats as central in the third
idea he draws from Wittgenstein's references to aspect perception
in the psychological domain:

> Wittgenstein's expression 'The human body is the best picture of
> the human soul' is an attempt to. . .express the idea that the soul
> is there to be seen, that my relation to the other's soul is as
> immediate as to an object of sight, or would be as immediate if,
> so to speak, the relation could be effected. But Wittgenstein's
> mythology shifts the location of the thing which blocks this
> vision. The block to my vision of the other is not the other's body
> but my incapacity or unwillingness to interpret or to judge it
> accurately, to draw the right connections. The suggestion is: I
> suffer a kind of blindness, but I avoid the issue by projecting this
> darkness upon the other.
>
> (*CR*, 368)

This diagnosis of the problem of other minds is, of course, based
upon a particular reading of the concept of aspect-blindness as we
first meet it in relation to the duck-rabbit:

> We may say that the rabbit-aspect is hidden from us when we
> fail to see it. But what hides it is then obviously not the picture
> (that reveals it), but our (prior) way of taking it, namely in its
> duck-aspect. What hides one aspect is another aspect, something
> at the same level. So we might say: what hides the mind is not
> the body but the mind itself – his his, or mine his, and
> contrariwise.
>
> (*CR*, 369)

And from this point Cavell enters into a stimulating and sophisticated discussion of the ways in which individuals might understand their separation from (and closeness to) other people as the result of particular stances of the mind rather than of metaphysical limitations. In effect, by exploring the sense in which people are responsible for everything that comes between them, he suggests that the relation to other minds might be more fruitfully conceptualized in terms of acknowledgement and denial rather than knowledge and ignorance.

The interest of Cavell's discussion must be left for the reader to explore, since the discussion itself defies summary; what is most pertinent for the purposes of this chapter is the question of how far Cavell's use of the concept of aspect-blindness matches or refines that of Wittgenstein. Cavell himself points out (*CR*, xv) that beyond a certain stage in his writings on acknowledgement, he no longer regards his citations of the *Investigations* as interpretations of it; in order to draw this chapter to a close, it would seem useful to attempt to identify the point of transition.

The crucial facet of the concept of aspect-blindness which Cavell's use of the notion *does* highlight is the sense in which the certainties and uncertainties involved in relations with other people should be seen as grammatically distinct from knowledge claims. The example employed earlier – our trust in the genuineness of a friend's expressions of unhappiness – reveals a relation between knowledge and certainty which mirrors that manifest in the role of *Weltbild* propositions: our certainty is so fundamental and open to so little serious questioning that it functions as a hinge around which our more specific dealings with the person concerned will revolve; and the revelation of its being erroneous (i.e. of our trust being misplaced) would entirely disrupt the world of our personal interrelationship which it helped found.

Two points flow from the role of imponderable evidence in grounding such certainties: first, that getting someone else to share our certainty is more akin to inducting them into a particular world-view (or rather, into a particular interpersonal world) than to presenting evidence to justify a hypothesis; and secondly, that doubts sufficient to disrupt the certainty can arise from evidence which patently has no intersubjective ground or strength. In all these respects, the case of Othello and Desdemona can stand as an exemplification of the issues at stake; it is no accident that Cavell's examination of the concept of acknowledgement in relation to other minds should culminate in a reading of that tragedy. And in this way, our recognition that concepts of the inner are aspect concepts can help us to see that continuous aspect perception – conceived of as involving the perceiver's unhesitating treatment of a person as the particular person he is – raises issues which may be correctly graspable only against the background of such discussions as those in *On Certainty* and other late texts.

The same notion of an attitude which is reflected in a familiar orientation within the world, and of the contrast between this subject–world relation and a relation of cognitive confrontation or knowledge claims is, however, also central to the Heideggerian contrast between presence-at-hand and readiness-to-hand as modes of relation to the world. Cavell's treatment of aspect perception in the sphere of other minds thus further suggests that a full understanding of aspect perception will involve plotting the relation between two texts which seem at first sight to inhabit entirely incommensurable philosophical traditions – namely, Section xi of the *Investigations*, and the first Division of *Being and Time*. This interpretative task is one that I will begin in the next chapter.

The *difficulty* which arises at this point for Cavell's interpretation of aspect-blindness is that he needs to read that notion in a way which conflicts with Wittgenstein if he wants to reach the conclusion at which he aims. We have already seen in rough outline the form which aspect-blindness in the psychological domain must take if it is to be modelled upon that disability as defined in other contexts. Just as the person who is blind to pictorial aspects regards paintings as we do blueprints, so the person blind to psychological aspects regards human behaviour as behaviour rather than as the field of expression of a heart and mind: he has to infer from the physical properties of a face the inner state which is thereby revealed. The problem for Cavell is not that aspect-blindness would have serious consequences for its sufferers; it is rather that according to Wittgenstein, those consequences take a form different from the one Cavell suggests.

To elucidate his own sense of these consequences, Wittgenstein hints at an analogy which might be used here in place of the reference to blueprints and pictures: the aspect-blind regard a human being's behaviour as we would the behaviour of a robot, of a construction whose behaviour is mechanical and thus describable by means of geometrical concepts (*RPP*,I, 324). The implications of this analogy are not easy to fathom, but once they are elucidated they can be seen to follow directions traced out in the previous section of this chapter. Whatever else one thinks of the idea of 'geometrical' concepts in the domain of descriptions of behaviour, this much at least is clear: they could not be concepts whose use relates to fine shades of behaviour and whose structure yokes elements into a loose, flexible *Gestalt*, because then they would lack the objectivity of application and the sharpness of boundaries which are characteristic of concepts in the field of geometry. The primary implication of the analogy would then seem to be that the aspect-blind cannot see (or regard) human behaviour in terms of the fine shades, the variety and the flexibility which our psychological concepts pick out and presuppose. They are incapable of applying our psychological concepts directly and unhesitatingly to behaviour and must instead infer its freight of human significance from those physical features of it that can in principle be described geometrically – and in the process of inference much of that freight is lost because it is not capturable in geometrical terms in the first place. In this sense, the aspect-blind would be blind to an aspect of the *humanity* of human behaviour, to part of what makes it behaviour expressive of mind.

A further element of significance in the robot metaphor lies in its purging of *individuality* as well as of humanity. Human behaviour does not consist in machine-tooled, precise repetitions of a limited repertoire of movements that is invariant between cultures or persons, but rather in irregularities and variations of texture which *inflect* culturally-relative paradigms of expressive behaviour in specific ways and which together produce a weave of behaviour with a particular *physiognomy* – an individual style or character. It follows that to regard someone as if he were a robot is to make use of a model which must deprive that person's actions of the fine shades and the sheer specificity which go to make up our sense of him as a *particular* human being. The capacity to register such individuality is manifest in the capacity to see a given piece of behaviour as significant in the context of one interpersonal world but not in another, as a variation of one paradigm rather than another; and such capacities presuppose an unhesitating recognition of the individual as a person – as someone whose behaviour is expressive of mind in the first place. As was hinted in the previous section, therefore, lacking the capacity to regard persons as persons condemns the aspect-blind to a failure to distinguish the individuality of the person with which they are dealing.

On this reading of the consequences of aspect-blindness in relation to concepts of the inner, Cavell's difficulty becomes obvious; for it is not easy to see how such a disability can lead us into the issues of acknowledgement and denial in quite the way Cavell proposes. He argued, for example, that when the rabbit aspect of the duck-rabbit is hidden from us, 'what hides it is then obviously not the picture (that reveals it), but our (prior) way of taking it, namely in its duck-aspect. What hides one aspect is another aspect, something at the same level' (*CR*, 369). This implies that it is some compound of the perceiver's and the perceived's states of mind which blocks vision, which causes aspect-blindness; and the implication that aspect-blindness is thus a function or reflection of how two persons relate to one another *as persons* is confirmed by the tenor of later passages:

> If something separates us, comes between us, that can only be a particular aspect or stance of the mind itself, a particular way in which we relate, or are related (by birth, by law, by force, in love) to one another – our positions, our attitudes, with reference to one another.
>
> (*CR*, 369)

It is difficult to imagine that a failed love-affair might lead to someone treating her ex-lover as if he were a robot; and this difficulty arises from Cavell's inclination to treat aspect-blindness as something '*on the same level*' as the aspect(s) to which one is blind. Of course, we are not meant to think of the aspect-blind as lacking the capacity to apply the relevant aspect concepts altogether: just as the original aspect-blind person could see that a schematic drawing was meant to represent a cube, so the person blind to psychological aspects is not incapable of drawing some inferences about the state of mind expressed in the behaviour he directly perceives. The defect of aspect-blindness is not so much an inability or unwillingness to draw the *right* conclusion (cf. *CR*, 368) – as if the aspect-blind simply relate in the wrong way to (mistreat?) another person – but rather the need to *draw* conclusions at all. The defect is thus not on the same level as the aspects to which one is blind: it is not a defective personal relationship that is involved in aspect-blindness, nor a complete inability to view the other as a person, but rather an inability *directly* to perceive the other as a person.

I have argued, then, that Cavell's desire to extend his reading of Wittgenstein on aspect perception into the realm of interpersonal acknowledgement and denial tends to contradict the primary thrust of his recognition that Wittgenstein uses aspect-blindness to highlight the sense in which continuous aspect perception is not a matter of knowing. Since I have already registered my intention to treat this latter theme as fundamental to Wittgenstein's purposes, the conclusion follows that the point at which Cavell's discussion of aspect perception stops being an explication of Wittgenstein is the point at which his interest in interpersonal acknowledgement and denial submerges his intermittent awareness that it is the immediacy rather than the distortions of such relations that is at stake in the Wittgensteinian text.

I should, however, make it clear that the problems I have unearthed in Cavell's treatment of this issue should not be seen as a condemnation of the insights with which his account is studded. In particular, the suggestion that the notion of continuous aspect perception may be analogous with, or otherwise related to, Heidegger's concept of readiness-to-hand is one which must be pursued in the next chapter. The interpretative anchor in such a project must be a sense of the nature of continuous aspect perception; and that sense is itself primarily determined by our picture of its contrast, aspect-blindness – a picture which I have tried to build up over the last three chapters. It therefore seems right that my final paragraphs should summarise the composite picture at which we have arrived by combining the results of the earlier chapters with those revealed by our examination of psychological concepts.

If, as Cavell suggests, the attitude of attachment to our words mirrors our attachment to ourselves and to other persons (a suggestion reinforced by noting that linguistic behaviour is a sophisticated domain of human behaviour in general), then those who lack the attachment to words will have a counterpart in those lacking the analogous attachment to other persons. Since this former attitude of attachment can be partly characterised as a familiarity with – an unhesitating capacity to move around within – language, and its lack as a form of linguistic stumbling (as if one's linguistic joints were in splints), we are led to conclude that an aspect-blind person's behaviour in relation to other persons is to be imagined as equally a matter of hesitation, stumbling, stiffness of joints. When we add to this stiffness the point made in Chapter 2 that the aspect-blind lack the second nature bequeathed to us by language (that range of spontaneous linguistic reactions which forms the substratum of certain language-games, experiences, or feelings), then it becomes clear that the behaviour of the aspect-blind will be just as robotic in nature as they take the behaviour of others to be. In other words, just as the aspect-blind regard another person's behaviour as we would that of a mechanical man, so their own behaviour must be regarded as similarly mechanical – as lacking in the variability and flexibility (the fine shades) which determine the individual physiognomy of human behaviour and provide the necessary logical multiplicity for the application of sophisticated psychological concepts. As we saw earlier, for example, their inability to comprehend the secondary meanings of terms is alone sufficient to deprive their behaviour of features which might ground the ascription of many feelings and states of mind to them.

Thus, by a reflexivity which is perhaps not surprising when one remembers the degree to which self-consciousness and consciousness of other selves have been linked in the history of philosophical treatments of these concepts, the aspect-blind person's blindness to the humanity in others parallels a dehumanizing blankness in himself; and it would seem to follow that philosophers who are prone to characterize the ordinary human relation to language and other people in terms which resemble Wittgenstein's characterization of aspect-blindness lay themselves open to the Kierkegaardian charge of denying their own humanity.

One might wonder whether such an extreme charge can be levelled at anything other than straw men. In fact, however, some philosophers *do* characterize the human relation to language and to other persons in that way; and to prove it, I shall begin the next chapter with an account of the theorizing of someone who is at the forefront of contemporary analytical philosophy and is vulnerable to precisely this charge. I shall, however, end the chapter by going on to show the ways in which Heidegger's system of thought (like

Wittgenstein's) is predicated upon an awareness of the need to avoid that type of error, and so might reveal further ranges of significance in the human attitude I have been calling continuous aspect perception.

4
OPPOSING TRADITIONS

DAVIDSON'S PHILOSOPHY OF LANGUAGE

Kurt utters the words 'Es Regnet' and under the right conditions we know that it is raining. Having identified his utterance as intentional and linguistic, we are able to go on to interpret his words: we can say what his words, on that occasion, meant. What could we know that would enable us to do this? How could we come to know it?

(*ITI*, 125)[1]

In this brief passage, Davidson defines the parameters of the task he sets himself within the domain of philosophy of language: he describes the specific empirical phenomenon with which he is concerned (everyday linguistic transactions) and highlights those aspects of the phenomenon which seem to him to require philosophical explanation.

It is important to note, however, that Davidson wishes to make a sharp distinction between empirical and conceptual issues in his project. In a recent paper, he makes this very clear:

[C]laims about what would constitute a satisfactory theory [of interpretation] are not...claims about the propositional knowledge of an interpreter, nor are they claims about the details of the inner workings of some part of the brain. They are rather claims about what must be said to give a satisfactory description of the competence of the interpreter. *We* cannot

---

1 D. Davidson, *Inquiries into Truth and Interpretation*, (Oxford: Oxford University Press, 1983) – hereafter known as *ITI*.

describe what an interpreter can do except by appeal to a theory of a certain sort.

('A nice derangement of epitaphs', 10–11)[2]

There is a detectably Kantian ring to this emphasis: the very possibility of human mastery of a language would be unintelligible unless one made reference to a theory of a certain sort. Davidson's concern is with the array of concepts which apply to this human capacity; he wants to 'consider in advance of empirical study what shall count as knowing a language, how we shall describe the skill or ability of a person who has learned to speak a language' (*ITI*, 7–8). Once the philosopher has prepared the conceptual highway, the field-workers in linguistics and psychology can direct their empirical bandwagons on to the most fruitful route to their goal of giving accounts of particular languages.

We must therefore reinterpret Davidson's two original questions (in my opening quotation) as being hypothetical in form: 'given a theory that would make interpretation possible, what evidence plausibly available to a potential interpreter would support the theory to a reasonable degree?' (*ITI*, 125). To understand why his conceptual question takes this particular form, however, we must be aware of which aspects of human mastery of a language seem so particularly mysterious to Davidson that he feels required to explain the very grounds of their possibility.

The first such aspect is one which seems mysterious to a great many other philosophers and linguists: the capacity to understand new sentences. Davidson couches the issue in terms of how we are to account for the fact that languages must be learnable; 'the fact that, on mastering a finite vocabulary and a finitely stated set of rules, we are prepared to produce and to understand any of a potential infinitude of sentences' (*ITI*, 17), i.e. that we can learn the language, must be given a philosophical explanation. The mystery can only be solved, Davidson claims, by presupposing that the meanings of sentences depend upon the meanings of sub-sentential components:

> When we can regard the meaning of each sentence as a function of a finite number of features of the sentence, we have an insight not only into what there is to be learned; we also understand

[2] In E. LePore (ed.), *Truth and Interpretation: Perspectives on the Philosophy of Donald Davidson* (Oxford: Basil Blackwell, 1986).

how an infinite aptitude can be encompassed by finite accomplishments. For suppose that a language lacks this feature; then no matter how many sentences a would-be speaker learns to produce and understand, there will remain others whose meanings are not given by the rules already mastered. It is natural to say such a language is *unlearnable*.

(*ITI*, 8)

The general philosophical conclusion to be drawn from meditating on this mystery, therefore, is that any language must be capable of being described as a recursive structure; 'every true expression may be analysed as formed from elements (the "vocabulary"), a finite supply of which suffice for the language, by the application of rules, a finite number of which suffice for the language' (*ITI*, 57).

In order to go beyond this general presupposition and into the question of precisely what *sort* of recursive structure ought to be employed in our description, Davidson needs to make further theoretical assumptions. He starts from the notion that one way of giving the meaning of a sentence is to give its truth conditions (which does not involve equating 'meaning' and 'truth conditions' – cf. *ITI*, 56, 1982 footnote). This would suggest that the meanings of sentences might be analysed as being composed in *truth*-relevant ways from the elements of a finite stock; and this in turn suggests that first-order predicate calculus with identity might be the best analytical tool for representing those modes of composition.

Since, Davidson claims, anyone armed with such a recursively structured description of a language could – in principle – understand all utterances couched in that language, the provision of an adequate description satisfying these constraints would allow us to understand how interpretation is possible (i.e. would answer the first part of Davidson's original hypothetical question); but the second part of that question remains. What evidence plausibly available to a potential interpreter would support the theory to a reasonable degree? This query also demands an answer, since we would once again be unable to make sense of the possibility of one person interpreting another person's speech behaviour unless we could show that it would at least be conceivable for him to do so successfully purely on the basis of the evidence available within the context of any such linguistic transaction. We must, in other words, explain how it might be possible for an interpreter to confirm his hypotheses about what a given utterance might mean.

Davidson is concerned to emphasize that any potential source of evidence must be non-linguistic in form:

> In radical interpretation. . .the theory is supposed to supply an understanding of particular utterances that is not given in advance. . . To deal with the general case, the evidence must be of a sort that would be available to someone who does not already know how to interpret utterances the theory is designed to cover: it must be evidence that can be stated without essential use of such linguistic concepts as meaning, interpretation, synonymy, and the like.
>
> (*ITI*, 128)

The relevant evidence must therefore consist entirely of facts about the behaviour and attitudes of speakers in relation to their utterances – but the issue yet to be resolved is whether this evidence should mesh with the theory at the level of sub-sentential components (i.e. words), or at the level of sentences. Davidson rejects the former alternative, since it has a historical track-record of complete failure and goes against the intuition that words have no function save as they play a role in sentences. Accordingly, he proposes the sentence as the appropriate focus of empirical interpretation, and the most useful attitude with which to relate it as being 'the attitude of holding a sentence true, of accepting it as true' (*ITI*, 135).

The procedure of radical interpretation is thus revealed to have a clear structure:

> First we look for the best way to fit our logic. . .on to the new language; this may mean reading the logical structure of first-order quantification theory (plus identity) into the language. . ., treating this much of logic as a grid to be fitted on to the language in one fell swoop. The evidence here is classes of sentences always held true or always held false by almost everyone almost all of the time (potential logical truths) and patterns of inference. The first step identifies predicates, singular terms, quantifiers, connectives and identity; in theory, it settles matters of logical form. The second step concentrates on sentences with indexicals; those sentences sometimes held true and sometimes false according to discoverable changes in the

world. This step in conjunction with the first limits the possibilities for interpreting individual predicates. The last step deals with the remaining sentences, those on which there is no uniform agreement, or whose held truth value does not depend systematically on changes in the environment.

(*ITI*, 136)

A tendency towards holism is already implicit in this picture; for, of course, taken on an individual basis, the evidence for a theorist's hypothesis that a given utterance should be linked to a given set of truth conditions (i.e. that the Tarskian biconditional correctly gives the meaning of the uttered sentence) is exceedingly thin. Davidson's solution to this difficulty is that the totality of T-sentences (i.e. of biconditionals of the form '"snow is white" is true iff snow is white') should optimally fit the evidence about sentences held true by native speakers: 'we compensate for the paucity of evidence concerning the meanings of individual sentences not by trying to produce evidence for the meanings of words but by considering the evidence for a theory of the language to which the sentence belongs' (*ITI*, 225). Knowledge of the theory as a whole would tell us not only the T-sentence for the sentence to be interpreted, but also the T-sentences for all other sentences of the language, together with all their proofs, i.e. together with an account of their recursive generation from the finite vocabulary and the transformation rules. We would therefore see the place of the sentence in the language as a whole, be aware of the role of each significant part of the sentence, and grasp logical connections between this sentence and others.

The work of the theory therefore consists in what it reveals about the ways in which the meanings of sentences depend systematically upon the meanings of their parts together with the mode of composition; it reveals nothing new about the conditions under which the given sentence is true, but rather uses that sentence as the point of contact between the theory and available empirical evidence. As Davidson puts it:

> The analogy with physics is obvious: we explain macroscopic phenomena by postulating an unobserved fine structure. But the theory is tested at the macroscopic level. Sometimes, to be sure, we are lucky enough to find additional, or more direct, evidence for the originally postulated structure; but this is not essential to

the enterprise. I suggest that words, meanings of words, reference and satisfaction are posits we need to inplement a theory of truth. They serve this purpose without needing independent confirmation or empirical basis.

(*ITI*, 222)

The articulation of sentences into singular terms, quantifiers, predicates, connectives, and the logical form attributed to them, must be treated as so much theoretical construction; and since these sub-sentential components are treated as primitive by the theory, we can expect no illuminating analysis of them.

The belief that empirical evidence need only enter at the level of the sentence allows Davidson to admit an element of indeterminacy into his project, since there is clearly no guarantee – given his emphasis on the *pattern* of truth-condition assignments – that the empirical and formal constraints on the theory of truth will yield only one adequate theory. For Davidson, it is precisely the aspect of sentence meaning which would be invariant as between rival acceptable theories that is the concern of his project:

The meaning (interpretation) of a sentence is given by assigning the sentence a semantic location in the pattern of sentences that comprise the language. Different theories of truth may assign different truth conditions to the same sentence (this is the semantic analogue of Quine's indeterminacy of translation), while the theories are (nearly enough) in agreement on the roles of the sentences in the language.

(*ITI*, 225)

Indeterminacy on this level cannot be of any concern, since it goes beyond the scope of any available empirical evidence, and so in fact reveals that certain apparently significant distinctions we might have been tempted to make (e.g. between 'rabbits' and 'undetached rabbit parts') have no bearing on the aspect of linguistic meaning under analysis.

Davidson's choice of the attitude of holding a sentence to be true as the basis of the interpreter's task tends to generate holism in another respect.

A speaker who holds a sentence to be true on an occasion does so in part because of what he means, or would mean, by an utterance of that sentence, and in part because of what he

> believes. If all we have to go on is the fact of honest utterance,
> we cannot infer the belief without knowing the meaning, and
> have no chance of inferring the meaning without the belief.
>
> (*ITI*, 142)

In addition to this difficulty, Davidson emphasizes the claim that it is impossible to make sense of the attribution of one belief in isolation from a general belief-structure:

> Beliefs are identified and described only within a dense pattern
> of beliefs. I can believe a cloud is passing before the sun, but
> only because I believe there is a sun, that clouds are made of
> water vapour, that water can exist in liquid or gaseous form; and
> so on, without end. No particular list of further beliefs is
> required to give substance to my belief that a cloud is passing
> before the sun; but some appropriate set of related beliefs must
> be there.
>
> (*ITI*, 200)

It follows that, just as the capacity to understand a single utterance presupposes a theory for the language in which the utterance is made, so an attribution of a single belief requires the attribution of a general belief-structure. Given this interrelation of belief and meaning, it would seem most fruitful to regard the interpreter's task as one of constructing a single general theory about the speaker, within which the attributions of beliefs and meanings are necessarily intertwined.

How is it possible, however, for an interpreter to deliver simultaneously a theory of belief and a theory of meaning? Davidson's answer to this query parallels his response to a similar query about the evidential base for constructing a theory of truth for a language as a whole. The evidence available to support the attribution of a given belief in the case of a specific utterance and its hypothesized meaning is slim; it is the potential infinity of specific attributions and hypotheses which makes the difference, for a strong theory weakly supported (but at enough points) may yield all the information needed. As Davidson puts it when discussing a parallel situation in decision theory:

> Support for the explanation doesn't come from a new kind of
> insight into the attitudes and beliefs of the agent, but from more
> observations of preferences of the very sort to be explained. In

brief, to explain (i.e. interpret) a particular choice or preference, we observe other choices or preferences; these will support a theory on the basis of which the original choice or preference can be explained.

(*ITI*, 146)

The problem is solved, therefore, if we view actual utterances in interpretation as analogous to actual choices in decision theory.

The view that beliefs and meanings are interrelated constructs in a single theory also allows Davidson to set his face against conceptual relativism:

> If I suppose that you believe a cloud is passing before the sun, I suppose you have the right sort of pattern of beliefs to support that one belief, and these beliefs I assume you to have must, to do their supporting work, be enough like my beliefs to justify the description of your belief as a belief that a cloud is passing before the sun. If I am right in attributing the belief to you, then you must have a pattern of beliefs much like mine. No wonder, then, I can interpret your words correctly only by interpreting so as to put us largely in agreement.
>
> (*ITI*, 200)

It would be wrong to object to this point by saying that, whilst good interpretation breeds concurrence, it does not guarantee that what is agreed upon is true.

> The basic claim is that much community of belief is needed to provide a basis for communication or understanding; the extended claim should then be that objective error can occur only in a setting of largely true belief. Agreement does not make for truth, but much of what is agreed must be true if some of what is agreed is false.
>
> (*ITI*, 200)

The anti-relativist conclusion follows at once from this:

> In sharing a language, in whatever sense this is required for communication, we share a picture of the world that must, in its large features, be true. It follows that in making manifest the large features of our language, we make manifest the large features of reality. One way of pursuing metaphysics is therefore to study the general structure of our language.
>
> (*ITI*, 199)

Davidson's sense of a theory of linguistic interpretation as being connected with a theory of the person speaking leads to one further conclusion which should be pointed out.

> Someone who utters the sentence 'The candle is out' as a sentence of English must intend to utter words that are true if and only if an indicated candle is out at the time of utterance, and he must believe that by making the sounds he does he is uttering words that are true only under those circumstances.
>
> (*ITI*, 155)

If we recognize that interpretation of utterances presupposes reference to thoughts, intentions, beliefs, and so on, it is also important to recognize that talk of sayings and of thoughts belongs to a familiar mode of explanation of human behaviour. This recognition in effect acknowledges that linguistic behaviour is a form of human behaviour in general, but its consequences for Davidson's understanding of his own project are crucial:

> [I]t should not be thought that a theory of interpretation will stand alone, for...there is no chance of telling when a sentence is held true without being able to attribute desires and being able to describe actions as having complex intentions. This observation does not deprive the theory of interpretation of interest, but assigns it a place within a more comprehensive theory of action and thought.
>
> (*ITI*, 162)

In other words, the type of theory of interpretation which Davidson has advanced as the only conceivable way of understanding 'how communication by language is possible' (*ITI*, 222) demands that we provide, and determines the form in which we can provide, an understanding of human behaviour in general.

THE METAPHYSICAL FOUNDATIONS

Up to this point in my exposition, I have refrained from critical assessment of the framework Davidson offers for the philosophy of language; the intention has rather been to show the strengths of that framework. If the reader can be persuaded to view as problematic those aspects of language mastery which Davidson finds mysterious (viz. our capacity to understand new sentences, and more generally our capacity to understand utterances on the basis of the meagre evidence available in speech transactions), then he will find the direction, scope, and form of the explanatory framework Davidson offers as a response to those problems to be both plausible and powerfully consistent.

The exposition was also intended to suggest, however, that a huge amount of weight correspondingly falls on Davidson's initial descriptions of the everyday phenomenon of linguistic transactions which it is the concern of his theory to render comprehensible. For if those descriptions are simply misleading, then the impression of mystery which is engendered in the reader may be generated by this inaccuracy rather than by the real nature of the phenomenon described – and once the impression of mystery dissolves, the need for an explanatory framework (of whatever sophistication) dissolves with it. The pressing question now becomes: how accurate are Davidson's accounts of the everyday activity of communication by language?

Two terminological points arise at once. First, Davidson continuously uses the terms 'interpretation' and 'understanding' as synonyms; he says, for example, that 'What is essential to my argument is the idea of an interpreter, someone who understands the utterances of another' (*ITI*, 157), and takes as the basis of his account of language mastery the assumption that someone who understands a given utterance has successfully interpreted it. Second, and in parallel with this, he refers to anyone who successfully interprets utterances as the possessor of a 'theory' of interpretation. It is no part of Davidson's position to claim that the theory of truth he offers as the best model of this interpretative capacity is known to any speaker in the form of propositional knowledge of its vocabulary and rules; but it is (and must be) essential to his project that unless an interpreter possesses a body of knowledge corresponding to, and similar in form to, such a theory, his ability to interpret becomes incomprehensible. The theory he offers takes the form it does precisely because we could not render intelligible our human capacity to successfully interpret the utterances of others without describing it in such a way: we must see the interpreter as a theorizer if we are to make sense of what he does.

To see why 'interpreting' and 'theorizing' go together at all, we might look at the definition of 'interpretation' provided in the *Concise Oxford Dictionary*:

Interpret. 1. vt. Expound the meaning of (abstruse or foreign words, writing, dreams, *etc.*); make out the meaning of; bring out the meaning of, render, by artistic representation or performance; explain, understand in specified manner ('we interpret this as a threat').

Someone interpreting a dream expresses the meaning of the dream in another medium, that of language; someone interprets a foreign word by giving its meaning in our native tongue; an abstruse word may be interpreted by explaining its meaning in less technical terms. In all these examples, the process of interpretation is linked with a transition between languages or between sectors of the same language; the point is to clarify meaning by giving it expression in another way, and the presupposition is that the original expression of that meaning was obscure, problematic, or difficult to understand. 'Interpretation' thus conjures up an image of translation from one domain to another, from one mode of description or expression to another; and it implies that this transition is necessary for understanding.

It is this image, and this implication, which Davidson builds into his conceptualization of *all* linguistic transactions:

> We interpret a bit of linguistic behaviour when we say what a speaker's words mean on an occasion of use. The task may be seen as one of redescription. We know that the words 'Es schneit' have been uttered on a particular occasion and we want to redescribe this uttering as an act of saying that it is snowing. What do we need to know if we are to be in a position to redescribe speech in this way, that is, to interpret the utterances of a speaker?
>
> (*ITI*, 141)

Once the task of interpretation is explicitly conceptualized as a movement from one level of description to another, it becomes clear why an interpreter is likely to be viewed as a theorizer: 'in passing from a description that does not interpret (his uttering of the words "Es regnet") to interpreting description (his saying that it is raining), we must introduce a machinery of words and expressions (which may or may not be exemplified in actual utterances)' (*ITI*, 126). It seems natural to assume that such a systematic capacity to redescribe must involve a 'machinery', a set of systematized rules governing the transition between descriptive levels; and how else ought we to model a system of translation rules except as a theory? 'To belong to a speech community – to be an interpreter of the speech of others – one needs, in effect, to know. . .a theory [of truth], and to know that it is a theory of the right kind' (*ITI*, 161).

The presumption that interpretation should be seen as a species of redescription is reinforced by the sense in which Davidson embeds a theory of interpretation within a more general theory of human behaviour and by the form he assumes such a more general theory should take:

> A theory of interpretation, like a theory of action, allows us to redescribe certain events in a revealing way. Just as a theory of action can answer the question of what an agent is doing when he has raised his arm by redescribing the act as one of trying to catch his friend's attention, so a method of interpretation can lead to redescribing the utterance of certain sounds as an act of saying that snow is white.
>
> (*ITI*, 161)

If all behaviour requires redescription in order to be grasped as human action (with its freight of intentions, beliefs, and desires), then that segment of behaviour which involves the utterance of sounds also requires redescription in order to be understood as a linguistic utterance with a specific meaning. The more primitive behavioural evidence requires organization by linguistic and semantic concepts; and once again the notion of organizing evidence seems to demand the use of the terms 'theorizing' and 'theory'. This is why Davidson feels justified in regarding everyday references to linguistic meaning (e.g. in reporting what someone said) as a mode of theory-building – or, as he puts it: 'Everyday linguistic and semantic concepts are part of an intuitive theory for organizing more primitive data. . . .If our ordinary concepts suggest a confused theory, we should look for a better theory, not give up theorizing' (*ITI*, 143).

Davidson gives this redescriptive picture plausibility by focusing on examples of utterances in a foreign language. At the very beginning of his paper 'Radical interpretation',[3] for example, we are presented with a German uttering a sentence in German, and it

3 In *Inquiries into Truth and Interpretation*.

would seem natural to say that we are interpreting such an utterance when we say what it means in English – indeed, the *Concise Oxford Dictionary* definition we examined earlier uses translation from a foreign tongue to exemplify the use of the term 'interpretation'. This does not, however, license us to regard a fellow-German's comprehension of Kurt's utterance as being the product of interpretation, precisely because Kurt's utterance is not in a language foreign to his compatriot. To say to a German 'Es regnet' just *is* to say 'It is raining'; and once the gap between speaker's and hearer's native tongues is closed, there is no room for the concept of interpretation because there is no reason for presupposing the need for a redescription of the utterance.

Davidson suggests a reason for rejecting this conclusion. 'The problem of interpretation is domestic as well as foreign: it surfaces for speakers of the same language in the form of the question, how can it be determined that the language is the same?' (*ITI*, 125) As Ian Hacking has noted,[4] however, the difficulty with this suggestion is its flagrant implausibility; it is as if every time I enter into conversation with another English speaker, I have to hold before me the possibility that he is an alien. Davidson's illustrative examples tend to involve cases of incorrect or non-standard use of certain English words – for instance, I may on a specific occasion be uncertain whether you are using the words 'yawl' and 'ketch' correctly (cf. *ITI*, 196); but such examples cannot do the work he requires of them. First, my uncertainty about the correct use of such abstruse or technical terms may well lead me to bluster because I fear that I am confused rather than you; but this is definitely not a worry about whether we are speaking the same language. Second, the scepticism Davidson invokes gives the impression of approaching paranoia because it simply lacks any grounds which might justify the generality he claims for it. Given the sense of interpretation outlined above, we may say that someone listening to a complex poem or a flow of abstruse terminology is interpreting what he hears; we may even stretch a point and say that our comprehension of malaprops and other linguistic errors involves interpretation – but if someone remarks that 'it is raining', and raindrops are running down the window-

---

4 In a paper entitled 'A parody of conversation', in E. LePore (ed.), *Truth and Interpretation: Perspectives on the Philosophy of Donald Davidson*, Oxford, Basil Blackwell, 1986.

pane, it makes no sense at all to say that I am interpreting his utterance. The vast majority of things said in everyday linguistic transactions between members of the same linguistic community are not interpreted at all; there can therefore be no mystery about how such universal interpretation is possible, or on what evidence it might be based.

I want to suggest that Davidson's underlying reason for his illicit extension of the notion of interpretation goes beyond the arguments he explicitly cites: it is rooted in a certain conception of what we hear when we listen to another person's speech. In one discussion, he considers the question of what might be said to recur in a sequence of linguistic transactions:

> The only candidate for recurrence we have is the interpretation of sound-patterns: speaker and hearer must repeatedly, intentionally and with mutual agreement, interpret relevantly similar sound-patterns of the speaker in the same way. (*ITI*, 277)

Here, Davidson implies that what we *really* hear when we listen to another speaker (even an English speaker) is a sequence of sound-patterns. Once this assumption is made, it follows that radical interpretation must begin at home, for clearly a process of systematic redescription is needed to effect the transition from sound-patterns to utterances with a specific meaning – and here is where the 'machinery' of words and expressions comes into its own. This assumption of bare sound as the interface between speakers is paralleled by Davidson's more general view of bare movement as the interface between human actors:

> We wonder why a man raises his arm; an explanation might be that he wanted to attract the attention of a friend. . . . [This] explains what is relatively apparent – an arm-raising – by appeal to factors that are far more problematical – desires and beliefs.
> (*ITI*, 158–9)

Only someone who believed that, when looking at another human being's actions, all we *really* perceive are bare movements could suggest that what is most apparent in such encounters is an 'arm-raising' rather than a wave.

What we therefore find at the foundations of Davidson's philosophy of language – what, in effect, we need to presuppose in order to make sense of his illicit and otherwise unintelligible use of the term 'interpretation' – is a metaphysics which is most easily expressed in quasi-ontological terms. In order to say anything philosophically instructive or revealing about language, we must assume that when a human being speaks to us, we hear sound-patterns; when he acts we see bare movements. The world we really perceive is radically devoid of any human significance, until we use our interpretative theorizing to organize this primitive data into units of human meaning – words, actions, gestures. Within this generally alien world, we are alienated in particular from language and from human behaviour as a whole, for the significance and the humanity we find in those phenomena of our everyday life are a result of our reading our concepts into the data we directly apprehend. Every language is at root a foreign tongue, every person an alien; a world which requires radical interpretation from its human residents is a world in which they can never be at home.

Davidson's commitment to the notion of bare sounds and bare movements as the experiential basis from which any understanding of human speech and action must arise is strikingly analogous to empiricist sense-datum theories of knowledge. In both, it is presupposed that everyday experience of the world can be illuminatingly viewed as a logical or theoretical construction out of brute data – 'the given'; and in both an unsubstantiated belief in the possibility of a systematic redescription of the everyday world in terms of this postulated category of brute data is held to reveal something fundamental about the ontology of that world – about its metaphysical structure, as it were.

Davidson discusses certain aspects of the empiricist world-view when analysing the dualism of conceptual scheme and empirical content:

> I want to urge that this second dualism of scheme and content, of organizing system and something waiting to be organized, cannot be made intelligible and defensible. It is itself a dogma of empiricism, the third dogma. The third, and perhaps the last, for if we give it up it is not clear that there is anything distinctive left to call empiricism.
>
> (*ITI*, 189)

In light of the fact that we can only make sense of Davidson's descriptions of everyday linguistic transactions as involving 'interpretation' and 'theorizing' by invoking a metaphysics which runs precisely parallel to that of the empiricists, such explicitly anti-empiricist declarations as the one just quoted assume more than a hint of irony. Even those who lead the hunt for empiricist dogmas can find that the task of extirpation must begin at home.

For the purposes of this book, however, it is important to note that this metaphysics of the given – revealed as it is by Davidson's emphasis upon the concept of 'interpretation' – exemplifies to perfection the stance of the interlocutor in Section xi of the *Philosophical Investigations*. Incapable of finding a home for the notion of continuous aspect perception in his framework of thought, Davidson describes the everyday phenomenon of perceiving words and other human beings as if aspect-blindness were the normal human state. His emphasis on processes of theorizing as necessary in order to organize bare sounds and movements into words and actions could stand as a paradigm of that reliance upon an activity of inferring or reading-off which characterizes the interlocutor of Section xi; and it commits him implicitly to a general notion of visual perception as divisible into what is really seen and what is interpreted, i.e. as divisible in precisely the way Wittgenstein rejects in the remarks we have been examining. The example of Donald Davidson therefore shows not only that Wittgenstein's target in his work on aspect perception is no straw man, but also that any attempt to take Wittgenstein's strictures to heart would result in a fundamental change in the guiding framework of much contemporary analytical philosophy.

A CONTINENTAL PERSPECTIVE

If nothing else, this exploration of Davidson's guiding presuppositions in his philosophy of language has revealed the emptiness of one possible way of defining the difference between the Anglo-American and the Continental traditions of philosophy. For if one of the leading exponents of analytical philosophy must draw upon a metaphysical vision of the relations between an individual and his natural language (*and* between that individual and other human beings) in order to preserve the intelligibility of his theorizing, then the utility of suggesting that these two philosophical traditions differ because one spurns a commitment to metaphysics which the other embraces, becomes very unclear. A more useful, and (or because?) a more specific, contrast might rather be drawn in terms of the divergent thrust which is evident in the metaphysical outlooks adopted by emblematic figures within the two traditions. In matters of quite specific detail, Davidson's picture of human existence as involving confrontation with a world which is radically devoid of human significance until an individual's interpretative theorizing organizes it into units of human meaning (such as words, actions, or gestures) is one that is directly contradicted by the general structure of Heidegger's metaphysics, as well as by the aspects of everyday existence which that metaphysics draws upon and foregrounds. An extended quotation should make this clear:

> Hearkening is phenomenally still more primordial than what is defined 'in the first instance' as 'hearing' in psychology – the sensing of tones and the perception of sounds. Hearkening too has the kind of Being of the hearing which understands. What we 'first' hear is never noises or complexes of sounds, but the creaking waggon, the motor cycle. We hear the column on the march, the north wind, the woodpecker tapping, the fire crackling.
>
> It requires a very artificial and complicated frame of mind to 'hear' a 'pure noise'. The fact that motor-cycles and waggons are what we proximally hear is the phenomenal evidence that in every case Dasein, as Being-in-the-world, already dwells *alongside* what is ready-to-hand within-the-world; it certainly does not dwell proximally alongside 'sensation'; nor would it first have to give shape to the swirl of sensations to provide the springboard from which the subject leaps off and finally arrives at a 'world'. Dasein, as essentially understanding, is proximally alongside what is understood.
>
> Likewise, when we are explicitly hearing the discourse of another, we proximally understand what is said, or – to put it more exactly – we are already with him, in advance, alongside the entity which the discourse is about. On the other hand, what we proximally hear is *not* what is expressed in the utterance. Even in cases where the speech is indistinct or in a foreign language, what we proximally hear is unintelligible words, and not a multiplicity of tone-data.
>
> (*Being and Time*, Sect. 34, p. 207)[5]

5 M. Heidegger, *Being and Time*, trans. J. Macquarrie and E. Robinson (Oxford: Basil Blackwell, 1962) – hereafter known as *BT*.

In the above paragraphs – as the frequent use of 'proximally' (*zunachst*) indicates – Heidegger is focusing attention on aspects of everyday experience by proffering those descriptions of it which are most natural and obvious at an uncritical or pre-philosophical level. They are not, however, to be dismissed on that account as superficial or misleading forms of description, as if they are merely subjective and impressionistic accounts of how perception appears to the perceiving subject, which can then be swept aside by the findings of cognitive psychology or other related sciences. On the contrary: true to the tradition of phenomenological analysis established by Husserl, Heidegger regards ordinary experience as the domain within which the essence of human existence is manifest:

> ...the problem of obtaining and securing the kind of access which will lead to Dasein, becomes even more a burning one. To put it negatively, we have no right to resort to dogmatic constructions and to apply just any idea of Being and actuality to this entity, no matter how 'self-evident' that idea may be; nor may any of the 'categories' which such an idea prescribes be forced upon Dasein without proper ontological consideration. We must rather choose such a way of access and such a kind of interpretation that this entity can show itself in itself and from itself. And this means that it is to be shown as it is *proximally and for the most part* – in its average *everydayness*. In this everydayness there are certain structures which we shall exhibit – not just any accidental structures, but essential ones which, in every kind of Being that factical Dasein may possess, persist as determinative for the character of its Being. Thus by having regard for the basic state of Dasein's everydayness we shall bring out the Being of this entity in a preparatory fashion.
>
> (*BT*, Sect. 5, pp. 37–8)

What, then, can we learn about the essence of human existence in the world by attending to those aspects of our ordinary experience of language and the world which Davidson's metaphysics ignores or denies? Heidegger reminds us of them in order to illustrate his claim that everyday human modes of sense-perception are always already founded in an understanding of the world, and to forge a link between such an analysis of understanding and the more general claim that the essence of

Dasein is Being-in-the-world. These aspects of ordinary experience show us, he claims, that Dasein already dwells alongside what is ready-to-hand within-the-world. In order to appreciate the force of this claim, however, we must first analyse the precise type of person–world relationship Heidegger is attempting to capture in the term 'Being-in-the-world'.

To say that a person exists in the world, and then to treat such a statement as analogous to claiming that a volume of water is in a glass, would – for Heidegger – involve a twofold misrepresentation of the essential difference between human existence and the Being of non-human entities. In the first place:

> Being-in is not a 'property' which Dasein sometimes has and sometimes does not have, and *without* which it could *be* just as well as it could with it. It is not the case that man 'is' and then has, by way of an extra, a relationship-of-Being towards the 'world' – a world with which he provides himself occasionally. Dasein is never 'proximally' an entity which is, so to speak, free from Being-in, but which sometimes has the inclination to take up a 'relationship' towards the world. Taking up relationships towards the world is possible only *because* Dasein, as Being-in-the-world, is as it is. This state of Being does not arise just because some other entity is present-at-hand outside of Dasein and meets up with it. Such an entity can 'meet up with' Dasein only in so far as it can, of its own accord, show itself within a *world*.
>
> (*BT*, Sect. 12, p. 84)

Secondly, however, even if we recognize that existence within a world is a *necessary* structure of Dasein, we must also take care to grasp correctly the *nature* of that embeddedness:

> As an *existentiale*, 'Being-alongside' the world never means anything like the Being-present-at-hand-together of Things that occur. There is no such thing as the 'side-by-sideness' of an entity called 'Dasein' with another entity called 'world'. Of course when two things are present-at-hand-together alongside one another, we are accustomed to express this occasionally by something like 'The table stands "by" the door' or 'The chair "touches" the wall.' Taken strictly, 'touching' is never what we are talking about in such cases, not because accurate re-

examination will always eventually establish that there is a space
between the chair and the wall, but because in principle the
chair can never touch the wall, even if the space between them
should be equal to zero. If the chair could touch the wall, this
would presuppose that the wall is the sort of thing 'for' which a
chair would be *encounterable*. An entity present-at-hand within the
world can be touched by another entity only if by its very nature
the latter entity has Being-in as its own kind of Being – only if,
with its Being-there, something like the world is already revealed
to it, so that from out of that world another entity can manifest
itself in touching, and thus become accessible in its Being-
present-at-hand.

(*BT*, Sect. 12, p. 81)

Unlike entities which are 'worldless' – such as tables and chairs –
Dasein is Being-in-the-world in such a way that it can understand itself as bound up in its existence with the Being of those entities which it encounters within its own world. Heidegger's concepts of 'encountering' and of 'touching' (in its 'strict' sense) are meant to imply that part of what it means to be embedded in the world in a human way is that we relate to non-human entities in a specific manner – as ready-to-hand rather than present-at-hand.

We can elucidate this crucial dichotomy by reference to Heidegger's example of the hammer, an example which also illustrates his claim that Being-in-the-world is proximally a matter of concernful dealings with entities within-the-world, of manipulating equipment rather than theoretically cognizing things.

> The hammering does not simply have knowledge about the
> hammer's character as equipment, but it has appropriated this
> equipment in a way which could not possibly be more
> suitable. . .the less we just stare at the hammer-Thing, and the
> more we seize hold of it and use it, the more primordial does our
> relationship to it become, and the more unveiledly is it
> encountered as that which it is – as equipment. The hammering
> itself uncovers the specific 'manipulability' of the hammer. The
> kind of Being which equipment possesses – in which it manifests
> itself in its own right – we call *readiness-to-hand*. Only because
> equipment has *this* 'Being-in-itself' and does not merely occur, is
> it manipulable in the broadest sense and at our disposal. No

matter how sharply we just *look* at the 'outward appearance' of Things in whatever form this takes, we cannot discover anything ready-to-hand. If we look at Things just 'theoretically', we can get along without understanding readiness-to-hand. But when we deal with them by using them and manipulating them, this activity is not a blind one; it has its own kind of sight, by which our manipulation is guided and from which it acquires its specific Thingly character.

(*BT*, Sect. 15, p. 98)

It is not difficult to see the aspects of ordinary experience upon which Heidegger is drawing here: most people, when using tools or sports equipment, will have felt the essential suitability of their racquet or chisel for the task in hand, and will have marvelled at the deeds of sportsmen or craftsmen able to utilize the 'kind of sight' appropriate to their activity. Can such feelings be rejected as irrational intuitions?

> The kind of Being which belongs to these entities is readiness-to-hand. But this characteristic is not to be understood as merely a way of taking them, as if we were talking such 'aspects' into the 'entities' which we proximally encounter, or as if some world-stuff which is proximally present-at-hand in itself were 'given subjective colouring' in this way.
>
> (*BT*, Sect. 15, p. 101)

To deny that entities are primordially encountered as equipment is to render oneself incapable of accounting for the distinctive way in which any human being's embeddedness in the world must be conceptualized; the notion of 'equipment' is merely the necessary complement of Heidegger's insight that human existence is essentially manifest in praxis, that the world is the domain for human practical activity. But how might this complementarity be spelt out?

To begin with, for Heidegger it makes no sense to talk of *an* equipment; what makes a given entity a piece of equipment is its place within a totality of equipment. This location involves more than simply its belonging to other equipment, in the sense in which a pen presupposes a relationship to ink, paper, blotting pad, and table if it is to be thought of as equipment for writing; we must also take account of what Heidegger refers to as the 'towards-which' of its usability and the 'whereof' of which it consists.

> The work to be produced, as the '*towards-which*' of such things as the hammer, the plane, and the needle, likewise has the kind of Being that belongs to equipment. The shoe which is to be produced is for wearing, the clock is manufactured for telling the time. The work which we chiefly encounter in our concernful dealings – the work that is to be found when one is 'at work' on something – has a usability which belongs to it essentially; in this usability it lets us encounter already the 'towards-which' for which *it* is usable.
>
> (*BT*, Sect. 15, p. 99)

Using tools involves more than a reference to a usable product, however, for the production itself is a using of something for something.

> In the work there is also a reference or assignment to 'materials': the work is dependent on leather, thread, needles and the like. . ... Hammers, tongs, and needle, refer in themselves to steel, iron, metal, mineral, wood, in that they consist of these. In equipment that is used, 'Nature' is discovered along with it by that use.
>
> (*BT*, Sect. 15, p. 100)

The essence of any given piece of equipment is thus constituted by the multiplicity of reference- or assignment-relations which define its place within a totality of equipment; because, for Heidegger, equipment is essentially 'something in-order-to. . .', its essential structure is one of an assignment or reference of something to something – 'The work bears with it that referential totality within which the equipment is encountered' (*BT*, Sect. 15, p. 99). However, just as – in everyday dealings with the world – our concern focuses not so much on the tools themselves as on the work for which they are ready-to-hand, so the work itself does not bear that referential totality on its face for us. The assignment becomes explicit only when it is disturbed: if, for example, a tool is damaged or missing, or an entity is encountered as an obstacle to work.

> When an assignment to some particular 'towards-this' has been thus circumspectively aroused, we catch sight of the 'towards-this' itself, and along with it everything connected witn the work – the whole 'workshop' – as that wherein concern always dwells.

The context of equipment is lit up, not as something never seen before, but as a totality constantly sighted beforehand in circumspection.
(*BT*, Sect. 16, p. 105)

Circumspection (i.e. the sight guiding our everyday praxis) comes up against emptiness, and sees for the first time what the missing article was ready-to-hand *with*, and what it was ready-to-hand *for*; in this way, Being-in-the-world is revealed as amounting to a circumspective absorption in references or assignments constitutive for the readiness-to-hand of a totality of equipment.

For our purposes, it is crucial to note that when the worldhood of the world announces itself in a disturbed assignment, the constitutive role of understanding for Being-in-the-world is simultaneously made clear. To say that the Being of the ready-to-hand has the structure of assignment or reference means that it has in itself the character of having been assigned or referred; with any such entity there is an *involvement* which it has in something, and the possibility of encountering any given entity as involved presupposes the prior discovery of a totality of involvements, since its readiness-to-hand presupposes such a referential totality:

> With the 'towards-which' of serviceability there can again be an involvement: *with* this thing, for instance, which is ready-to-hand, and which we accordingly call a 'hammer', there is an involvement in hammering; with hammering, there is an involvement in making something fast; with making something fast, there is an involvement in protection against bad weather; and this protection 'is' for the sake of providing shelter for Dasein – that is to say, for the sake of a possibility of Dasein's Being.
> (*BT*, Sect. 18, p. 116)

The totality of involvements is always 'earlier' than any single item of equipment but it is ultimately grounded in a reference-relation in which there is *no* further involvement – a 'for-the-sake-of-which' which pertains to the Being of Dasein.

Here, Heidegger invokes his claim that Dasein is an entity which in its Being has this very Being as an issue:

> In each case, Dasein *is* its possibility, and it 'has' this possibility, but not just as a property, as something present-at-hand would.

And because Dasein is in each case essentially its own
possibility, it *can*, in its very Being, 'choose' itself and win itself;
it can also lose itself and never win itself; or only 'seem' to do so.
(*BT*, Sect. 9, p. 68)

The existentialist view that what one does and who one is are
internally related issues is here expressed in the claim that the
modes of practical activity which are an essential aspect of human
existence are rendered intelligible only by presupposing their
contribution to specific ways of existing within the world. At the
root of praxis lies Dasein's essential capacity to understand its
existence in terms of a potentiality-for-Being for the sake of which
it itself is; and in thus understanding itself, it understands the
world.

That wherein Dasein understands itself beforehand in the mode of
assigning itself is *that for which* it has let entities be encountered
beforehand. *The 'wherein' of an act of understanding which assigns or
refers itself, is that for which one lets entities be encountered in the kind of
Being that belongs to involvements; and this 'wherein' is the phenomenon of
the world.*
(*BT*, Sect. 18, p. 119)

Once again, the relationship of mutual implication between
human being and world is emphasized: to say that Dasein exists in
the world is to say that the act of understanding through which
Dasein grasps its own Being and potentiality-for-Being must
always encompass the world in which it is, i.e. must always relate
to the environment which the referential totality constitutes, and
which alone furnishes the equipmental domain within which
human purposes can be achieved:

Dasein as such is always something of this sort; along with its
Being, a context of the ready-to-hand is already essentially
discovered: Dasein, in so far as it *is*, has always submitted itself
already to a 'world' which it encounters, and this *submission*
belongs essentially to its Being.
(*BT*, Sect. 18, pp. 120–1)

Before going on to analyse in more depth the content of
Heidegger's claim that the world is always already understood in
terms of what he calls its 'significance' (i.e. the referential totality

which constitutes its worldhood), we must grasp the relation between Dasein and another type of entity it encounters within that world – other human beings. Our account of the world as 'workshop' left out the fact that the work produced also has an assignment to the person who is to use it or wear it; the work is cut to his figure, he 'is' there along with it as the work emerges:

> The Others who are thus 'encountered' in a ready-to-hand, environmental context of equipment, are not somehow added on in thought to some Thing which is proximally just present-at-hand; such 'Things' are encountered from out of the world in which they are ready-to-hand for Others – a world which is always mine too in advance. . ... Thus Dasein's world frees entities which not only are quite distinct from equipment and Things, but which also – in accordance with their kind of Being *as Dasein* themselves – are 'in' the world in which they are at the same time encountered within-the-world, and are 'in' it by way of Being-in-the-world. These entities are neither present-at-hand nor ready-to-hand; on the contrary, they are *like* the very Dasein which frees them, in that *they are there too, and there with it.*
> (*BT*, Sect. 26, p. 154)

Being-with is not, of course, equivalent to the contingent occurring together of several 'subjects':

> Being-with is an existential characteristic of Dasein even when factically no Other is present-at-hand or perceived. Even Dasein's Being-alone is Being-with in the world. The Other can be missing only in and for a Being-with. Being-alone is a deficient mode of Being-with; its very possibility is the proof of this. . ... Being missing and 'Being away' are modes of Dasein-with, and are possible only because Dasein as Being-with lets the Dasein of Others be encountered in its world.
> (*BT*, Sect. 26, p. 157)

If Being-with-Others belongs to the Being of Dasein, then – as Heidegger's reiteration of the term 'encountered' suggests – those Others must already have been disclosed in their Dasein, i.e. they must be encounterable. 'With their Being-with, their disclosedness has been constituted beforehand; accordingly, this disclosedness also goes to make up significance – that is to say, worldhood' (*BT*, Sect. 26, p. 160). This entails that other human beings are never proximally present-at-hand as free-floating subjects along with other entities; but the contribution of other Daseins to the significance of the world also implies something about our understanding of other people:

> Because Dasein's Being is Being-with, its understanding of Being already implies the understanding of Others. This understanding, like any understanding, is not an acquaintance derived from knowledge about them, but a primordially existential kind of Being, which, more than anything else, makes such knowledge and acquaintance possible. . ... It operates. . .by an acquaintance with that which Dasein, along with the Others, comes across in its environmental circumspection and concerns itself with – an acquaintance in which Dasein understands.
> (*BT*, Sect. 18, p. 161)

To summarize Heidegger's point: when analysing the issue of understanding the 'psychical life of Others', we should not take phenomena such as empathy to be the first ontological bridge between two self-contained subjects, but rather recognize that empathy (or indeed misunderstanding) becomes possible only on the basis of Being-with. We share the world with other people, not merely with organisms whose human status is in doubt.

Even if we can now see that the world's significance is constituted by Others as well as by entities ready-to-hand, we need to explore further the structure of the human understanding which Heidegger regards as the necessary complement to that world's worldhood. In understanding, as we have seen, the Being of Dasein discloses in itself what its Being is capable of; and Heidegger terms the structure of this understanding 'projection'. In other words, he conceives of Dasein as necessarily understanding itself in terms of its possibilities, which are grasped in their essence as possibilities and which permit Dasein to say to itself 'Become what you are'. Since these potentialities-for-Being presuppose a world in which they can be realized and an implicit grasp of Dasein's relation to that world and the entities within it, understanding necessarily involves an awareness of those items which are constitutive for Dasein as Being-in-the-world, i.e. Being-alongside the world and Being-with Others. This self-transparency is what Heidegger labels 'sight'; but it is only when such transparency is related to the concept of interpretation that we can appreciate the full essence of understanding.

The projecting of the understanding has its own possibility –
that of developing itself. This development of the understanding
we call 'interpretation'. In it the understanding appropriates
understandingly that which is understood by it. In
interpretation, understanding does not become something
different. It becomes itself.

(*BT*, Sect. 32, p. 188)

What is revealed explicitly in cases of interpreting the world (e.g. examining a tool in order to repair it) is the structure of something *as* something. The circumspective question as to what a given entity is ready-to-hand for receives the answer that it is for such-and-such a purpose – we *see* the entity *as* a table, a door, a carriage, or a bridge. Since, however, interpretation is simply an explicit mode of understanding, the seeing-as structure must also be the essence of all our encounters with the world:

In interpreting, we do not, so to speak, throw a 'signification'
over some naked thing which is present-at-hand, we do not stick
a value on it; but when something within-the-world is
encountered as such, the thing in question already has an
involvement which is disclosed in our understanding of the
world, and this involvement is one which gets laid out by the
interpretation.

(*BT*, Sect. 32, pp. 190–1)

Any pure perception of the ready-to-hand is an encounter which is understood in terms of a totality of involvements; it is simply that the assignment-relations which belong to that totality are hidden. Thus, Davidson's metaphysical assumptions of bare sound and movement, of a world devoid of significance, are directly contradicted by Heidegger's Cavell-like use of 'interpretation' as a synonym for a type of continuous seeing-as; and the ultimate ground of our comprehending perceptions is to be found in the realm of language and meaning, as Heidegger goes on to point out.

When entities within-the-world are discovered along with the Being of Dasein (i.e. when they have come to be understood), they are said to have meaning; but this 'meaning' is not a property those entities possess so much as the field wherein the intelligibility of something maintains itself – the framework in terms of which something becomes intelligible as something. It is thus internally related to projective understanding, and must be regarded as an essential facet of Dasein's Being-in-the-world:

> Meaning is an *existentiale* of Dasein, not a property attaching to entities, lying 'behind' them, or floating somewhere as an 'intermediate domain'. Dasein only 'has' meaning, so far as the disclosedness of Being-in-the-world can be 'filled in' by the entities discoverable in that disclosedness. *Hence only Dasein can be meaningful or meaningless.* That is to say, its own Being and the entities disclosed with its Being can be appropriated in understanding, or can remain relegated to non-understanding.
>
> (*BT*, Sect. 32, p. 193)

At the heart of understanding we find the formal-existential framework of meaning; but this framework is bequeathed to us not through language but rather through the existential-ontological foundation of language, i.e. 'discourse'.

> The intelligibility of something has always been articulated, even before there is any appropriative interpretation of it. Discourse is the Articulation of intelligibility. Therefore it underlies both interpretation and assertion. That which can be Articulated in interpretation, and thus even more primordially in discourse, is what we have called 'meaning'. That which gets articulated as such in discursive Articulation, we call 'totality-of-significations'.
>
> (*BT*, Sect. 34, pp. 203–4)

Discourse, as the necessary structure of the field of meaning, is the ground for the intelligibility of Being-in-the-world. It permits the disclosedness of entities within-the-world by Articulating that disclosedness according to significations, and it allows Being-in-the-world (as Being-with) to maintain itself in some definite way of concernful being-with-one-another, e.g. in assenting, refusing, interceding. The Articulations of discourse also permit Dasein, in talking, to express itself:

> Being-in and its state-of-mind are made known in discourse and indicated in language by intonation, modulation, the tempo of talk, 'the way of speaking'. In 'poetical' discourse, the communication of the existential possibilities of one's state-of-mind can become an aim in itself, and this amounts to a disclosing of existence.
>
> (*BT*, Sect. 34, p. 205)

All these structures of Being are to be seen in language, of course; but it is discourse – as the structure of the field of meaning – which makes it possible for language to do this at all. 'Language is a totality of words – a totality in which discourse has a "worldly" Being of its own; and as an entity within-the-world, this totality thus becomes something which we may come across as ready-to-hand' (*BT*, Sect. 34, p. 204). Language is the way in which discourse is expressed, but it is discourse which – in grounding the intelligibility of the world – accounts for the comprehending modes of perception (the hearing of waggons and words rather than tone-data) which Davidson ignores or denies.

What leads Davidson to down-play or explain away such revelatory aspects of everyday experience is his emphasis on theoretical cognition (on knowing) as the primary mode of human relations to the world – a mode in which, for Heidegger, entities are encountered simply as material objects rather than (e.g.) as tools. Heidegger does not, of course, deny that entities which are ready-to-hand can become present-at-hand, but he does claim that the latter mode of encountering the world is derivative and deficient. To take a specific example, Heidegger admits that language 'can be broken up into word-Things which are present-at-hand' (*BT*, Sect. 34, p. 204), but argues that such a possibility presupposes that readiness-to-hand is more primordial. Knowing is a capacity belonging to Dasein, and so must be conceptualized as a mode of Being-in-the-world; it is constitutive for Dasein's Being that it is always already-alongside-the-world, and this means that entities are proximally encountered as ready-to-hand:

> If knowing is to be possible as a way of determining the nature of the present-at-hand by observing it, then there must first be a *deficiency* in our having to do with the world concernfully. When concern holds back from any kind of producing, manipulating, and the like, it puts itself into what is now the sole remaining mode of Being-in, the mode of just tarrying alongside. . ... Such looking-at enters the mode of dwelling autonomously alongside entities within-the-world. In this kind of *dwelling* as a holding-oneself-back from any manipulation or utilization the *perception* of the present-at-hand is consummated.
>
> (*BT*, Sect. 13, pp. 88–9)

This perception amounts to interpretation in the broadest sense (a term central to Davidson's project), a making determinate which can be expressed in propositions; but such perceptive retention of assertions is itself a way of Being-in-the-world (not a mechanical procedure of conceptualizing bare sense-data), and must – in the last resort – be seen as founded on a more practical relationship to that world. Unlike the radical interpreter, Heidegger's human beings are at home in the world in precisely the way a labourer is at home in his workshop. Praxis without theory has its own sight.

PRELIMINARY FINDINGS

The preceding juxtaposition of Davidson and Heidegger in terms of their contrasting attitudes to a specific facet of ordinary experience (viz. our comprehending perception of the world), is of relevance to this book because – as I have argued in earlier chapters – Wittgenstein's account of aspect perception has the central aim of shedding some light on precisely that area of our lives. Since Davidson's metaphysics is structured in just such a way as to avoid treating such phenomena as important, it seems clear that any conceivable convergence or parallelism of philosophical approach evident in Wittgenstein's account and those of our two metaphysicians will involve Heidegger rather than Davidson. This conclusion can be further strengthened by noting that Heidegger's phenomenological methodology – in its presumption that those structures which it is the goal of philosophy to illuminate are to be found in Dasein's everyday experience – has a certain affinity with the Wittgensteinian emphasis on the grammatical structures manifest in ordinary language. The structures are differently conceived, but the return to the everyday is crucial for both.

More specifically, however, it is striking that Heidegger's description of the structures which underlie and make possible the phenomena with which we are concerned can be seen as resembling the form in which Wittgenstein's account of these same phenomena is given. Heidegger tells us that the notion of pure, bare perception as the primordial medium of our interaction with the world, with values and conceptual significations being projected upon it, is to be rejected in favour of an awareness that such perceptions always already involve human understanding and reveal the world as manifesting complex structures of intelligibility on an immediate level. The existence of specialized contexts in which entities in the world are encountered as present-to-hand (i.e. in terms of how they look, their bare shape and colour – as material objects) and are *then* interpreted, does not – we are told – prove that all perception is a matter of such interpretation. Rather, the seeing-as structure which *dawns* on certain occasions (e.g. when a tool is damaged and our attention thereby directed to the relations and assignments which constitute it as the kind of thing it is) should be seen as an explicit variant of a similar structure (a type of continuous seeing-as) which informs all of our relations with the world, and which is an element of our understanding of it. This structure is implicit in our encounters with any entities in the world, and so is necessarily involved in our relationship with language as a totality of concrete symbols. However, even when the entities concerned are not words, our mode of understanding and encountering them is ultimately to be grasped in terms of language, since the readiness-to-hand they manifest rests on those structures which constitute the essence of language (i.e. discourse). These essential linguistic structures are also – it is claimed – what permits linguistic behaviour to function as a mode of manifesting an individual's state of mind or feelings, and as a means of sharing those thoughts and reactions with others: they can thus be seen as grounding the various *aspects* of linguistic behaviour. And in the last resort, this multiplicity of interrelated issues concerning human relationships to language, other people and the world – a totality which can only be correctly grasped via the essential structures of language – reveals that human existence in the world should be seen as a mode of dwelling rather than of spatial location, as a matter of familiarity and at-homeness which is rooted in praxis rather than theoretical cognition. As Heidegger puts it:

> Nor does the term 'Being-in' mean a spatial 'in one-anotherness' of things present-at-hand, any more than the word 'in' primordially signifies a spatial relationship of this kind. 'In' is derived from '*innan*' – 'To reside', '*habitare*', 'to dwell'. '*An*' signifies 'I am accustomed', ' I am familiar with', 'I look after something'. It has the signification of '*colo*' in the senses of '*habito*' and '*diligo*'.
>
> (*BT*, Sect. 12, pp. 79–80)

In this respect, our understanding of the world is not a matter of knowing.

It is no part of my intention to make the naïve claim that Heidegger and Wittgenstein are 'saying the same thing' – as if the necessary criterion of identity which such a claim presupposes were obvious or unproblematic. The function of this chapter is much more tentative. First, since – as our analysis of Davidson's metaphysics showed – the issues at stake in Wittgenstein's treatment of aspect perception are standardly ignored or downplayed in Anglo-American philosophy, the sketch of Heidegger's treatment of those issues just given is designed to show that a certain tradition of philosophical thought *does* take them seriously – and furthermore, regards them as capable of bearing the weight of a complex and intriguing metaphysics. Second, the precise details of Heidegger's treatment are such that a summary of them might legitimately function as an additional means of orientation within the relevant philosophical terrain: the aspects of ordinary experience he invokes, and the deployment of related concepts (such as 'understanding', 'language', 'equipment') he effects, can cast light on the account Wittgenstein gives of these issues as well as being illuminated *by* that account.

Third, and most importantly, however, the working assumption which this chapter reflects (that in locating Wittgenstein's treatment of aspect perception in the space between a Davidsonian and a Heideggerian approach, we can cast some light upon its complexities) raises an issue which will occupy us for the rest of this book. Can the scope and depth of interest Heidegger attributes to the issues involved in aspect perception be preserved or enhanced by a philosophical treatment which explicitly presupposes that metaphysics is the shadow of grammar? Can a Wittgensteinian approach to this topic retain any semblance of Heidegger's sense that profound questions about the most appropriate way to characterize a specifically human mode of existence in the world are at stake when we attempt to give an account of these matters? In the following chapter, I shall begin to explore the answer to these questions.

5
GRAMMAR, METAPHYSICS, AND CONCEPT-MASTERY

After such a detailed examination of alternative philosophical perspectives on the central issues of this study, it may be worth re-emphasizing the two central themes that emerged from our earlier investigation of Wittgenstein's own remarks on aspect perception. First, I have argued that, notwithstanding the fact that Wittgenstein typically illustrates his remarks by reference to pictures or schematic figures, his observations are also applicable to words and people, i.e. that concepts of linguistic meaning and psychological concepts can be fruitfully regarded as aspect concepts. Second, I have emphasized the point that – again contrary to appearances – Wittgenstein's primary concern in this area is not the concept of aspect-dawning but rather that of continuous aspect perception (or 'regarding-as', as Wittgenstein sometimes labels it). In order to support this controversial conclusion, I have attempted to show not only that the mode of aspect-dawning appropriate to each of the three domains of aspect perception identified above is accompanied by a parallel mode of continuous seeing-as, but also that the capacity to experience aspect-dawning is of importance primarily because it manifests the general attitude or relation to symbols and people which the concept of continuous aspect perception picks out. In other words, the behaviour which manifests the experience of aspect-dawning is also a criterion for attributing the attitude of continuous seeing-as to a given individual.

The task of delineating the grammar of these concepts, however, is much more difficult in the case of continuous aspect perception than in that of aspect-dawning. This is primarily because, although one of the criteria for the applicability of continuous aspect perception is the capacity to experience aspect-dawning, continuous seeing-as is an *attitude* rather than an experience – and experiential concepts, for obvious reasons, are the more easily and the more strikingly illustrated. For example, the most revealing experiences of aspect-dawning in relation to pictures and words are to be found in aesthetics (cf. the examples of iconicity to be cited in Chapter 6), but more mundane examples are not hard to come by (cf. the example of 'living' pictures in Chapter 1, or the case of often-repeated words becoming mere sounds and a variety of other experiences of meaning examined in Chapter 2); and Chapter 3 touched upon the striking impression sometimes made by a human facial expression or gesture (cf. *RPP*,I, 267–8). The task of describing the concept of continuous aspect perception, on the other hand, must perforce be prosecuted in the absence of striking experiential illustrations.

The grammar of this latter concept emerged most clearly by contrasting it with the concept of aspect-blindness, a contrast which Wittgenstein often examines under the heading of a distinction between seeing and knowing or interpreting. In the case of pictures, the contrast is between someone who directly perceives an arrangement of colour-patches on canvas which he then interprets as a representation of a landscape and someone whose gestures and verbal behaviour reveal his taking it for granted that the basic elements of what he sees (the ones he directly perceives) are representations of elements of the landscape – trees, houses, and so on. With respect to language, continuous aspect perception involves directly perceiving the written and spoken elements of language as meaningful words and sentences rather than inferring their linguistic meaning from a direct perception of bare sounds or marks. In the domain of psychological concepts, continuous seeing-as involves seeing a friendly glance in another's eye rather than directly perceiving shapes, colours, and movements which are then interpreted to mean that the glance is a friendly one.

We might therefore redescribe the claim that the standard human relationship with pictures, words, and people is one of continuous aspect perception as the recognition that in these respects we encounter the world as always already saturated with human meaning. With respect to people, the force of this phrasing is obvious; and with respect to pictures and words it becomes obvious if we think of symbolic representation and expression as a function of human conventions and practices. I attempted to clarify the importance of this claim in Chapter 4 by presenting Davidson's philosophical system as an example of a diametrically opposed position. As his fundamental reliance upon the concept of interpretation indicates, Davidson assumes that when a human being speaks to us we hear bare sounds, and when he acts we perceive bare movements – the world is devoid of any human significance until we use our interpretative theorizing to organize this primitive data into units of human meaning, i.e. words, actions, gestures. Wittgenstein's conception of the ordinary human relationship with entities in these domains opposes and undermines such a vision of the human race as a tribe of aspect-blind beings, a vision of a world in which every language is at root a foreign tongue and every person an alien.

However, I also argued in Chapter 4 that Heidegger's conception of the basic human relationship towards such things as words, speech, and people paralleled Wittgenstein's position by being defined in direct opposition to such views as those of Davidson, and that Heidegger's metaphysics grounded this opposition by – again like Wittgenstein – allotting a fundamental role to the concept of seeing-as. Given this parallel, the implications conveyed by the terms in which Heidegger expresses his own position become very significant:

> What we 'first' hear is never noises or complexes of sounds, but the creaking waggon, the motorcycle. We hear the column on the march, the north wind, the woodpecker tapping, the fire crackling.
>
> It requires a very artificial and complicated frame of mind to 'hear' a 'pure noise'. The fact that motorcycles and waggons are what we proximally hear is the phenomenal evidence that in every case Dasein, as Being-in-the-World, already dwells alongside what is ready-to-hand-within-the-world; it certainly does not dwell proximally alongside 'sensation'; nor would it first have to give shape to the swirl of sensations to provide the springboard from which the subject leaps off and finally arrives at a 'world'. Dasein, as essentially understanding is proximally alongside what is understood.
>
> (*BT*, Sect. 34, p. 207)

As this quotation illustrates (by its attempt to take the battle against the interpretative or inferential model from the restricted field of symbols and other people into the domain of perception *per se*), and as my delineation of the way in which Heidegger treats seeing-as as a basic structure of Being-in-the-world confirms, for Heidegger the relationship between human beings and objects or phenomena *in general* must be conceptualized in terms of aspect perception. It is the concern of this present chapter to reveal those grammatical features of the concept of aspect perception which might have led Heidegger to universalize its role in this way, and to evaluate the validity of that universalization.

THE UNIVERSALITY OF ASPECT PERCEPTION

The direction of Heidegger's thought in this area has already been traced in some detail, but it may be of some use to summarize it here. Briefly, Heidegger begins from the Kantian problematic, i.e. the fact that human experience is of a coherent, intelligible world of objects rather than a blooming, buzzing confusion, and adds the claim that the entities in this world are encountered as ready-to-hand rather than present-at-hand (as akin to tools rather than merely material objects). The accessibility or intelligibility of the world to human understanding can be comprehended only on the assumption that the structures of intelligibility that the world manifests are in essence the structures which constitute language (i.e. discourse); and the claim that this accessibility or discoverability of entities is primordially one of readiness-to-hand (i.e. the particular *mode* of their accessibility) can be comprehended only if the relevant omnipresent structures of intelligibility are conceptualized in terms of an inexplicit (continuous) seeing-as structure. Thus we can say that the *centrality* of the concept of seeing-as in Heidegger's analysis is a function of the centrality of the category of readiness-to-hand; but the *generalization* of that concept's explanatory role is a function of the generalized and indispensable role allotted to language in the attempt to comprehend the fact that human beings perceive an intelligible world at all. Seeing-as pervades all our encounters with things just because language does so too.

It has already been argued in Chapter 2 that language occupied a central place in Wittgenstein's treatment of aspect perception; indeed, a transition to the realm of words, whether from that of pictures or from that of other people, seems forced upon us. Once it is established that aspect perception is at stake with respect to pictures and schematic figures, the question of whether the same can be said of specifically *linguistic* symbols (words and sentences uttered or written) arises immediately; and once psychological concepts in their application to human behaviour are seen to be aspect concepts, it follows that human linguistic behaviour (considered as a sub-set of human behaviour in general) must be similarly related to issues of aspect perception.

In both respects, however, the terms 'language' and 'linguistic' are simply picking out facets of specific types of entity within the world: linguistic meaning as an aspect of ink-marks or sounds, and linguistic meaning or import as an aspect of a particular sort of human behaviour. Heidegger posits a connection between seeing-as and language where 'language' refers to the bearer of conceptual structures which inform all experience – which can be said to constitute the world. The question now becomes: does language in this second sense play a similarly general and important role in Wittgenstein's treatment of aspect perception?

In one obvious way, an affirmative answer could be returned to this question simply on the basis of Wittgenstein's methodology. Any philosophical investigation was, for him, a grammatical investigation, i.e. a process of delineating the conceptual structures pertinent to the issues and confusions under examination; and, as the label 'grammatical' implies, such a process necessarily involved attention to linguistic matters. We might summarize his view as one in which concepts are constituted by the rules for the use of the corresponding concept-term; but in addition these grammatical rules – which determine what it makes sense to say about any given category of phenomena – are held to be autonomous, i.e. they do not reflect but rather constitute the essential nature of the corresponding phenomena.

This is what I take to be the import of Wittgenstein's remark that essence is expressed by grammar (*PI*, 371); and it entails a view of language as the bearer of conceptual structures which alone determine the bounds of sense in experience, which provide the only content that can be given to the idea of the *essence* of entities and processes. This treatment of the notion of essence differs radically from that of Heidegger as it is developed in his later philosophy, where the essence of beings is never *fully* exhausted by the resources of language. However, as a vision of linguistic structures and the way they inform all human experience by determining what it makes sense to say of the world, it is strikingly analogous to that of Heidegger.

This methodological emphasis upon language is, of course, evident in Wittgenstein's treatment of aspect perception as we have outlined it so far; and it is evident on two levels. First, in order to investigate the nature of aspects, he examines the nature of aspect concepts, which involves looking at the grounds for describing any given concepts as aspect concepts. Second, his investigation of the nature of the experience of aspect-dawning and its correlative phenomenon of continuous aspect perception in the domains of pictures, of words and of people is always couched in terms of eliciting the grounds for applying the concepts of aspect-dawning and of continuous aspect perception to a given person. For example, the question of whether the rabbit aspect of a duck-rabbit has dawned for someone is seen to be determined by the way in which that person employs a specific form of words as an *Ausserung*.

It would seem to follow that, before we can regard our investigation of the notion of continuous aspect perception as teaching us *general* lessons about the manner in which human beings relate to the world, we must first show that it is legitimate to regard any given set of concepts as *aspect* concepts. For if that label can only be applied to the concepts we examined in earlier chapters, then even if we *can* apply the concept of continuous aspect perception to human behaviour in relation to the objects to which those concepts apply, we could not extend it *beyond* those precise contexts. The question we must now ask, accordingly, is whether the notion of an aspect concept picks out a fixed or specific sub-set of all concepts; and whether it does so in such a manner that what can validly be observed about aspect perception can be applied to perception and experience involving concepts other than the ones to which our investigation has been restricted thus far.

To talk of psychological concepts and concepts of pictorial representation and linguistic meaning as aspect concepts encourages the following vision of the domains to which those concepts apply. The basic ontology in each is a type of material object or entity (an arrangement of lines and colour-patches, an ink-mark, a particular kind of organism); and in applying the appropriate aspect concepts to these things we are simply picking out particular features they can be said to possess when used or viewed in a particular way. Such a vision may well have a salutary effect on one type of philosophical confusion, since it discourages the notion that – for example – ink-marks become meaningful by being associated with mental acts of meaning or with concepts conceived of as existing in some ethereal third realm, or that psychological phenomena are private objects or processes existing in a world within the subject. In other words, to talk of these concepts as aspect concepts discourages the ontological excesses inherent in a view of such concepts as referring to phenomena in a linguistic or psychological realm which is distinct from the material one.

However, the alternative which this vision seems to entail is that aspects have an ontologically secondary status: that – unlike properties such as colour, shape, length – they are features that entities possess only when viewed from a particular perspective. Put in grammatical terms, the claim would be that aspect concepts are logically secondary in comparison with concepts of material properties, since the former involve human projections of significance upon the world whereas the latter refer to properties which entities possess in their own right. It would be a consequence of this view that aspect concepts *do* form a specific sub-set of all concepts, and that accordingly lessons derived from a study of them could not be generalized.

As I tried to show in some detail in Chapters 1 and 2, however, this interpretation of the difference between aspect concepts and those of material properties is precisely the one Wittgenstein is concerned to combat, since it entails the view that aspects are features of objects which are not really seen (for they are not 'objectively' there to be seen) but are rather interpretations of the immediate material properties of the relevant entities. In short, the contrast between continuous aspect perception and knowing or interpreting is designed specifically to reveal that this inferential model of aspect perception is erroneous.

But it must be admitted that such a model is merely one proffered *interpretation* of the difference between aspect concepts and other concepts: and it is undeniable that Wittgenstein does on occasion emphasize the distinctive nature of aspect concepts by contrasting them with material property concepts. When discussing the issue of seeing the glance or look of an eye, he puts it this way:

> Certainly I too say that I see the glance that you throw someone else. And if someone wanted to correct me and say I don't really *see* it, I should hold this to be a piece of stupidity. On the other hand, I have not *admitted* anything with my way of putting it, and I contradict anyone who tells me I see the eye's glance 'just as' I see its form and colour.
>
> (*RPP*,I, 1101)

The basic question of this chapter can therefore be refined: given that the label 'aspect concept' is used to pick out certain concepts in contrast to others, are such contrasts timeless and absolute or are they context-relative? Is the label 'aspect concept' inalienable?

When attempting to elucidate the nature of aspect concepts in Chapter 1, I argued that, whereas an object's properties of colour and shape can be explained by means of an exact copy of the object of sight, no such reproduction of what is perceived could make manifest the aspect of a given object that one suddenly perceives. What is rather necessary is an attempt to convey certain references and relations which are not purely material. This, I suggested, was related to a key remark of Wittgenstein's which runs as follows:

> The colour of the visual impression corresponds to the colour of the object (this blotting paper looks pink to me, and is pink) – the shape of the visual impression to the shape of the object (it looks rectangular to me, and is rectangular) – but what I perceive in the dawning of an aspect is not a property of the object, but an internal relation between it and other objects.
>
> (*PI*, 212a)

In other words, when we notice a new aspect of an object, we do not suddenly see a property, part, or element of it which we had previously failed to register (e.g. a particular patch of colour) but rather become aware that a new *kind* of description might be made of the object as a whole. We perceive that it can be seen as another sort of object altogether.

Part of the content of the claim that we see something as a different sort of object altogether is that we are capable of using a different set of concepts to describe its basic elements, properties, or parts. When the rabbit aspect of the duck-rabbit dawns, we see that the duck's bill can also be described as the ears of a rabbit, and so on; when we suddenly perceive the face in a puzzle-picture, we realize that a randomly organized collection of lines can be described in terms of facial features. In thus perceiving the applicability of a certain system of concepts, one perceives a relation between the object and those objects to which that set of concepts is also applicable; and since this relation has been established via conceptual or grammatical structures, it can validly be called an internal relation – one pertaining to the essence or identity of the relata. For Wittgenstein, as we mentioned earlier, grammar is that which tells us what kind of an object anything is.

The posited unique status of material property concepts emerges more clearly as a result of this formulation of the nature of aspects, for it permits the following restatement: seeing something as something involves seeing one kind of object as another kind of object. However, to describe something as a particular *kind* of object necessarily presupposes that it is an object (i.e. that it is a something); and objecthood – the applicability of the general concept of an object *per se* – is partially defined by the applicability of material property concepts. Part of what it *means* to describe something as an object at all is that it possesses some determinable colour, shape, length, etc. The system of material property concepts thus necessarily applies to anything we might see as something, whereas any other system – given that it defines a particular kind of object, and thus applies to a sub-set of objects in general – need not do so.

However, much less follows from this distinction than might be thought. First, the very fact that the concepts of objecthood and of material properties are internally related means that the statement 'All objects have some specifiable colour and spatial dimensions' (together with its companion 'This object has some specifiable colour and spatial dimensions') conveys no information: they are expressions of a grammatical rule, not empirical propositions. Thus no metaphysical conclusions can be derived; no support is given, for example, to the idea that all phenomena are reducible to material phenomena. We might say that it licenses the view that, for any set of concepts which pick out a particular kind of object to have application, the set of material property concepts must have application, i.e. there must exist some objects – but this again reduces to a grammatical remark.

Second, it might be thought that if the concept of seeing something as something presupposes the applicability of material property concepts (i.e. presupposes the existence of a something that is being seen as something else) then the set of material property concepts will – if in play at all – always occupy the first place in the 'seeing x as y' schema. And since it is occupation of the *second* place in that schema that confers the label of aspect concepts upon a given set of concepts (i.e. since aspect concepts are standardly thought to be the ones in terms of which we see something), it follows that the set of material property concepts can never be described as aspect concepts.

This view is quite simply erroneous. The point – one emphasized by Heidegger when he says that encountering beings as present-at-hand is a derivative mode of Being-in-the-world – is that we do not encounter things as exemplars of objecthood in general but rather as specific *kinds* of object. The things I directly perceive on my desk are books, envelopes containing letters consisting of words and sentences, a group photograph, a lamp, a pen and ruler; they are not most immediately encountered simply as material objects of varying form and colour. I can, of course, take up a perspective from which I can see these things as bare arrangements of colour and shape (I can try to see the photograph as an array of colour-patches); but then the set of material property concepts occupies that second place in the schema 'seeing x as y' which permits us to label it as picking out an aspect of the object (its material aspect). Furthermore, the very multiplicity of kinds of objects with which the world is populated and which we directly encounter entails a multiplicity of different sets of concepts occupying the first place in the seeing-as schema and a consequent restriction of the occasions upon which the set of material property concepts occupies that first place.

Here, it is important to remember that on my interpretation of the concept of continuous aspect perception, Wittgenstein introduced that concept precisely to pick out the potential multiplicity of types of conceptual framework that can occupy that first place in the seeing-as schema. The central thrust of his treatment of the domains of pictures, words, and people is directed against the idea that we directly perceive the entities we encounter in those domains as mere material objects. For example, continuously to see the (or a) pictorial aspect of a figure was defined as treating it as a picture, directly perceiving it in terms of its pictorial elements rather than drawing conclusions about what it was supposed to represent from its specific colour-shape properties; and another way of putting this is to say that we would have to make an effort in order to perceive the picture as a material object in its own right. Analogous work is done by the notion of continuous seeing-as with respect to words and people: in all three domains, the claim is that the set of material property concepts could secure application in the conceptual structure of seeing-as only by occupying the second place in the schema.

So a difficulty now arises for our attempt to analyse the nature of aspect concepts – or, more accurately perhaps, illumination is cast on our difficulties in understanding that label. For if the concepts of pictorial and linguistic meaning as well as psychological concepts are the paradigmatic examples of aspect concepts, and yet in their own domain can generally be used in the conceptual structure of seeing-as only by occupying the first place in the schema, then the paradigms of aspect concepts fail to fulfil the first criterion for 'aspecthood' that we have been relying upon – viz. that they occupy the second place in that schema, that they provide the framework in terms of which we see something. Indeed, once they occupy the first place in the schema it would be impossible for them to occupy the second place as well, for the same set of concepts cannot be employed in both places of that schema at once: it makes no sense to say, for example, 'I'm seeing the knife and fork as a knife and fork' (*PI*, 195b). Is Wittgenstein arguing that the paradigmatic aspect concepts are not aspect concepts at all?

One qualification of the terms of this seeming contradiction must be acknowledged at once: for some of the examples of seeing-as upon which Wittgenstein concentrates in his treatment relate not so much to primary applications of the relevant set of concepts as to secondary ones – to extensions or modifications of those language games. His examples are sometimes of schematic drawings rather than fully-fledged pictures, of words considered in isolation rather than in the context of uttered sentences or extended texts, of psychological concepts in their relation to the multiplicity of human facial expressions rather than to their 'core' application to the behaviour of a person in context. In such secondary cases, it is more easy to perceive the material aspect of the symbol or the physical aspect of the face – and correspondingly more likely that a given observer might have to make an effort in order to see the relevant entity in terms of those aspect concepts. Nevertheless, the major part of Wittgenstein's discussions relate to fully-fledged pictures, to poetry and conversations, and to sequences of human actions; so this qualification does not eradicate the pertinence of our question.

However, the postulated contradiction vanishes when we recognize that these paradigmatic aspect concepts fall under the label of aspect concepts in two different senses, i.e. that the category of aspect concept has a double function in Wittgenstein's investigation. On the one hand, the label relates to those concepts which occupy the second place in the seeing-as schema, i.e. to those concepts in terms of which we are coming to perceive a given kind of object, in experiences of aspect-dawning or of trying to see an aspect. On the other hand, by making us aware that we can see an entity as a new kind of object, such experiences thereby highlight the fact that we are already regarding it as a particular kind of object, i.e. they focus our attention upon the set of concepts occupying the first place of the seeing-as schema.

This 'regarding as' is *also* conceptualized as a mode of aspect perception by Wittgenstein: partly because it emerged as a philosophical topic via an investigation of aspect-dawning, and partly because the label 'aspect concepts' in its first sense picks out systems of concepts which furnish a kind of description of objects as a whole (i.e. determine a kind of object) – and exactly the same can be said of systems of concepts eligible to occupy the first place in the seeing-as schema. The three paradigmatic systems of aspect concepts can, as we have seen, occupy either place in the seeing-as schema, and therefore can intelligibly be labelled aspect concepts in the second sense of that term even in contexts where it is logically impossible for them to occupy the second place in the schema. Accordingly, no contradiction exists in Wittgenstein's treatment of those concepts.

The crucial point for the purposes of this chapter, of course, is that the capacity shared by our three paradigm sets of concepts to occupy either place in the seeing-as schema (in an appropriate context) is one possessed by *any* set of concepts which determines a kind of object. The ability to perceive a given kind of object as another kind of object (i.e. in terms of another set of concepts) is limited only by the powers of the human imagination – which is simply another way of saying that we can place no logical constraints upon *what* we might see any given object *as* (apart, of course, from requiring that the perceiver be capable of giving an intelligible explanation of how one might see the object as he sees it).

It is also the case, however, that the intelligibility of using any such set of concept words in that way is dependent upon their being able to occupy the first place in the seeing-as schema, i.e. upon it being possible for us to describe some entities as *being* the kind of thing we can *see* other entities *as*. This is an issue Wittgenstein is commenting upon when he remarks that mastery of an existent conceptual technique is a logical condition of someone's having an experience of aspect-dawning (*PI*, 208e,f), and also when he points out that words can be used in a secondary sense only if they already have a primary sense (*PI*, 216e). The reason for this is as follows: if someone says 'I'm seeing this as a y' and another person asks what he means by 'a *y*', the first speaker must be capable of explaining the meaning of his words – and he cannot do so by (e.g.) pointing to the object he is seeing *as* a *y*, since that would explain nothing. He can only point to something which *is* a *y* – that is, make some reference to a domain within which the relevant set of concepts would occupy the first place of any seeing-as schema. If, however, any set of concepts determining a kind of object can occupy the second place in the schema, and if any such set must be capable of occupying that schema's first place, then it follows that any such set of concepts is capable of falling under the heading of 'aspect concepts' in either sense of that phrase.

At this stage we must recall that the form of words I have been using to distinguish the two different senses of the phrase 'aspect concept' (viz. the schema 'I am seeing something as something') has a very precise and limited range of intelligible application – namely, contexts of giving expression to the experience of the dawning of a new aspect. As we saw earlier, that form of words is simply not applicable in contexts of everyday visual perception, for any attempt to do so would involve using the same set of concepts in both places of the schema, e.g. saying 'I'm seeing the cutlery as cutlery.' If the category of 'aspect concept' is defined by reference to such contexts, must it not therefore follow that it cannot be employed in contexts of everyday visual perception, no matter *which* of its two senses we wish to stress, and so that the conclusions of our investigations into aspect perception cannot be generalized?

In order to address this anxiety, we must look at the two different senses of the term 'aspect concept' in turn. A given set of concepts can be said to function as aspect concepts in the *first* sense of that phrase only if they provide the terms in which someone is seeing a certain entity (i.e. are presently occupying the second place in the seeing-as schema). The point that they can intelligibly be so used only when a different set of concepts occupies the first place in the schema is indeed equivalent to saying that concepts can be regarded as aspect concepts in this first sense only when involved in an experience of aspect-dawning. Since this experience is a very specific and relatively rare one, it seems clear that any conclusions we might draw concerning aspect concepts in *this* sense of the term 'aspect' could *not* be viewed as generalizable to the relationship between human beings and objects or phenomena in general.

If generalization along the lines implied by Heidegger's text is thus effectively blocked on the first interpretation of the category of aspect concepts, what of the *second* sense of that term? At first sight, a similar impediment exists in this quarter, since I defined aspect concepts in the second sense as those eligible to occupy the first place in the seeing-as schema, and the intelligible use of that form of words is – as we have seen – restricted to (because partially constitutive of) the experience of aspect-dawning. Such an impression is, however, misleading; for in this case, the experience of aspect-dawning merely highlights a set of relations which must manifest themselves in contexts other than this specific one. This conclusion follows from the fact that any particular experience of aspect-dawning, in making us aware that we can see a given entity as a *new* kind of object, thereby highlights the fact that we are *already* regarding it as a particular kind of object – the kind determined by the set of concepts occupying the first place in the seeing-as schema.

For example, on the one hand seeing a painting as an array of colour-patches is merely one way of seeing a painting, it is *one* experience we can have when we encounter paintings. Accordingly, if we focus upon the way the *new* set of material property concepts relates to the object and to our perceptual experience of it, we restrict ourselves to a special mode of the relation between concepts and experience because we are restricting ourselves to a special experience (i.e. aspect-dawning). On the other hand, even if seeing a painting as an array of colour-patches is a particular sort of experience – is one unusual way of perceiving the painting – it necessarily involves perceiving a painting, and thus exemplifies the relation between 'painting' concepts and experience which applies in the whole domain of paintings even when no experience of aspect-dawning is at stake. So, if we focus upon the way the *old* set of concepts (that which occupies the first place of the schema) relates to the object and to our perceptual experience of it, we are studying an exemplification of a universal relation between concepts, the world, and experience, viz. that between concepts determining an object of kind x, objects of kind x, and our perception of such objects in so far as it involves such concepts.

I can therefore simplify my initial definition of aspect concepts in this second sense. Aspect concepts are not so much any set of concepts capable of occupying the first place in the seeing-as schema, but rather any set of concepts determining any kind of object, i.e. determining what it is for an object to be an object of a given kind. If one adds to this the fact that when people – language-users – perceive and encounter particular objects, those encounters will necessarily involve a set of concepts which determine those objects as objects of a particular kind (otherwise it would make no sense to describe what takes place as (e.g.) someone perceiving some particular thing), it follows that a study of continuous aspect perception can legitimately be viewed as a philosophical investigation of human relationships with objects or phenomena *in general*.

GRAMMAR AND METAPHYSICS

The above conclusion – one derived from Wittgenstein's treatment of aspect perception – runs precisely parallel to that reached by Heidegger in the first Division of *Being and Time*, where – as I have already argued – he claims that the relationship between human beings and objects or phenomena *in general* must be conceptualized in terms of aspect perception. The next task in this chapter is to investigate what – if anything – this tells us about the *nature* of that general relation.

As I mentioned earlier, Wittgenstein's methodology is determined by the two interlinked principles that essence is expressed by grammar and that grammar is autonomous. From this perspective, the meaning of the claim that human beings encounter objects in a particular way (or of the corresponding claim that our experience of those objects has a certain form) is given by an account of what it is in human behaviour (linguistic and non-linguistic) relating to those objects that would justify the application of that particular form of words. For Heidegger, the category of 'readiness-to-hand' is intended rather to capture the being of the *entities* we encounter; but he also takes those features to reveal something about the essence of Dasein, and it will be my claim in the remainder of this chapter that he can execute just such a change of focus in his analysis precisely because the features his notion of 'readiness-to-hand' captures are in fact the criteria in human behaviour which justify our applying the concept of 'continuous aspect perception' to it.

As I noted at the beginning of this chapter, Heidegger is led to argue that the structures of intelligibility which constitute the essence of language must be conceptualized in terms of seeing-as primarily because to do so is our only way of comprehending the particular way in which human beings encounter things in the world. In other words, his invocation of seeing-as is intended to be a restatement on a deeper level of the claim that readiness-to-hand is the category in terms of which we standardly encounter things in the world. In Chapter 4, I offered a detailed examination of this category, but it may be worth reiterating some of the features this category is intended to highlight.

To begin with, readiness-to-hand is presented as a contrast to presentness-at-hand, the latter being that mode of encountering things which is appropriate to theoretical cognition and which involves treating an entity as a material object in its own right. Treating this mode of encountering entities as basic or fundamental entails the view that one's awareness of the entity as whatever particular kind of object it is (a hammer, shoes, a desk), is the result of interpreting what is immediately seen in terms of a set of subjective categories. Clearly, in regarding readiness-to-hand as the more basic of the two categories, Heidegger is opposing just the sort of inferential or interpretative model of perception and understanding against which Wittgenstein defines his concept of continuous aspect perception:

But [readiness-to-hand] is not to be understood as merely a way of taking [entities], as if we are talking such 'aspects' into the 'entities' which we proximally encounter, or as if some world-stuff which is proximally present-at-hand in itself were 'given subjective colouring' in this way.

(*BT*, Sect. 15, p. 101)

The fact that such a vision of human relationship with objects and phenomena can be seen to pervade central strands of contemporary philosophy, including the Davidsonian approach, makes it clear that Wittgenstein and Heidegger are not combating straw men or passé philosophical outlooks.

But how are we to understand the contrasting vision they offer? What, if anything, is involved in the claim that we directly perceive and encounter hammers, shoes, and desks rather than a material world-stuff upon which subjective meanings are projected? Heidegger lays emphasis upon the way in which human life involves practical activity, i.e. upon the point that the things we meet with in the world are not simply treated as objects in their own right but as things which relate in different ways to the context and goals of human purposive activity:

If we look at things just 'theoretically', we can get along without understanding readiness-to-hand. But when we deal with them by using them and manipulating them, this activity is not a blind one; it has its own kind of sight, by which our manipulation is guided and from which it acquires its specific Thingly character.

(*BT*, Sect. 15, p. 98)

The point here is that objects are things which we use and manipulate in our daily life, and the ways in which a given object is utilized manifest the kind of object it is – a hammer is the sort of thing we use for knocking in nails, a desk is something we rest on when writing letters.

Such an observation seems unobjectionable; but the *additional* point that the notions of readiness-to-hand and continuous aspect perception bring out is that objects are absorbed into human practical activity in a particular way, a smooth unhesitating way which manifests the complete absence of room for doubt about the kind of object any given thing may be. Whenever we encounter hammers and desks, we do not continually have to stop and ask ourselves what kinds of object they may be, there is no inferential or interpretative process at work: when, in the middle of the task of erecting shelves, some nails need to be knocked in, we reach at once for the hammer rather than breaking off from the task to examine all the contents of our tool-box.

Another way of putting this is to say that we sight *through* the objects, that the particular activity in which we are engaged orients us towards a particular goal upon which we are focused directly, and the things in our environment – according to the *kind* of thing they are – are treated as means towards that goal. Treating them as material objects in their own right (i.e. making the object the goal or end of our activity by contemplating it) involves a completely different orientation and suspends the unhesitating way they were absorbed into our activities as means.

This point, in its application to paintings, words, and people, was what I was alluding to in Chapters 1 and 2 when I characterized continuous aspect perception as a relation to these three kinds of thing which took their specific nature ('[their] specific Thingly character') for granted. For example, I defined that relation to paintings as one in which the basic elements of what is seen (the ones directly perceived) are representations of (e.g.) a landscape – trees, houses, and so on – rather than colour-patches on canvas; and another way of expressing this would be to say that we see straight through the painting to that which it is intended to represent rather than being directly concerned with it as a material object. Similarly, an apt way of characterizing a relation of continuous aspect perception towards *language* would be to say that, in it, words are ready-to-hand for the speaker or author or audience. We do not have to remember that 'tree' means tree, texts and speeches directly convey information and express emotion rather than confronting us with symbols requiring interpretation; in short, words are available to us as a particular means of achieving our purposes and goals – just as a hammer is unhesitatingly utilized when our goal is hammering nails.

Those features of our relation to objects which I am attempting to characterize here under the heading of readiness-to-hand are most evident when the objects under consideration are paradigmatic examples of tools. Heidegger's favoured illustrations are those of craftsmen and farmers precisely because in such ways of life the equipmental relation between objects and human practical activity is dominant. In claiming that we should conceptualize human relationships with objects in general along similar lines, however, it should not be thought that I am claiming that all objects are tools. The point is rather that, to some degree or other, things tend to be seamlessly woven into human practical activity when encountered in everyday life rather than being treated as objects of theoretical contemplation – and that is simply a way of describing one of the features of everyday life picked out by the claim that we *regard* entities as particular *kinds* of objects (as desks, hammers, shoes) rather than simply as objects. It is therefore important to remember that continuous aspect perception refers to more than perception or contemplation of an object. To say that someone directly perceives an object in a given way is a description whose applicability is judged *inter alia* by the specific ways in which that object's being the kind of object it is is manifest in the ways it is woven into that person's verbal and non-verbal practical activities.

Heidegger traces two paths from the claim that human beings encounter entities as ready-to-hand, paths which I followed in some detail in Chapter 4 but which can now be used to throw further light upon the notion of continuous seeing-as. First, then, for Heidegger it makes no sense to talk of an entity as a piece of equipment when it is considered in isolation; what makes a given entity a piece of equipment is its place within a totality of equipment. Partly, this location consists in its relationship with other pieces of equipment: if a pen is to be thought of as a pen, i.e. as equipment for writing, this presupposes a relationship to ink, paper, blotting pad, and desk.

This point, I want to suggest, is paralleled in the way Wittgenstein regards aspect perception as relating a given entity to other entities in a particular way; for people who see the same object differently show this, amongst other ways, in the differing types of contrast and comparison which make sense to them or which they take for granted. To take an example Wittgenstein employs in passing: seeing a chair as being in the style of Louis XIV (*LW*,I, 750) involves locating it very precisely within the general category of furniture. Not only would one relate it to other Louis XIV chairs, one would treat it as being like tables or stools which exemplify the same style but unlike chairs which exemplify other styles – whereas someone who does not recognize it as being in any sort of style would draw precisely the opposite comparisons and contrasts, would in effect know his way around within the world of furniture in very different ways.

The guiding principle here is that perceiving such an aspect – treating the entity as that particular *kind* of object – involves a set of concepts, a framework or system which organizes a domain of the world; and, as I mentioned in Chapter 3, this means that grasping one concept within the set involves grasping the set as a whole. In conveying one particular way in which objects can vary, can differ from and resemble one another, such a set of concepts provides a dimension of variation. This general dimension is itself defined by the various points along it, and each specific point is given by its difference from the other points: to say that a chair was in the style of Louis XIV would mean something very different if our furniture-style concepts picked out only two different styles. Heidegger's talk of an equipmental totality thus expresses in material mode a grammatical point about the nature of aspect concepts.

Heidegger goes on, however, to trace a second feature of such totalities, one which he refers to as the 'towards-which' of its usability. In simple terms, this refers to the work to be produced by human utilization of the relevant totality of equipment within a particular environment; and he emphasizes the fact that this product typically also has the being of equipment, e.g. a shoe is produced for wearing, a clock for telling the time. Once again, the direction of his thought is being shaped by the grammatical point that to describe an entity as a given kind of object is to relate it to human purposes in some way – in the sense that a vase is something we fill with flowers in order to decorate a room, or a lamp is something we use to illuminate (e.g.) a work-surface.

However, Heidegger wishes to go further than this:

With the 'towards-which' of serviceability there can be an involvement: with this thing, for instance, which is ready-to-hand, and which we accordingly call a 'hammer', there is an involvement in hammering; with hammering, there is an involvement in making something fast; with making something fast, there is an involvement in protection against bad weather; and this protection 'is' for the sake of providing shelter for

Dasein – that is to say, for the sake of possibility of Dasein's Being.

(*BT*, Sect. 18, p. 116)

Here, Heidegger is invoking his existentialist claim that Dasein is an entity which in its Being has this very Being as an issue, i.e. that Dasein has an essential capacity to understand its existence in terms of a particular potentiality-for-Being for the sake of which it itself is. This capacity is held to be at the root of all human praxis, since many modes of such practical activity are rendered intelligible only by presupposing their contribution to specific ways of existing within the world. As I summarized this tortuous argument in Chapter 4: for Heidegger, to say that Dasein exists in the world is to say that the act of understanding through which Dasein grasps its own Being and potentiality-for-Being must always encompass the world in which it is, i.e. must always relate to the environment which the equipmental totality constitutes, and which alone furnishes the equipmental domain within which human purposes can be achieved.

Needless to say, Wittgenstein produces no such baroque metaphysical structures from his claim that human relations towards objects and phenomena in general should be seen in terms of continuous aspect perception. For him, part of what is *meant* by saying that we directly perceive things as kinds of object rather than as pieces of world-stuff which must then be interpreted is that our verbal and non-verbal behaviour in relation to such entities takes a distinctive form, one in which their status as a particular kind of object is taken for granted. One ubiquitous example of such taking-for-granted is the smooth and unhesitating way in which objects are taken up as means into the flow of human activity when they are appropriate for the task in hand; and one way of expressing this smoothness is to say that our focus is on the goal or purpose rather than upon the objects considered as material objects in their own right. In saying all this, however, we are simply transforming expressions according to grammatical rules, connecting expressions with the criteria for their application, or offering alternative characterizations of certain phenomena; no metaphysical *discoveries* can emerge from such grammatical explorations.

We might characterize the position we have reached in the following way. Heidegger, having been perceptive enough to focus upon the features that continuous aspect perception is meant to pick out, and having seen their importance as a means of dislodging erroneous philosophical world-views, attempts to utilize those features as proof of a metaphysical conception of the essence of human existence. The only way of showing that Heidegger's choice of the metaphysical route is to be avoided is to show that the features of human relationships with objects which we have isolated do not require the truth of his metaphysical doctrine in order to be explicable; and the material we need for such a route-blocking enterprise is precisely what Wittgenstein's investigation provides.

As I noted earlier, Wittgenstein's methodology presupposes that philosophical investigations are always and only grammatical investigations, i.e. are always pitched at a conceptual level. We can therefore assume that in examining the ordinary human relationship towards objects in general, Wittgenstein is in fact examining the way in which human beings manifest their grasp of the relevant concepts in their practical activity. In other words, those features of human relationships towards objects and phenomena which I have so far been attempting to express in material mode should be seen as marking aspects of the grammar of concepts relating to human behaviour. What I want to suggest here is that those features might be given expression by saying that concepts *inform* human experience rather than interpreting it for us; and the best way of seeing what this formulation encapsulates is to approach it by means of a philosophical worry about issues in the area of conceptual relativism.

In attempting to illustrate and defend his views on the autonomy of grammar Wittgenstein often hypothesizes the existence of tribes with differing concepts from our own. In one case he imagines a world in which certain shapes tend always to go with certain colours, and points out that in such a context a tribe's having a linguistic technique of colour-shape concepts but no terms for colour as opposed to shape (e.g. for the colour which two differently shaped objects share) would be both intelligible and natural. The question then arises: to what extent can we make such alien sets of concepts intelligible to ourselves?

In one sense, this example is a relatively amenable one, for it seems to be a case where the alternative concepts can be mapped without remainder onto our own – the categories provided by our language are merely grouped differently, they are not cut across or jettisoned. On the other hand, however, how can we justify a description of the alien concepts as referring to combinations of colour and shape while simultaneously denying that this tribe possesses colour concepts or shape concepts? To put the worry another way: although we can intelligibly describe the alien conceptual structure of colour-shape combinations, teach the alien technique to others and learn to employ it as does the alien tribe, we cannot – as it were – see the world through their eyes; we cannot experience the world according to a language which makes no distinction between concepts of colour and concepts of shape. At best, it might be said, we can continue to perceive our world of colours and shapes, and then reinterpret that experience in terms of the alien concept words; when the aliens speak, we will know what they mean but we will not be able to see the world like that. The fact that concepts *inform* our experience rather than simply functioning as a means of describing it locks us out of the experience of others who have even minimally divergent concepts.

Clearly, there are some problematic aspects to this philosophical worry as it has just been articulated. To begin with, the issue is presented as though we are locked out from the alien's world of consciousness – as if from their subjectivity, the quality of their day-to-day experience of the world – when the very notion of a 'world of consciousness' is left unexplained and vulnerable to philosophical attack. Furthermore, the failure of accessibility involved is seen as an empirical barrier, an ultimate brute fact resulting from the way in which our concepts are deeply engrained in our experience by means of some combination of nature and socialization processes. And yet, the implicit sense that this empirical (and therefore contingent) barrier could not possibly be removed suggests that the roots of our awareness of a limitation may well lie in the realm of grammar (i.e. of rules determining what it makes sense to say and think) rather than of experience. Indeed, if we reinterpret the problem as a misinterpretation of real conceptual distinctions then the insights which this worry embodies in a confused way will be revealed.

For it is surely striking that the above sketch of our position *vis-à-vis* alien tribes with divergent concepts resembles that of the phenomenon of aspect-blindness provided by Wittgenstein. As I argued in Chapter 1, the aspect-blind person is not rendered incapable of learning, employing, and even teaching a given conceptual technique; when, for example, he looks at a picture of a landscape, he can discern what is being depicted and provide what he knows to be the conventional description of it (*PI*, 201e). He will know what the drawing and pictures are intended to represent but he can at best *interpret* them in these terms; and the fact that he must read the picture like a blueprint is what leads us to say that he merely knows what the picture represents – he cannot *see* it as a pictured animal or landscape (*PI*, 203–4). To put this in terms of the present discussion: the meaning-blind person's relationship to language is such that the linguistic technique *stands between* him and the world. The concepts it provides do not inform his experience, but rather interpret it; and this, it is held, is how we stand in relation to the world of a tribe with even minimally divergent concepts.

To begin with, then, we can say that this worry about alien concepts does correctly perceive that the normal role of concepts in our lives takes a form different from that of aspect-blindness, i.e. that it is misrepresented if couched in terms of an inferential or interpretative model. The additional gain in translating the worry into the terms of Wittgenstein's discussion of continuous aspect perception, however, is that it reveals the difference between aspect-blindness and continuous aspect perception to be a matter of conceptual rather than empirical/psychological distinctions, to be marked by criteria rather than references to the different subjective 'feel' of an alien world of consciousness. My contention is that the claim 'concepts inform our experience' is another way of saying 'our relationship towards objects in general is one of continuous aspect perception', i.e. the content of that former claim is exhausted by the features of the ordinary human relationship with objects which the notion of continuous aspect perception picks out.

Wittgenstein refers to several criteria for the application of the latter notion, i.e. to several features of everyday human verbal and non-verbal behaviour in relation to objects in general. He highlights the inclination to choose particular forms of words and intonation-patterns (*PI*, 201e), the tendency to find a given type of description of an object natural and unavoidable rather than conventional, as well as precluding certain types of mistake (*PI*, 203–4), and in particular the distinctive ways in which our behaviour and activities in relation to entities manifest our taking it for granted that the entity is the kind of object it is (i.e. the features I have dwelt on in this chapter).

On this interpretation, references to subjective 'feels' and worlds of consciousness drop out in favour of verbal and non-verbal behavioural criteria – as might be expected in any Wittgensteinian foray into the philosophy of psychology. And it follows that the only relevant evidence for the claim that we cannot see the world as the alien tribe sees it must consist in our failure to manifest the fine shades of behaviour which go together in the behaviour of that tribe's members and which reveal that they do not merely interpret the world according to their conceptual scheme. However, there seems to be nothing in the criteria which marks the distinction between the alien tribe's relation towards its concepts and our own relation to them that entails its being logically impossible for one of us to attain a 'tribal' or 'natural' relation to those concepts. Questions about the importance of upbringing and habituation as parts of the process of inculcating the relevant forms of behaviour remain open, of course; but these empirical matters are the domain of the relevant sciences. On the *conceptual* level – the only level at which necessary (logical) constraints become manifest and to which intuitions about inconceivability can be traced – there is nothing to suggest that a combination of imaginative projection and interaction with native speakers could not allow us to see the world as the tribe sees it. In short, Wittgenstein's examination of aspect perception – by revealing that the notion of concepts informing our experience refers not to the physiological or psychological imposition of brute constraints upon the subjective quality of our world of consciousness, but rather to a particular distinction in our relationship to certain concepts which is marked in the logic of our linguistic practices – provides the material necessary for the diagnosis and dissolution of a particular philosophical worry concerning conceptual relativism.

The above detour into issues of conceptual relativism also contributes to the clarification of the notion of continuous aspect perception, however. By revealing that the content of a claim that concepts inform human experience is in fact precisely these features of human attitudes towards things in general which the notion of continuous aspect perception is meant to pick out, it shows that this form of words is merely an alternative way of expressing the significance of that latter notion. Most importantly, however, it adds a further dimension to our sense of the nature of continuous aspect perception – one which confirms (by further specifying) the picture of it which I sketched at the end of Chapter 3. We can see this most easily by reminding ourselves of the criteria in *linguistic* behaviour that we used to distinguish 'native' from 'alien' modes of understanding the tribal concepts.

That distinction emerged as follows. The interpretative model of perception (i.e. aspect-blindness) was, for example, characterized by a failure directly to perceive a given object as having a particular set of basic elements; but this failure is manifest in linguistic behaviour in such things as hesitancy or stumbling when giving a description of the object in those terms, uncertainty in relating another person's description of the object to that object when it is couched in such terms, or a momentary hesitation over pointing to that object when asked to explain the meaning of such words. It is in precisely those three dimensions of linguistic behaviour – modes of use of the word, modes of response to the word's use by others, modes of explanation of the word's meaning – that the criteria for understanding a given term are made manifest. So it would seem to follow that part of what it means to say that a given concept *informs* someone's experience of the world is that his understanding of the relevant concept word takes a particular form. In other words, his understanding of the corresponding linguistic technique is thereby characterized as having a particular depth or ease, as displaying a certain smoothness and absence of stumbling or hesitation (*RPP*,II, 259).

One might say that such a man speaks the language like a native, that the language has become second nature to him – that he has assimilated it. This is the point which I stressed in Chapter 2. But what *this* chapter shows is that such native *linguistic* behaviour hangs together with the forms of non-verbal behaviour in relation to objects picked out by 'continuous aspect perception'. All of the features of our relation to the world which Heidegger aims to capture under the label of 'readiness-to-hand' might be summed up by saying that the ways in which objects are woven into our practical activity manifest precisely the smoothness (the seamlessness and absence of stumbling or hesitation) that is also evident in our purely linguistic behaviour (*RPP*,I, 295). One might say that the world is the native element of human beings, that we and it absorb one another. To be at home in a language is but one central part of being at home in the world.

The seamlessness of the human relation to the world is exceedingly difficult to characterize, whether in terms of linguistic or of non-linguistic behaviour, because it is not a specific feature or property of that behaviour but rather an *aspect* of it. It is, however, implicitly registered in the general form of psychological concepts – in the relation between behaviour and background which we summarized by talking of behavour-in-context. Wittgenstein suggests that we regard such concepts as describing our irregular and variable behaviour against that background of regular patterning which the world provides (*LW*,I, 206); and this highlights the fact that our relation to the world is not one which we conceptualize independently of conceptualizing human behaviour as expressive of mind.

What is emerging now, however, is the *mode* of that relation, its form or physiognomy – the physiognomy of human linguistic and non-linguistic behaviour in the world: what is emerging is the physiognomy of the human. The claim is that our sense of words and of other people as having familiar physiognomies, because it reflects the way in which we have assimilated the world of that word and that person, instantiates the way in which we are absorbed in and by the world in general. It thus makes manifest the physiognomy of our own human behaviour in relation to the world – the form or style, the character, which distinguishes human behaviour from that of an automaton. The aspect-blind view others as if they were robots, and their own behaviour has the stiffness, the absence of fine shades and flexibility, the stumbling and hesitation, of a robot. Philosophers who characterize human life as if humans were aspect-blind thereby reveal themselves to be blind to an aspect of that life which helps to make it distinctively human. In failing to accord importance to this smoothness and spontaneity, to the grace in human practical activity which is the very negation of stumbling and hesitation, they manifest their blindness to a crucial aspect of what we mean by specifically human behaviour.

To summarize: on Wittgenstein's view, continuous aspect perception picks out the basic or fundamental way in which human beings relate to the world around them through their linguistic and non-linguistic behaviour. The interpretative model of the linguistic dimension of this relationship may well characterize the standard human relation to alien concepts which have not yet been assimilated (e.g. may apply to an anthropologist's grasp of a primitive tribe's concepts); but such a model presupposes the existence of a more basic set of concepts the role of which in the subject's experience of the world it is incapable of characterizing.

For example, in the case of someone who is blind to the pictorial aspect of a painting, that person directly perceives the painting as an array of colour-patches on canvas; but in order to characterize the relation between those colour and shape concepts and his experience as an interpretative or aspect-blind one, we would require a further and distinct set of concepts in terms of which the array of colour-patches is directly perceived. Since the interpretative model must always presuppose such an existent set of concepts and is in principle incapable of giving an account of their direct or immediate relation to the concept-user's experience (on pain of infinite regress), it follows that this model cannot be universalized or regarded as explanatorily fundamental. It cannot adequately characterize the way in which a human being's basic or native conceptual framework (whichever framework that might be) relates to the world and his or her experience of it.

This native relationship is what Wittgenstein refers to as continuous aspect perception. It is manifest in those features of human *verbal and non-verbal* behaviour in relation to objects and phenomena met with in the world that have been emphasized in this chapter. Heidegger's concept of readiness-to-hand helped in the attempt to delineate this syndrome; but his attempt in turn to claim that these features are explicable only if we presuppose the truth of his existentialist concept of the essence of human subjectivity has been shown to be less than compelling. This is because those features lose their air of mystery when it is recognized that they constitute the characteristics which help to make *human* behaviour the kind of behaviour it is. We are not discovering a metaphysical truth about human essence: we are reminding ourselves of an aspect of the grammar of the concepts with which we describe human life.

It may seem that we have come a long way from the duck-rabbit and the often seemingly trivial experiences of aspect-dawning with which Wittgenstein laces his text; but in fact the distance is not so great. As we saw earlier, the intelligible use of the 'seeing *x* as *y*' schema is limited to such experiential contexts, and its grammar is such that different sets of concepts must occupy the two places in the schema. In other words, such experiences presuppose the existence of a set of concepts which define what the something *is* that we are seeing as something else, and thus bring to our attention the more direct or immediate relation between that set of concepts and the object of our gaze – a relation which is not typically the focus of our everyday concerns.

When Heidegger is analysing the equipmental totality of which any piece of equipment is a part, and arguing that this totality includes references or assignments to the purpose or goal 'towards-which' it is a means, he emphasizes a related point. Just as, in our everyday dealings with the world, our concern focuses not so much on the tools themselves as on the work for which they are ready-to-hand, so the work itself does not bear the referential totality on its face for us. The assignment, he claims, becomes explicit only when it is disturbed: if, for example, a tool is damaged or missing, or an entity is encountered as an obstacle to our work.

> When an assignment to some particular 'towards-this' has been thus circumspectively aroused, we catch sight of the 'towards-this' itself, and along with it everything connected with the work – the whole 'workshop' – as that wherein concern always dwells. The context of equipment is lit up, not as something never seen before, but as a totality constantly sighted beforehand in circumspection.
>
> (*BT*, Sect. 16, p. 105)

Heidegger's use of the phrase 'lighting up' here is suggestive; for the phrase 'aspect-dawning' itself translates a German expression more literally rendered as 'the lighting up of an aspect'. In short, the connection between aspect-dawning and continuous aspect perception might be seen more clearly if we regard aspect-dawning as a context in which our normal focus on the purposes for which objects are ready-to-hand is disturbed and shifted to the objects themselves, thus lighting up that conceptual framework and revealing the fact that it *informs* our everyday encounters with them.

A TRANSITIONAL DIAGNOSIS

Even when drawing upon Heidegger's text to explicate continuous aspect perception, I made it clear that he parted company with the Wittgensteinian view that essence is expressed by grammar, since for Heidegger the essence of beings is never fully exhausted by the resources of language. And in these last paragraphs, I have emphasized the infinite regress to which the interpretative model of perception falls prey when applied to the relation between basic conceptual frameworks and the world – a regress avoidable only by hypothesizing a nameless, pre-conceptualized world-stuff which could be interpreted in terms of the basic concepts. What I wish to suggest – as a conclusion to this chapter and as a transition to the issues in aesthetics to be dealt with in the final chapter – is that both of these philosophical mythologies could be regarded as variants of the same human response to a vivid and quite specific sort of experience. The responses take different forms depending upon the philosophical vocabulary one inherits (analytic or continental), but the root experience can best be described as one of aspect-dawning *without* a change of aspect.

The possibility of such a variant of aspect-dawning was mentioned in Chapter 1, and exemplified by occasions when one wants to say that a photograph or painting makes a striking impression on us, but that what strikes us is – as it were – its pictoriality: we do not suddenly see it as an array of colour-patches, it lives for us (*PI*, p. 205g–i). Such experiences can, however, occur with respect to any object of our perception and that set of concepts which defines the sort of thing it is. In Sartre's novel *Nausea*, it occurs when Roquentin encounters the twisted black roots of a chestnut tree in a park:

> The roots of the chestnut tree sank into the ground beneath my bench. I could not remember it was a root anymore. Words had vanished, and with them the meanings of things, the way things are to be used, the feeble points of reference which men have traced on their surface.
>
> (*Nausea*, 170–2)

As in all aspect-dawning experiences, one feels that a separation between concept and object has been effected, one has a heightened awareness of the conceptual framework one can impose upon that object. However, when – as in this case – the set of concepts involved is that which determines the object as being the sort of thing it is, it can seem that we have stripped away even the most minimal and basic conceptual framework and achieved a perception of what lies beyond those conventions of human language and its structures of intelligibility:

> The root, the park gates, the bench, the sparse bits of grass, all that had vanished: the diversity of things, their individuality, were only an appearance, a varnish. This varnish had melted, leaving soft, monstrous lumps, in naked disorder, with a frightful and obscene nakedness.
>
> (*Nausea*, 170–2)

Here we see the nameless world-stuff required by the analytic philosopher, the existentialist perception of a Being which transcends language and makes a given object cohere in its unique individuality as *that one there*. The difficulty with the philosophical claims that have been erected upon such perceptions, however, should be clear: for if they are indeed *experiences* of such ineffable Being, then whatever has been experienced in such moments is indeed conceptualizable and therefore accessible to language, since it has been experienced and can be described, talked about, considered and thought about.

To query the intelligibility of such philosophical claims, however, is not to deny the fact that there is a type of experience to which they are an understandable human response. Indeed, the very fact that we are inclined to use forms of words such as those Sartre employs to express that experience helps to clarify its nature very precisely. I want to suggest that such experiences have two key features: they involve a sense of having penetrated beyond language, and in doing so what is encountered is not a void but something (Being, stuff) that is external to – other than – language.

Experiences of aspect-dawning, I would claim, are such as to produce just that type of response. By making us aware of a new set of concepts in terms of which we might describe a given type of object, aspect-dawning helps – as we have seen – to highlight the fact that for us language-users even such unusual encounters with such an object primarily involve that set of concepts which determines what it is for something to be an object of that kind. However, in those rare cases where the conceptual framework of which we gain an awareness is that which pertains most basically to the perceived object (e.g. the rootness of the root, the pictoriality of the picture), then one might well be inclined to express one's sense of a separation being effected between *that* set of concepts and the object as a stripping away of all language from the thing itself.

This inclination will be reinforced by the further fact that aspect-dawning experiences bring us to focus upon a given entity as an object in its own right. In such contexts, its nature is not taken for granted or subordinated to the tasks we usually perform with it; and since it is a part of our concept of a material object (of material reality) that such entities do not come into existence with the invention of language or the evolution of concept-using animals, it will be natural to think that the experience of aspect-dawning confronts us directly with something that is other than and alien to language.

Thus, the myth of rare direct perceptions of Being, of fleeting uncapturable glimpses of the essence of reality, is born – but it emerges only because of a confused perception of the grammar of the concept of aspect-dawning: for, of course, to confront an entity simply as a material object in its own right rather than as a specific *kind* of thing, is not to strip away all conceptual structures. It is *one* way of regarding an object, and for concept-using creatures such as ourselves *all* such encounters necessarily involve that set of concepts which determines an object as being an object at all, i.e. material property concepts. Roquentin takes himself to have encountered a reality which is alien to language precisely because the conceptual structures involved in that encounter determine things as having an existence which is not dependent upon the existence of language; his *experience*, however, is not language-transcendent.

If my suggested diagnosis is correct, we can reject the philosophical claims arising from such experiences without denying that human beings have such experiences, and without leaving opaque the ways in which such experiences lead to philosophical claims of precisely that sort. In the final chapter of this study, I shall apply the diagnostic techniques exemplified here to certain theoretical pronouncements on aesthetics made by literary critics as well as philosophers. The purpose of this exercise is twofold: first, it will permit me to take up the one strand of Wittgenstein's treatment of aspect perception which we have hitherto only glanced at – namely, his conception of the relevance of aspect perception to aesthetics. Secondly, it will provide a way of further testing the validity of the juxtaposition I have effected between Wittgenstein's and Heidegger's writings on aspect perception, by demonstrating whether a similar process of 'grammatical reduction' can be carried out upon Heidegger's later writings on art-works.

Before moving on to this final task, however, I want to end by pointing out that the diagnosis offered above can also stand as a summary of the ways in which a philosophical analysis of aspect-dawning might legitimately lead to issues pertaining to the relation between basic conceptual frameworks and human experience (issues we have subsumed under the heading of continuous aspect perception). The reason for this is simple: according to that diagnosis, even those experiences of aspect-dawning which do *not* involve a change of aspect reveal the sense in which language is inescapable, the sense in which conceptual structures determine the 'essence' of reality rather than reflecting its pre-existent nature; and to this extent, those who experience the dawning of an aspect experience thereby the autonomy of grammar.

6
ICONS, GESTURES, AND AESTHETICS

At several points in his treatment of aspect perception, Wittgenstein appears to presuppose a close link between the issue and a constellation of related topics in the domain of aesthetics. He asserts, for example, that the concept of 'seeing something as something' is very frequently formed, and felt as a need, when we are talking about a work of art (*RPP*,I, 91); and he characterizes the aspects in a change of aspects as being those which a figure might sometimes have permanently in a picture (*PI*, 201b). However, in order to utilize such references as a means of deepening our comprehension of the issues involved in aspect perception, we must grasp the relevant contours of Wittgenstein's treatment of aesthetics; and those contours are difficult to map in their own right, particularly in the case of his frequent reliance on the concept of a 'gesture'.

Accordingly, if we are to break into the circle, this chapter must take on a dialectical form and function, oscillating between the topics of aesthetics and aspect perception and attempting thereby to cast light upon both. The guiding thread which turns out to be most suited to this purpose is a facet of aesthetic experience that has frequently been seized upon by literary critics and philosophers alike – namely, the inclination to characterize major works of art as iconic embodiments of their meaning or significance.

Within the domain of aesthetic experience, confrontation with a great work of art can often involve a sense that it *embodies* that which it depicts or signifies. For example, on those occasions when we become particularly absorbed in a performance of Beethoven's Ninth Symphony, we can feel that the fourth movement is not so much a musical representation or evocation of joy as a direct manifestation of that emotion. Similar feelings can be evoked in other media: a masterful interpretation of Iago can make us feel that pure evil has come to inhabit the stage, a late Hopkins sonnet can seem to be a verbal incarnation of human agony, a portrait glimpsed in the gallery at Pemberley may be said to strike Elizabeth Bennet as if the master of the house were in her presence. The experience these examples are intended to evoke is characterized precisely by our sense – when undergoing it – that to express it in terms of the work of art being a 'good' or 'accurate' or even 'skilful' representation of its subject would be precisely to fail to articulate the essential nature of that experience. Our inclination in such circumstances is to talk of incarnation or immediate embodiment, to regard the work of art as if the joy or agony, the person or quality it depicts had become manifest in the work itself.

The crucial point to be remembered, however, is that we are here dealing with what we are *inclined to say* when attempting to articulate such experiences. In this respect, the precise form such verbal expressions characteristically take should be regarded as philosophical raw material rather than as a proto-theory about the 'essential nature' of great works of art; to take such incarnation metaphors simply at face value is likely to guarantee philosophical confusion about their significance. On the other hand, it is equally important to recognize that what we are inclined to say when articulating or evoking such experiences counts as a partial *characterization* of those experiences. These forms of words are not descriptions of particular phenomena in our inner world of private consciousness (and so not open to the charge of being *mis*-descriptions), but rather constitute the most apt direct expressions or manifestations of that experience.

Accordingly, any attempt to achieve philosophical clarity concerning the nature of the experiences thus evoked must pay careful attention to the precise form that the verbal expressions of these experiences tend to assume; for the criteria which justify our ascribing that type of experience to someone and refusing to ascribe it to another person standardly relate to similarities and differences in the form of the verbal expression (in the type of metaphor or picture) which the given person regards as an apt articulation of his experience. How else, for example, would one give content to the claim that those responding to Beethoven and Hopkins in the manner quoted earlier were expressing analogous experiences with respect to different media except by reference to their both finding such rhetorical pictures as incarnation to be apt means of articulating what they experienced?

The treatment accorded to those texts (works by Heidegger and Steiner) which I use to exemplify literary-critical and philosophical attempts to delineate and analyse the nature of this aesthetic experience therefore conforms to the two methodological principles just outlined. First, I treat those texts as if they are, to a large degree, simply more complex and sophisticated articulations or evocations of the aesthetic experience under scrutiny rather than theoretical descriptions of the nature of such experience whose truth depends upon their literal meaning. For example, Elizabeth Bennet's inclination to say that Darcy's portrait struck her as embodying the personality of the sitter does not commit her to the claim that a conjuring trick has translated a human being's character into a prison of varnish and paint. And in the same way, Heidegger's assertion that a work of art is the site for strife between world and earth should be viewed as a means of evoking crucial features of the relevant aesthetic experience (one which relies upon connotations and associations woven around the concepts of 'world' and 'earth' by his text and by his metaphysical framework) rather than as a quasi-scientific claim to have discerned new forces of nature. In so far as this treatment fails to accord with the relevant author's conception of the significance of their writings and of the appropriate way to read them, my position is simply that adopting this approach is the best way in which I am able to extract intelligible and potentially significant content from their texts.

The above point virtually exhausts the significance of Steiner's text for the purposes of this chapter. I eschew any criticism of his prose style: this is partly because such questions of literary taste are irrelevant to the philosophical issues at stake, and partly because it is precisely his rhetorical tendencies that make the relevant text such an unselfconscious and correspondingly revealing articulation of the experience with which I am concerned. Steiner's constant restatements of the same points in different terms, together with the complexity and detail of the restatements, permit me to identify more clearly the nature of the relevant experience by showing the logical multiplicity of form or structure necessary to convey its distinctive characteristics.

The case of Heidegger's text is more complex, because the lectures I examine perform a twofold function in this chapter. On one level, their scope and complexity permits a fine-grained identification of the defining features of the experience they articulate and with which I am concerned, as already mentioned above; and in this respect I would claim that a recognition of the degree to which the structure of these lectures is anchored in the type of aesthetic experience from which they take off provides a crucial interpretative principle for anyone interested in comprehending Heidegger's meaning and purposes. Unlike Steiner, however, it is clear that Heidegger is concerned to utilize this type of aesthetic experience as a means of confirming and refining the metaphysical framework first set out in *Being and Time*; it follows that any attempt to render his lecture intelligible will presuppose a preliminary grasp of that framework, and in this respect my exegetical work in Chapter 4 is taken for granted in the exposition to be provided here.

Since the metaphysical structures invoked as explanatory tools by Heidegger can, I believe, most fruitfully be viewed as grammatical or conceptual structures seen through a glass darkly (and more particularly as metaphysical versions of precisely the grammatical structures identified by Wittgenstein), the Heideggerian text can be seen as an intermediate case. It effects a transition from what I take to be a complex evocation of an experience (Steiner) to a philosophical treatment of such evocations designed to reveal the grammatical articulations which define the role and significance in our lives of the concepts we employ in that field of experience (Wittgenstein). In order to justify this claim to find structural parallels in Heideggerian and Wittgensteinian thought, however, my exposition of Heidegger's writings must focus primarily upon the structure and interrelations of the metaphysical elements which are central to his project, and thus forgo any serious attempts to evaluate the claim that the essential nature of reality is thereby being displayed to the reader. Indeed, given my other assumption that these metaphysical structures can be fruitfully viewed as an alternative and sophisticated articulation of a type of experience rather than as a description of reality, such an evaluation becomes irrelevant.

This methodological decision should not, therefore, be interpreted as a sign that I regard Heidegger's writings as containing nothing but truth about these matters. Nor should the reader be disconcerted by the result of this decision – namely, the fact that long stretches of this chapter move entirely within the charmed circle of Heideggerian metaphysics and poetry in order to display their internal structure. The reader should rather regard the account of Wittgenstein's corresponding grammatical investigations which follows the exposition of Heidegger as an exhaustive summary of the intelligible content which can be extracted from Heidegger's metaphysics as it has application to (and draws sustenance from) this facet of our lives. In short, one should regard the structure of this chapter as an exemplification of the belief that one can approach certain Continental modes of philosophy in a productive way only if one treats such texts as sophisticated articulations of key human experiences and attitudes embedded in metaphysical theorizing whose form mirrors the grammatical (conceptual) structures at work in the relevant areas of our lives.

ICONS

The idea of labelling our chosen facet of aesthetic experience 'iconicity' derives in the first instance from George Steiner (although this label can be traced back to the writings of Peirce). In a recent article[1] he attempts to distinguish between the roles of critic and of reader by reference to the presuppositions which inform the differing attitudes they adopt towards works of art (primarily literary texts), and in the process he provides an analysis of the experience of confronting major works of art. In adopting the attitude of a reader rather than of a critic, Steiner argues, 'what is implicit is the notion and expression of "real presence". The reader proceeds *as if* the text was the housing of forces and meanings, of meanings of meaning, whose lodging within the executive verbal form was one of "incarnation"' (*GSR*, 85).

As the reliance on such terminology as 'incarnation' suggests, Steiner has in mind an attitude whose structure is manifest in the role played by sacred texts in religious traditions:

---

[1] 'New literary history' (1979), in *George Steiner: A Reader* (Harmondsworth: Penguin, 1984). All page references are to this collection, hereafter known as *GSR*.

The relevant presumption is that of an inherence, however
esoteric, however eroded or possibly falsified by human
transcription, of a 'spirit' in, 'behind', the letter. It is just this
presumption which underwrites the concept of the 'iconic', the
belief that the icon is not so much a representation of the sacred
person or scene as it is the immediate manifestation, the
epiphany of that person or scene. In other words, the latter are
'really present' to the beholder not by virtue of a voluntary
imaginative concession or transposition on the beholder's part,
but because they have taken dwelling in the icon.

(*GSR*, 85)

The real presence referred to, then, is the embodiment in the artwork of the scene, object, or emotion that the art-work depicts or expresses.

For Steiner, the ascription of real presence to the text is a model or trope which captures two crucial aspects of aesthetic experience. First, it highlights a movement of simultaneous discovery and withdrawal:

The reader opens himself to the autonomous being of the text.
The dialectic of encounter and of vulnerability (the text can
bring drastic hurt) is one in which the ontological core of the
text, its presentness of inward being, both reveals and makes
itself hidden. This pulsing motion is a familiar one. As we come
to know the text, the painting, the piece of music better, as we
become more at home in its idiom, there is always more which
seems to elude us.

(*GSR*, 86)

Secondly, however, the presumption of real presence is made only 'when the true source of this apparently contradictory pulse of disclosure and concealment is assigned to the text, to the work of art' (*GSR*, 86–7). For Steiner, these two aspects are the fundamental concern of any important aesthetics:

Such essential excess of meaning characterises the order of texts
or art forms with which the reader engages. All serious aesthetics
aims to elucidate what can be termed, to borrow a Marxist
econometric vocabulary, the phenomenon of 'surplus value', of
the 'forces' in and beyond 'sense' generated by art.

(*GSR*, 87)

Steiner goes on to characterize further the notion of an iconic text in terms of its irreducibility:

> 'Irreducibility' signifies 'non-paraphrasability', the untranslatability of an iconic presence into any other form without loss and estrangement (where 'sense' can be preserved, 'force' cannot). As lived by the true reader, the text is irreducible to, inexhaustible by, even the most penetratively diagnostic, explicative of visions.
>
> (*GSR*, 87)

Here, the polemical purpose of Steiner's analysis becomes obvious. If art-works manifest a real presence which is irreducible to analytic summation and resistant to judgement in precisely the sense in which the critic can and must judge, then criticism is necessarily incapable of grasping or matching the essence of art, and modern (primarily structuralist and poststructuralist) critics should learn to accept their secondary (if valuable) role in relation to the work of art. For my purposes, however, the outcome of this polemical struggle is irrelevant: the interest of Steiner's article lies rather in the clarity with which he gives expression to a specific facet of aesthetic experience. He provides the raw material from which our philosophical investigation of aspect perception and aesthetics can take its departure.

Steiner's own instinct – the normal instinct for any philosophically inclined literary critic, one might say – is to attempt to give a theoretical explanation which accounts for the facets of aesthetic experience he has delineated:

> The evident reason for the irreducibility of the iconic is that that which declares and conceals itself in the text or canvas or musical structure is of the order of being rather than of meaning, or, more accurately, that it has force incarnate in but also in excess of sense. . . .. It is this immediate infolding of meaning into force of being which makes of music the most 'iconic', the most 'really present' essence known to man. It follows that music is also that which most absolutely resists paraphrase or translation. But infolding and resistance of this kind characterise all living texts and art.
>
> (*GSR*, 88)

If we wish to explicate this explanatory model of meaning

inhering in *being*, we must return to an earlier position of Steiner's paper in which he cited various literary/philosophical models for the notion of real presence he wishes to employ:

> A third-model of 'inherence' is that provided by the application of an absolute philosophic ontology to aesthetics. It is that which justifies Heidegger's ascription of a total Dasein, of a total 'presentness of being', to the worn pair of boots in the Van Gogh painting. As Heidegger urges, the 'real presence' of these boots on or 'within' the canvas is of an order and intensity, of a phenomenological necessity, denied not only to this or that actual pair of boots but denied as well to the most rigorous chemical-functional analysis of 'what it is that boots are made of and for'.
>
> (*GSR*, 86)

The force of this reference to Heidegger may seem obscure; and since it is also clear that by the end of his paper Steiner is treating Heideggerian ontology as not only an enabling model which authorizes a reader to assign iconic status to his text but also as the *reason* for the iconicity of an iconic text, we have a dual motive for turning to Heidegger's text in search of a fuller understanding of aesthetic real presence.

Van Gogh's painting of a pair of peasant shoes stands as a central example of great art in Heidegger's lectures 'The Origin of the Work of Art';[2] and the power and beauty of Heidegger's account of the painting is such that it deserves quotation in full:

> As long as we can only imagine a pair of shoes in general, or simply look at the empty unused shoes as they merely stand there in the picture, we shall never discover what the equipmental being of the equipment in truth is. From Van Gogh's painting we cannot even tell where these shoes stand. There is nothing surrounding this pair of peasant shoes in or to which they might belong – only an undefined space. There are not even clods of soil from the field or the field-path sticking to them, which would at least hint at their use. A pair of peasant shoes and nothing more. And yet –

---

2 Collected, in abbreviated form, in Martin Heidegger: *Basic Writings*, ed. D. F. Krell (London: Routledge & Kegan Paul, 1977). All page references are to this collection, hereafter known as *BW*.

From the dark opening of the worn insides of the shoes the toilsome tread of the worker stares forth. In the stiffly rugged heaviness of the shoes there is the accumulated tenacity of her slow trudge through the far-spreading and ever-uniform furrows of the field swept by a raw wind. On the leather lie the dampness and richness of the soil. Under the soles slides the loneliness of the field-path as evening falls. In the shoes vibrates the silent call of the earth, its quiet gift of the ripening grain and its unexplained self-refusal in the fallow desolation of the wintry field. This equipment is pervaded by uncomplaining worry as to the certainty of bread, the wordless joy of having once more withstood want, the trembling before the impending childbed and shivering at the surrounding menace of death. This equipment belongs to the *earth*, and it is protected in the *world* of the peasant woman. From out of this protected belonging the equipment itself rises to its resting-within-itself.

(*BW*, 163)

As an example of a genuine and insightful aesthetic response to a particular work of art, this passage makes an immediate impact upon the reader – an impact which is assisted by the structure and location of the passage in the lecture as well as by its specific content. The process of reading mimics the movement of thought of a spectator in front of the canvas, of a viewer whose detached awareness of certain superficial properties of the painting is suddenly transformed when a more profound impression of the world of farm and countryside strikes. Given this combination of quality of response and the capacity to mirror the form of experience in language, it is hardly surprising that Steiner should regard such a passage as a paradigm for the type of attentive and careful 'reading' he is attempting to characterize.

What should also be clear is that the passage exemplifies the phenomenon of ascribing real presence to an art-work; for Heidegger goes on to say:

Van Gogh's painting is the disclosure of what the equipment, the pair of peasant shoes, *is* in truth. This being emerges into the unconcealedness of its Being. The Greeks called the unconcealedness of beings *aletheia*. We say 'truth' and think little enough in using this word. If there occurs in the work [of art] a disclosure of a particular being, disclosing what and how it is,

then there is here an occurring, a happening of truth at work.
(*BW*, 164)

The Being of the particular thing depicted in the art-work (the peasant woman's shoes) is conceived of as present in the art-work itself, as being available for discovery 'in' the painting in a way which does not apply to an encounter with the shoes themselves;

> The equipmental quality of equipment was discovered. But how? Not by a description and explanation of a pair of shoes actually present; not by a report about the process of making shoes; and also not by the observation of the actual use of shoes occurring here and there; but only by bringing ourselves before Van Gogh's painting. This painting spoke.
> (*BW*, 164)

Not merely the thing itself depicted by the artist but rather the *essence* of that thing has taken dwelling in the iconic work.

Of course, a further motive for Steiner's placing such reliance upon this Heideggerian text is provided by the fact that, in the process of developing the ontology of Being which that philosopher takes as having been proven by (or revealed through) such aesthetic experiences and attitudes, Heidegger touches upon issues of irreducibility and disclosure/withdrawal which we have already seen to be central to Steiner's own theory of art. An exploration of the Heideggerian text can therefore help to provide further raw material for our philosophical investigation as well as deepening our comprehension of the material already provided. In addition, such an exploration can permit us to test the correlation between aesthetic judgement and philosophical insight which the quality of Heidegger's response to Van Gogh's painting might have led us (as it led Steiner) to posit.

The key to Heidegger's understanding of the work of art lies in the two concepts which we saw him introduce at the end of his reading of the Van Gogh painting, viz. the notions of 'world' and of 'earth'. In the context of that particular painting, these terms might easily be taken to refer to the psychological world of the peasant and to the countryside respectively, particularly since it is the existence of such connotations in this context that allows the relevant concepts to emerge so smoothly from the passage. In fact, however, Heidegger has something of more general import in mind; and this becomes clearer when he turns to a discussion of non-representational art in the second part of his lecture.

The concept of world emerges as follows when a Greek temple is the work of art under examination:

> By means of the temple, the God is present in the temple. This presence of the God is in itself the extension and delimitation of the precinct as a holy precinct. The temple and its precinct, however, do not fade away into the indefinite. It is the temple-work that first fits together and at the same time gathers around itself the unity of those paths and relations in which birth and death, disaster and blessing, victory and disgrace, endurance and decline acquire the shape of destiny for human being. The all-governing expanse of this open relational context is the world of this historical people. Only from and in this expanse does the nation first return to itself for the fulfilment of its vocation.
>
> (*BW*, 168)

In this context, the notion of the psychological world of an individual is overlaid by connotations of a cultural-social world and of the historical role of a people. Once again, however, Heidegger attaches a more specific meaning to the term 'world', as we can see from a crucial later passage which again requires extensive quotation:

> The world is not the mere collection of the countable or uncountable, familiar and unfamiliar things that are at hand. But neither is it a merely imagined framework added by our representation to the sum of such given things. The *world worlds*, and is more fully in being than the tangible and perceptible realm in which we believe ourselves to be at home. World is never an object that stands before us and can be seen. World is the ever non-objective to which we are subject as long as the paths of birth and death, blessing and curse keep us transported into Being. . . .. A stone is worldless. Plant and animal likewise have no world; but they belong to the covert throng of a surrounding into which they are linked. The peasant woman, on the other hand, has a world because she dwells in the overtness of beings. Her equipment, in its reliability, gives to this world a necessity and nearness of its own. By the opening up of a world, all things gain their lingering and hastening, their remoteness

and nearness, their scope and limits.

(*BW*, 170–71)

In effect, then, and despite the shifts in connotation noted above, the concept of world is clearly rooted in the notion as defined in *Being and Time*, where 'world' is the structural whole of significant relationships that Dasein experiences – with tools, things of nature, and other human beings – as Being-in-the-world. It is that already familiar horizon upon which everyday human existence confidently moves, that in which Dasein always has been and which is co-disclosed in all man's projects and possibilities.

Two facets of this concept are important in this context. First, Heidegger thinks that Dasein's having a world entails that (unlike stones and animals) it encounters the disclosedness of beings and thereby the openness of Being; and second – as we saw in Chapter 4 when explicating the notion of the worldhood of the world announcing itself – Heidegger views Dasein's worldliness as most intimately bound up with the category of things labelled tools or, more generally, equipment. To summarize that earlier analysis: to say that Dasein exists in the world is to say that the act of understanding through which Dasein grasps its own Being and potentiality-for-Being must always encompass the world in which it is, i.e. must always relate to the environment which the referential totality constitutes, and which alone furnishes the equipmental domain within which human purposes can be achieved.

If we wish to grasp the co-related concept of 'earth' as it is used in this lecture, however, we have no analysis in *Being and Time* to fall back upon, for that concept seems first to have been used in this present context. Our attempt to explicate it must therefore rely even more closely upon the shades of meaning and association which crystallize around the term in the passages where it is employed. The most accurate and efficient way of conveying such connotations is of course to display the term as embedded in the contexts of its use; and once more Heidegger's discussion of the Greek temple provides us with the necessary foothold.

> Standing there, the building rests on the rocky ground. This resting of the work draws up out of the rock the obscurity of that rock's bulky yet spontaneous support. Standing there, the building holds its ground against the storm raging above it, and so first makes the storm itself manifest in its violence. The lustre

and gleam of the stone, though itself apparently glowing only by the grace of the sun, yet first brings to radiance the light of the day, the breadth of the sky, the darkness of the night. The temple's firm towering makes visible the invisible space of air. The steadfastness of the work contrasts with the surge of the surf, and its own repose brings out the raging of the sea. Tree and grass, eagle and bull, snake and cricket first enter into their distinctive shapes and thus come to appear as what they are. The Greeks early called this emerging and rising in itself and in all things *physis*. It illuminates also that on which and in which man bases his dwelling. We call this ground the *earth*. What this word says is not to be associated with the idea of a mass of matter deposited somewhere, or with the merely astronomical idea of a planet. Earth is that whence the arising brings back and shelters everything that arises as such. In the things that arise, earth occurs essentially as the sheltering agent.

(*BW*, 169)

Once more, attention to the rhetorical form and structure of the lecture can help us to grasp the concepts of 'earth' and 'world' as Heidegger intends them to be read. His analysis of the essence of works of art, of aesthetic objects, took its departure in the first section of his lecture from a tripartite categorization of intra-mundane entities (excluding Dasein), from preliminary comparisons and contrasts between a work of art, things of nature, and tools; and in the process, Heidegger assigned to the latter two categories a definition of their essence – of the thingness of the thing and the equipmentality of equipment. After evaluating and rejecting certain orthodox definitions of the essence of objects of nature, Heidegger suggests that we exert ourselves to think this essence anew:

This exertion of thought seems to meet with its greatest resistance in defining the thingness of the thing; for where else could the cause lie of the failure of the efforts mentioned? The unpretentious thing evades thought most stubbornly. Or can it be that this self-refusal of the mere thing, this self-contained, irreducible spontaneity, belongs precisely to the essence of the thing?

(*BW*, 161)

Heidegger then moves on to other issues; but I believe that the concept of 'earth' introduced later is precisely the result of Heidegger's attempt to think the essence of things in a new way. This, I think, becomes clear by implication in such passages as the following:

> the work [of art, i.e. the temple] sets itself back into the massiveness and heaviness of stone, into the firmness and pliancy of wood, into the hardness and lustre of metal, into the lighting and darkening of colour, into the clang of tone, and into the naming power of the word. That into which the work set itself back and which it causes to come forth in this setting back of itself we called the earth.
>
> (*BW*, 171)

In a parallel way, the concept of 'world' can be seen to relate to Heidegger's view of the essence of tools, of that second category of entities. This view emerges in an extended passage in which he suggests that the misleading 'matter-form' analysis of things results from an illicit extension of that structure from its appropriate place in analysing the equipmentality of equipment:

> The self-contained block of granite is something material in a definite if unshapely form. Form here means the distribution and arrangement of the material parts in spatial locations, resulting in a particular shape, namely that of a block. But a jug, an axe, a shoe are also matter occurring in a form. Form as shape is not the consequence of a prior distribution of the matter. The form, on the contrary, determines the arrangement of the matter. Even more, it prescribes in each case the kind and selection of the matter – impermeable for a jug, sufficiently hard for an axe, firm yet flexible for shoes. The interfusion of form and matter prevailing here is, moreover, controlled beforehand by the purposes served by jug, axe, shoes. Such usefulness is never assigned or added on afterward to a being of the type of a jug, axe, or pair of shoes. But neither is it something that floats somewhere above it as an end.
>
> . . .A being that falls under usefulness is always the product of a process of making. It is made as a piece of equipment for something. As determinations of beings, accordingly, matter and form have their proper place in the essential nature of

equipment. This name designates what is produced expressly for employment and use. Matter and form are in no case original determinations of the thingness of the mere thing.

(*BW*, 158–9)

The essence of equipment, then, lies in its relation to human purposes and the means-end structure which that implies, i.e. its essence is constituted by the referential totality which informs Dasein's environment and which alone furnishes the equipmental domain that is the necessary arena for human purposive activity. As we saw earlier, it is this environment which is 'the world'.

These connections (between 'world' and equipment, 'earth' and things or materiality) are of crucial importance to Heidegger because he goes on to define the essence of a work of art in the following way:

> The setting up of a world and the setting forth of earth are two essential features in the work-being of the work. They belong together, however, in the unity of work-being. This is the unity we seek when we ponder the self-subsistence of the work and try to tell of this closed, unitary repose of self-support.
>
> (*BW*, 172)

To oversimplify, it seems that the essence of art-works (of the third of Heidegger's original tripartite categorization of entities) is being defined in terms of the essences of the other two types of entity. More precisely, the Being of the work of art lies in its providing a domain within which the world of human purposes and meanings meets the non-human horizon of any purposive activity. This meeting, however, is inherently one of conflict:

> World and earth are essentially different from one another and yet are never separated. The world grounds itself on the earth, and earth juts through world. But the relation between world and earth does not wither away into the empty unity of opposites unconcerned with one another. The world, in resting upon the earth, strives to surmount it. As self-opening it cannot endure anything closed. The earth, however, as sheltering and concealing, tends always to draw the world into itself and keep it there. The opposition of world and earth is strife.
>
> (*BW*, 172)

Heidegger's references to self-opening and sheltering become less obscure if we relate them to the essence of equipment and of tools. In Chapter 4, I noted Heidegger's view that the essence of any given piece of equipment is constituted by the multiplicity of reference-relations which define its place within a totality of equipment, by its location in the equipmental domain presupposed by any human practical activity. However, he also claimed that at the root of such praxis lies Dasein's capacity to understand itself in terms of its potentiality-for-Being, and that in thus understanding itself, it understands the world. Such understanding is grounded in structures of interpretation Heidegger labels 'totality of significations', frameworks of human meaning which underpin the intelligibility of Being-in-the-world; they permit the disclosedness of entities within-the-world by Articulating that disclosedness according to significations. Thus, in relating to the domain of human praxis, the concept of 'world' thereby relates to the structures of human understanding which go to make up Dasein's unique openness to Being – its capacity to encounter and grasp the Being of beings it meets with in the world. This is why the world can be said to be self-opening, to be striving to surmount anything closed.

Earth, however, relates to sheltering and concealing because it expresses the Being of things, the essence of their materiality. Here, Heidegger's seemingly by-the-way reference to the self-refusal of the mere thing (quoted earlier) becomes relevant. The material elements of the natural world do not constitute merely the field within which any human praxis must be involved, the provisions upon which human purposes must work; they also constitute an inexhaustible horizon of that which is non-human in the world. In other words, the earth is simultaneously available for use and constituted by the self-refusal of mere things, by their materiality which is other than and alien to Dasein. Furthermore, just as the concept of the world relates to human understanding as well as praxis, so the concept of earth relates to that in things which resists *comprehension* as well as employment, to that which stubbornly evades thought. Once these connections are seen, the necessity of strife between world and earth becomes clear, even though the grounds of their mutual need (Dasein's need for a world of things to employ and understand, the need of beings to manifest their Being) should also be borne in mind.

Why, however, does Heidegger regard this notion of strife between world and earth as the essential, defining feature of works of art? The answer lies in the characteristic of art-works to which Kant drew attention when he spoke of them as exemplifying purposiveness without purpose, as celebrating the human capacity to set and achieve purposes. Heidegger labels this quality 'createdness':

> In contrast to all other modes of production, the work is distinguished by being created so that its createdness is part of the created work. But does not this hold true for everything brought forth, indeed for anything that has in any way come to be? Everything brought forth surely has this endowment of having been brought forth, if it has any endowment at all. Certainly. But in the work, createdness is expressly created into the created being, so that it stands out from it, from the being thus brought forth, in an expressly particular way.
>
> (*BW*, 182)

This createdness has a further effect which makes the work of art differ from a piece of equipment:

> Because it is determined by usefulness and serviceability, equipment takes into its service that of which it consists: the matter. In fabricating equipment – e.g. an axe – stone is used, and used up. It disappears into usefulness. The material is all the better and more suitable the less it resists perishing in the equipmental being of the equipment. By contrast the temple-work, in setting up a world, does not cause the material to disappear, but rather causes it to come forth for the very first time and to come into the open region of the work's world. The rock comes to bear and rest and so first becomes the rock; metals come to glitter and shimmer, colours to glow, tones to sing, the words to say.
>
> (*BW*, 171)

By being fabricated without being intended as an object for practical use, an art-work calls attention to the materiality of its medium, to that which constitutes its existence as a thing. In the strife of the world and earth, it is this emergence of the essence of materiality that is expressed by the thrusting of the earth.

At the same time, however, a created thing is a human product;

and the work of art, in setting up a world, brings the necessary framework of human practical activity to our explicit attention as well. All praxis presupposes an equipmental domain; and, as we summarized earlier, this in turn manifests itself in a totality of reference-relations whose significance must be seen as constituted by frameworks of human meaning which underpin the intelligibility of the beings Dasein encounters in the world. The concept of world, in relating to the domain of human praxis, must also therefore be seen as expressing – as bringing forth explicitly – the structures which permit Dasein to apprehend the Being of beings; and this too is celebrated in the work of art.

> [T]he sculpture of the god, votive offering of the victor in the athletic games...is not a portrait whose purpose is to make it easier to realize how the god looks; rather, it is a work that lets the god himself be present and thus is the god himself. The same holds for the linguistic work. In the tragedy nothing is staged or displayed theatrically, but the battle of the new gods against the old is being fought.
>
> (*BW*, 169–70)

Here we can clearly see that Heidegger's notion of strife between world and earth takes up just those elements of aesthetic experience that are articulated in Steiner's concept of the iconic text, and reveals more clearly their interrelation. To say that the true reader proceeds as if the text was the housing of forces and meanings is to place simultaneous emphasis upon the text as dwelling-place *and* upon the meanings it houses. If one asserts that a given work of art manifests an emotion, person, or scene rather than 'merely' representing it, as if (e.g.) certain words *are* the emotion metamorphosed, then one's attention focuses just as much upon the text *as text* as it does upon the embodied forces or meanings. The reader's sense of a text's autonomous being (as Steiner puts it) refers to an awareness of the text as an entity in its own right, an existent object; and this is represented by the concept of earth in Heidegger. At the same time, however, the reader's direct encounter with that which has taken dwelling *in* the icon would, in Heideggerian terms, reveal the essential role of the world in the strife which is the work of art. To employ an example Steiner and Heidegger both favour, the possibility of experiencing the total presentness of being of the peasant shoes in Van Gogh's painting exists only because that painting, in setting up a world, thereby sets out the structures of intelligibility which constitute Dasein's capacity to apprehend the Being of beings.

Thus, the notion of real presence, of iconic texts, is meant to capture the sense in which works of art generate two opposing tendencies in their audience, directing their attention and awareness towards the text and towards that which it embodies, to both the medium and the message. Heidegger's notion of strife between world and earth also captures two key qualities Steiner attributed to those texts he categorized as iconic – that of such texts' inexhaustibility, and that of their irreducibility.

As we saw earlier, Steiner sees the former quality as reasonably self-evident: 'As we come to know the text, the painting, the piece of music better, as we become more at home in its idiom, there is always more which seems to elude us' (*GSR*, 86). As we begin to penetrate further into the complexity and layers of meaning in a particular work of art, so we discover ever-receding vistas of significance still to be grasped and articulated, as if the work contained a horizon of meaning(s). This sense of a constantly-present surplus of meaning is registered in Heidegger's concept of the world. As we have seen, the world of a work of art is the world of a given people or nation, an all-governing relational context provided by a nation's culture and history. The very term employed for this concept signals Heidegger's awareness of precisely this quality of inexhaustible fields of meaning manifest in works of art.

The second of the two key qualities mentioned by Steiner was irreducibility: 'the untranslatability of an iconic presence into any other form without loss and estrangement' (*GSR*, 87). This aspect of the aesthetic attitude – the sense of a work of art's uniqueness, the feeling that the slightest alteration or substitution within it would rupture its meaning – is captured in Heidegger's reading of that aspect of an art-work's createdness which relates to the role of earth within it:

> In general, of everything present to us, we can note that it *is*; but this also, if it is noted at all, is noted only soon to fall into oblivion, as is the wont of everything commonplace. And what is more commonplace than this, that a being is? In a work, by contrast, this fact, that it *is* as a work, is just what is

unusual. . . ..[T]he work casts before itself the eventful fact that the work is as this work, and it has constantly this fact about itself. The more essentially the work opens itself, the more luminous becomes the uniqueness of the fact that it is rather than is not.

(*BW*, 182–3)

Heidegger can talk of this uniqueness, of this strange solitariness, as expressive of the thrust of the earth precisely because it manifests that quality in things which resists comprehension as well as employment. That which resists the gathering and opening of the world is that which goes beyond any list of properties (of applicable concepts) and makes any given object *that one there*. The concreteness of concrete things, the essential sense in which things are, and must be, richer than any definition of them we might possibly frame, is brought to our attention when earth resists the surmounting of world in the work of art.[3]

In both Heidegger's and Steiner's texts, then, the concept of iconic presence draws together the defining qualities of works of art, their inexhaustibility and irreducibility. In addition, however, both authors regard the possession of such qualities by the artwork as an indication of the fact that such works manifest a total presentness of being, instigate a conflict in which the unconcealedness of beings is won. Such unconcealedness is what Heidegger understands as truth, as the essence of the true. I do not have the space in this chapter to unravel the complexities inherent in this concept of *aletheia*: suffice it to note that the qualities of inexhaustibility and irreducibility captured in Heidegger's emphasis on iconicity constitute an exemplification of the sense of unconcealedness he is attempting to convey by means of the Greek term. This is why he can say that truth happens in a work of art:

> Truth happens in Van Gogh's painting. This does not mean that something which is at hand is correctly portrayed, but rather that in the revelation of the equipmental being of the shoes

[3] Here we encounter the classic existentialist formulation of the ways in which essence is perceived to outrun language, a formulation quoted in its literary version at the end of Chapter 5. As we emphasized there, our interest in such formulations lies in their role as expressions of specific experiences to which language-users are prone and does not stretch to an endorsement of their philosophical rectitude.

beings as a whole – world and earth in their counterplay – attain to unconcealedness. . . .. The more simply and essentially the shoes are engrossed in their essence, the more directly and engagingly as all beings attain a greater degree of being along with them. That is how self-concealing Being is illuminated. Light of this kind joins its shining to and into the work. This shining, joined in the work, is the beautiful. *Beauty is one way in which truth essentially occurs as unconcealedness.*

(*BW*, 177–8)

By moving his final emphasis in these lectures from painting to poetry, moreover, Heidegger takes the phenomenon of iconicity to be equally revelatory of the essence of language:

Language is not only and not primarily an audible and written expression of what is to be communicated. It not only puts forth in words and statements what is overtly or covertly intended to be communicated; language alone brings beings as beings into the open for the first time. Where there is no language, as in the Being of stone, plant and animal, there is also no openness of beings.

(*BW*, 185)

Dasein's unique openness to being rests (as we have seen) upon the structures of intelligibility which constitute discourse, the essence of language; and in poetic uses of language, this essential characteristic is brought explicitly to attention and celebrated. 'Poetry is the saying of the unconcealedness of beings. Actual language is the happening of this saying, in which a people's world historically arises for it and the earth is preserved as that which remains closed' (*BW*, 185).

Heidegger's concluding references to language thus contain two crucial and general points. First, the primacy of poetry over other art-forms is held to be the product of two converging lines of thought. All non-linguistic art-forms (such as building and painting) always and only happen in the open region of saying and naming, i.e. within a world whose intelligibility and openness to Dasein presupposes the essential structures of discourse; and in addition – in so far as their essence is the instigation of strife between earth and world – they are partly constituted by precisely those structures (in the form of 'the world') manifesting themselves. Accordingly, they reveal a twofold dependence upon the essence of language, which is most directly manifest in poetry. In this sense, all art is in essence poetry.

Secondly, however, the iconicity of all works of art is taken to manifest the idea that truth is more fundamentally a matter of unconcealedness than of accurate correspondence or representation. This is because the unconcealedness of Being which such works manifest depends upon their drawing attention to the field of disclosure within which Dasein must always be supposed to exist if his capacity to grasp the Being of beings (and to express this comprehension in the form of linguistic propositions which correspond to beings in the world) is to be rendered intelligible.

So, in regarding the aesthetic experience of iconicity as a revelation of the essence of art and thereby of the essence of truth, language, and Being, Heidegger makes it abundantly clear that one's interpretation of iconicity can have crucial and wide-ranging philosophical consequences. We must now discover whether it can also provide a guiding thread for the dissolution of philosophical confusions in precisely those areas.

GESTURES

I can best begin to disinter the connections between the material examined in the first half of this chapter and the phenomenon of aspect perception by noting a restriction in the subject-matter of Heidegger's lecture, a restriction signalled only in passing: 'It is precisely in great art – *and only such art is under consideration here* – that the artist remains inconsequential as compared with the work' (*BW*, 167; my italics). The implication of such a remark seems to be that the best way of coming to understand the whole realm of aesthetics is to extract the essential character of all works of art from the phenomenology of human encounters with artistic *masterpieces*. Philosophical confusions may well lurk in the very notion of a universal essence of which all true art-works partake, but I shall set this worry aside for the moment in order to follow up a different consequence of Heidegger's choice of subject-matter. Wittgenstein puts it this way:

> When we talk of a symphony of Beethoven we don't talk of correctness. Entirely different things enter. One wouldn't talk of

appreciating the *tremendous* things in Art. In certain styles in
Architecture a door is correct, and the thing is you appreciate it.
But in the case of a Gothic Cathedral what we do is not at all to
find it correct – it plays an entirely different rôle with us. The
entire *game* is different. It is as different as to judge a human
being and on the one hand to say 'He behaves well' and on the
other hand 'He made a great impression on me'.

(*LC*, 7–8)[4]

Wittgenstein simultaneously notes the fact that great works of
art play a different role in our lives than do other sorts of art-work
(thus limiting the scope of any conclusions we might draw from
looking at the role of the former works), and suggests one useful
way of clarifying the nature of that difference: the greatness of a
work of art lies not in its conforming to a set of rules or principles
going to make up a canon of correctness, but in its direct impact
upon the individual members of its audience, the impression it
makes and the reactions it elicits. This would suggest, despite
Heidegger's emphasis on the work of art *itself* as the site on which
truth happens, that the structures and processes in terms of which
he characterizes the work of art will in fact be traceable to the
experience of the viewer, to the reaction and attitudes he adopts;
and indeed, Heidegger acknowledges this in his lectures. When
describing the way in which the work of art displaces its audience
from the realm of the ordinary, he says:

> To submit to this displacement means to transform our
> accustomed ties to world and to earth and henceforth to restrain
> all usual doing and prizing, knowing and looking, in order to
> stay within the truth that is happening in the work. Only the
> restraint of this staying lets what is created be the work that it is.
> This letting the work be a work we call the preserving of the
> work. . . Just as a work cannot be without being created but is
> essentially in need of creators, so what is created cannot itself
> come into being without those who preserve it.

(*BW*, 183)

Furthermore, the very starting-point of Heidegger's analysis of
art and art-works is the phenomenology of his response to the Van

---

4 *Lectures and Conversations on Aesthetics, Psychology and Religious Belief* (Oxford: Basil Blackwell, 1970) – hereafter known as *LC*.

Gogh painting, a response which was quoted earlier in this chapter. As I stressed then, the structure of that passage in the lecture mimics the experience of the viewer, mirroring that familiar reaction to a great work of art as its beauty and profound significance suddenly impress themselves upon us. This crucial facet of an aesthetic response to certain works of art is, I would suggest, a very clear example of the experience Wittgenstein refers to as the dawning of an aspect.

Naturally, the structural parallel here does not encompass all facets of the paradigmatic experience of aspect-dawning, namely that of suddenly noticing the rabbit aspect of the duck-rabbit; the suggestion is not, for example, that a viewer impressed by Van Gogh's painting suddenly notices that the painting represents a pair of shoes. Wittgenstein makes the connection in a very precise way, as follows:

> I say: 'We regard a portrait as a human being,' – but when do we do so, and for how long? *Always*, if we see it at all (and do not, say, see it as something else)? I might say yes to this, and that would determine the concept of regarding as – The question is whether yet another concept, related to this one, is also of importance to us: that, namely, of a seeing-as which only takes place while I am actually concerning myself with the picture as the object depicted. I might say: a picture does not always *live* for me while I am seeing it. 'Her picture smiles down on me from the wall'. It need not always do so, whenever my glance lights on it.
>
> (*PI*, 205g,h)

The best way to understand Wittgenstein's notion of a 'living' picture is to regard it as an attempt to characterize that feature of great art-works upon which Steiner and Heidegger concentrate, and which I have labelled 'iconicity'. This becomes clear in such passages as the following, in which Wittgenstein is discussing responses to a picture of a horse:

> But suppose it is said 'One *sees* the painted horse running!'. Here, however, I don't just mean to say 'I know that this represents a running horse'. One is trying to say something *else*. Imagine that someone reacted to such a picture by a movement of his hand and a shout of 'Tally ho!'. Doesn't that say roughly

> the same as: he *sees* the horse running? He might also exclaim
> 'It's running!' and that would not be the observation that it is
> running, nor yet that it *seems* to be running. Just as one says 'See
> how it runs!' – not in order to inform the other person; rather
> this is a reaction in which people are in touch with one another.
>
> (*RPP*,I, 874)

Just as such verbal reactions illustrate the way in which that picture conveys a sense of motion directly to the viewer, so Heidegger's more measured verbal response manifests the power of the Van Gogh painting to convey the world of the peasant woman in a very immediate way. In both cases, the viewer's aesthetic response signals the dawning of an aspect.

In order to buttress the claim that Heidegger and Wittgenstein are here concerned with the same phenomenon I must now highlight the manifold points of resemblance in their respective analyses of that experience. One initial difficulty must, however, be surmounted, for Wittgenstein's detailed discussions of aspect-dawning standardly invoke examples of that experience which are bound up with a *change* of aspects; and as we have already seen, no equivalent of the change from duck aspect to rabbit aspect in the case of the duck-rabbit figure can be said to exist with reference to those occasions when a painting can be said to live for us. Since, however, this issue has already been dealt with in our initial discussion of living pictures in Chapter 1, and further analysed at the end of Chapter 5, we need do no more at this point than note the disanalogy and make the necessary transpositions and adjustments.

The central point to preserve in *any* case of aspect-dawning is the paradoxical sense that it involves a change in the figure itself even though we know that no such change has occurred. Utilizing the analysis of this paradox presented in Chapter 1, we can say that, just as we are inclined to express the realization that one *picture* can be treated as a representation of two different entities in a way which suggests a change from one sort of *pictured object* to another, so we are sometimes inclined to express the impact a picture makes upon us in terms which imply the materialization of the pictured scene or object before us. Both inclinations manifest a tendency to regard a figure as if it *were* the thing it represents: to talk of real presence or of the disclosedness of the Being of the pictured object is to offer a similar if extreme form of such paraphrase, another appropriate set of terms in which to articulate the inclination we are examining.

A similar structural parallel is revealed by juxtaposing Wittgenstein's analysis of aspect-dawning in the case of linguistic symbols with the iconicity attributed by Steiner and Heidegger to literary texts. As we saw in Chapter 2, Wittgenstein attempts to define (and defuse) the puzzlement which might arise from our inclination to express the impression an isolated word can make on us in terms which suggest that it carries its meaning within itself, even though we might simultaneously acknowledge that what it means is primarily a function of how – and in what context – it is used (*PI*, 214d). His strategy involves comparing that inclination with the forms of words we find it appropriate to use when expressing our response to poetic uses of language: 'But if a sentence can strike me as like a painting in words, and the very individual word in the sentence as like a picture, then it is no such marvel that a word uttered in isolation and without purpose can seem to carry a particular meaning in itself' (*PI*, 215c). This juxtaposition of paraphrases reveals the structural analogy between them, i.e. the fact that the experiences they articulate share a certain feature which, as we have seen, has a parallel in the field of human relations to pictorial symbols. Whether we look at paintings or at poetry, then, it seems clear that the Heideggerian notion of presentness of Being in the art-work can best be understood as exemplifying the type of experiences Wittgenstein is concerned with under his rubric of aspect-dawning.

If, however, Wittgenstein's notion of aspect-drawing can serve as a means of illuminating the nature of Steiner's and Heidegger's discussions of art, we should also note that those discussions in turn cast light on the central metaphor Wittgenstein employs in his treatment of aspect perception. After suggesting a definition of the concept of an aspect as something which a figure or shape might have permanently in a picture (*PI*, 201b), Wittgenstein offers the following characterization of the typical human relation to pictures: 'Perhaps the following expression would have been better: we regard the photograph, the picture on our wall, as the object itself (the man, landscape, and so on) depicted there' (*PI*, 205e). Although – as I argued earlier – this remark is intended to characterize continuous aspect perception as well as aspect-dawning, it remains the case that the experience of an aspect of a picture dawning on us is a very clear example of the general relationship Wittgenstein has in mind. If, for example, someone responds to a picture of a horse by saying 'See how it runs!', he is reacting to the picture in the way he would to what it depicts, using a form of words which would be appropriate to the sight of a galloping horse in a field. The aspect of aesthetic experience upon which Steiner concentrates and from which Heidegger develops a complex metaphysics illustrates in the clearest way possible the phenomenon of human beings treating pictorial (linguistic etc.) symbols in certain respects as they would the objects represented; for it involves a sense of the real presence in the art-work of the scene, object, or emotion that the art-work depicts or expresses.

However, clarification of the notion of regarding-as is not all that is necessary at this point. If we are to grasp the *general* thrust of Wittgenstein's remarks on this facet of aesthetics we must also come to to understand the precise role played by the concept of a gesture in those writings. Wittgenstein's use of the term is ubiquitous: it is constantly interwoven with his attempts to paraphrase the experiences and inclinations involved in aesthetic understanding, and he seems happy to invoke it in such contexts regardless of whether the topic is music, architecture, or poetry (cf. *Culture and Value*, 22g, 42i, 73d).[5] In addition, its employment allows him to make smooth (if obscure) modulations from remarks concerning aspect perception or aesthetics to comments on the significance of rituals and ceremonies, and on the nature of religious belief (*RPP*,I, 33–6; *CV*, 45c). I want to suggest that Wittgenstein is using it to refer to experiences of aspect-dawning, to occasions when aesthetic objects or human behaviour or events in the natural world make a very striking impression upon us. My contention is, of course, precisely not that Wittgenstein is wedded to a gestural or expressive theory of art. It is rather that his use of the concept is intended to pick out a *specific* facet of aesthetic experience in general – as he puts it, not all purposive movements of the human body are gestures – and that he uses this concept because of certain key features of its grammar, attention to which might help dissolve our philosophical difficulties in this area.

5 L. Wittgenstein, *Culture and Value*, trans. P. Winch, (Oxford: 1980) – hereafter known as *CV*. The letter after the page number indicates the position on the page.

I can justify this postulated identity between the concepts of aspect-dawning and gestures in two different ways. The first rests on certain details of Wittgenstein's treatment of linguistic aspect perception, i.e. the idea that words carry a very particular physiognomy or atmosphere with them, an idea expressed in our inclination to talk of the if-feeling, for example. In discussing the if-feeling (cf. *PI*, 182; *LW*,I, 366–83), Wittgenstein appears to use the terms 'if-feeling' and 'if-gesture' interchangeably – as, for example, in the following sequence:

> The if-feeling cannot be something which accompanies the word 'if'. Otherwise it would accompany other things too. Suppose I were to speak of an if-gesture. Could another word make the same gesture? – Or 'would it then not be the same gesture'? The sound of the word 'if' is simply part of the if-gesture.
>
> (*LW*,I, 368–71)

This implication of synonymy is prima facie evidence that when Wittgenstein talks of a word or a building making a gesture, or of one's comprehension of a musical theme being best expressed in a gesture, he is attempting to capture the striking impression such works of art can make, and thus to provide a term which might be an apt expression of the aesthetic experience I have suggested should be viewed as an instance of aspect-dawning.

The second way of justifying this interpretation of Wittgenstein's concept of a gesture lies in the grammatical features that concept embodies. If we look in some detail at those features, we will be forced to make connections with issues raised by both Steiner and Heidegger in their analyses of iconicity – and in such a way that the structural parallels between this grammatical account and the metaphysical theory-building examined earlier irresistibly suggest that the two analyses are focused on the same phenomenon. It would then follow that, if it is correct to regard iconicity as a variant of aspect-dawning, we should regard the concept of a gesture in precisely the same way.

Once again, the example of experiencing the meaning of words can serve here as an analytical template: for the two crucial features of such phenomena as the if-feeling, on Wittgenstein's account, are the inseparability of the feeling from the word itself and the role of context in analysing the reasons for the particular impression the word makes. First, the very peculiarity of the experience lies in the fact that we are inclined to say that the if-feeling could not accompany any other word, that it is integrally bound up with just that element of the English language; although the feeling is not identical with the word itself (since we recognize that the word can be encountered without the feeling), on the occasions when we do experience the feeling we experience it as inseparable from the relevant word. And in thus focusing upon the context in which we are inclined to talk about the if-feeling, the second key feature of the notion emerges: for, as Wittgenstein points out (*LW*,I, 366–7), the glance the word casts at us – the gesture it makes – relates to that particular word spoken in a certain tone in a specific context.

The same two points can be made in the case of Wittgenstein's other favoured arenas for invoking the concept of a gesture. In a brief discussion of gestures in music and expressive gestures in religious ceremonies (*RPP*,I, 34–6), Wittgenstein remarks that, just as the way to achieve a clearer understanding of the precise significance of a musical phrase is to say a great deal about the surrounding of the phrase, the same is true of understanding an expressive gesture in a ceremony: 'in order to explain it, I should need as it were to analyse the ceremony. E.G. to alter it and show what influence that would have on the role of the gesture'. None of this, however, is taken to contradict the equally central point that it is the phrase itself which makes such a powerful impression: 'The question is really: are these notes not the best expression for what is expressed here? Presumably. But that does not mean that they aren't to be explained by working on their surrounding.'

A similar dual emphasis also characterizes Wittgenstein's account of poetic uses of language. He calls attention to the inseparability of the text's significance from the text itself by speaking of the way in which sentences tell us something *as examples* (*RPP*,I, 1091), by saying themselves; and he elucidates this phrase as follows:

> [Y]ou might say: the work of art does not aim to convey *something else*, just itself. Just as, when I pay someone a visit, I don't just want to make him have feelings of such and such a sort; what I mainly want is to visit him, though of course I should like to be well received too.
>
> (*CV*, 58f)

At the same time, in assessing the impression made by a particular word or line of poetry, one must explore the way in which that word or line relates to its context:

> It is possible – and this is important – to say *a great deal* about a fine aesthetic difference. – the first thing you say may, of course, be just: '*This* word fits, *that* doesn't' – or something of the kind. But then you can discuss all the extensive ramifications of the tie-up effected by each of the words. That first judgement is not the end of the matter, for it is the field of force of a word that is decisive.
>
> (*PI*, 219b)

And in a certain sense, this exploration of tie-ups with the word's surroundings can encompass the whole of the language:

> If a person is to admire English poetry, he must know English. Suppose that a Russian who doesn't know English is overwhelmed by a sonnet admitted to be good. We would say that he does not know what is in it at all. Similarly, of a person who doesn't know metres but who is overwhelmed, we would say that he doesn't know what's in it.
>
> (*LC*, 6)

It should now be evident that the two key features Wittgenstein is employing the concept of a gesture to emphasize are the same ones captured in his concept of aspect-dawning. The stress upon the art-work itself parallels the point that aspect-dawning experiences involve a concentration upon the object itself, an explicit preoccupation with it (*PI*, 197c); and the importance of context parallels the claim that aspect-dawning involves a sense of the object's internal relation with other objects, a capacity to surround it with a context (*PI*, 210c, 197a).

I shall return to these claims later; but at this stage it is of more importance to see that these two features which the concept of a gesture foregrounds are precisely the ones central to both Steiner's notion of iconicity and Heidegger's reference to art-works as the loci of strife between world and earth. As we saw earlier, in saying that the true reader proceeds as if the text was the housing of forces and meanings Steiner places simultaneous emphasis upon the text as dwelling-place *and* upon the meanings it houses; for example, treating certain words as if they *were* the emotion they express metamorphosed involves focusing one's attention as much upon the text *as text* as upon the embodied meaning. This dual focus was further characterized by Steiner as involving the inexhaustibility and the irreducibility of iconic texts; and this duality is the one emphasized in Heidegger's description of the conflict between world and earth. The role of earth within a work of art dramatizes the sense we have that a great work of art is unique, that the slightest alteration within it or attempt to translate it into another form would rupture its meaning; and it does so by treating it as a manifestation of the concreteness of existent things. The bare fact of its being the particular thing it is, that quality in any thing which resists comprehension and labelling, is seen as explicitly foregrounded by the createdness which is emphasized in all works of art. Similarly, Heidegger's concept of world captures the inexhaustibility of iconic texts by founding our capacity to discover ever-receding vistas of meaning and significance in the art-work upon an all-governing relational context provided by a nation's culture and history, a surrounding framework ultimately reliant upon the structures of intelligibility which constitute Dasein's capacity to apprehend beings in their Being.

This is the point at which my attempt at a 'grammatical reduction' can begin. For it is not just that Wittgenstein's concept of a gesture highlights precisely those qualities of inexhaustibility and irreducibility: it is also the case that it does so in service of a grammatical rather than a metaphysical account of aesthetics. Wittgenstein's emphasis upon a work's saying or conveying itself – calling attention to itself as an existent thing – parallels the element of irreducibility captured in the Heideggerian concept of earth; and his simultaneous emphasis on the importance of context, of familiarity with the cultural and linguistic world surrounding the art-work, matches the features central to Heidegger's notion of the world. Indeed, in the latter case, Wittgenstein is prepared to match the scope implicit in Heidegger's references to the world as the world of a whole people expressed in its history and culture: 'The words we call expressions of aesthetic judgement play a very complicated role, but a very definite role, in what we call a culture of a period. To describe their use or to describe what you mean by a cultured taste, you have to describe a culture' (*LC*, 8). In the case of both features, however, the role they play in Wittgenstein's account is to help dissolve philosophical problems rather than to provide a metaphysical solution to those problems.

Let us begin with the notion of an iconic text's inexhaustibility. Heidegger accounts for this as a function of the role of the world in the ongoing process of strife between metaphysical principles or forces within the art-work itself; but Wittgenstein suggests that we regard our inclination to describe such works of art as inexhaustible as a muddled recognition of the grammatical point that, in aesthetic contexts, there is in principle no fixed limit upon the degree to which tie-ups between the elements of the work of art and their surroundings in the culture may be relevant to a comprehension of the art-work's significance. If we use Heidegger's own response to the Van Gogh painting of peasant shoes as an example of aesthetic understanding, we can see that such an understanding is manifest in a grasp of the relation between features of the pictured shoes and facets of the world of peasant life for which they stand. In explaining what the painting means, Heidegger yokes the sheen of the leather to the rich dampness of soil, the worn insides of the shoes to the toil of a working day, and so on. In fact, his references to the surrounding world of peasant life seem to reach out indefinitely far; and yet, in so far as they articulate a response to the painting in which others can share and by means of which they can clarify their own sense of why the painting is so impressive (i.e. if the explanation is of a sort they can accept – *LC*, 18, fn.5), they can count as relevant to an understanding of the picture.

A similar preliminary 'translation' of metaphysics into grammar can also be provided for the notion of an iconic text's irreducibility. Heidegger regards this property of the art-work as an element arising from the thrusting of earth, as its self-closing refusal of the openness of the work's world celebrates the essence of materiality by calling attention to the fact that the art-work is *this thing here*. Wittgenstein's account suggests two more mundane features of the notion of iconicity (or of a gesture) which may account for our inclination to describe great works of art in such terms. First – and perhaps paradoxically – it would seem that the notion of world rather than earth plays a role here. This is due to the fact that one's impression of a work of art's uniqueness is likely to be strengthened the more wide-ranging and specific a set of tie-ups between work and world is provided in our attempts to grasp that art-work's significance (this point is perhaps mirrored in Heidegger's warning that the belligerence of earth and world reveals the essential reliance of the one upon features of the other – *BW*, 177).

Secondly, however, Wittgenstein suggests that attributions of irreducibility to the art-work are in fact reflections of the attitude of the audience (*LW*,I, 712). The description of such an art-work as irreducible, the refusal to accept any other art-work or any change in its constituents as a legitimate substitution – these reactions are all manifestations of the way in which the viewer/reader has assimilated the work of art and come to treat it as if it were unique. Note that this is not an attempt to give a reductive explanation of the property of irreducibility, or to impugn the reality of this facet of our experience of art-works. Rather, by emphasizing that objects come to be characterized as aesthetic objects because of the role they play in our form of life and the attitudes we adopt towards them, the intention is to render inert the will to ascribe mysterious metaphysical properties to a certain class of entities in order to quieten our misunderstandings of this aspect of our lives.

This excursion into the exegetical issue of how one is to interpret Wittgenstein's concept of a gesture has thus given us a preliminary framework within which to locate the phenomenon of iconicity and neutralize its capacity to generate philosophical confusion. The task of clarification can now be furthered by picking up another element in the grammatical structure of the concept of aspect-dawning – an element which is particularly evident in the case of experiencing the meanings of words. The key example of such experiences that Wittgenstein invokes is the feeling of a word losing its meaning and becoming a mere sound when repeated in isolation ten times over (*PI*, 214d); in other words, we are inclined to express ourselves in such a context in a way which implies a sudden separation of the meaning of the linguistic symbol from the symbol itself (conceived of as a material object). This inclination is paralleled in the paradigmatic experiences of aspect-dawning in relation to pictorial symbols. In attempting to articulate the feelings involved, Wittgenstein talks of the experience of aspect-dawning as a matter of entering into the relevant aspect, immersing oneself in it (*RPP*,I, 1033), as a phenomenon by means of which the aspect is detached from the rest of the seeing (*RPP*,I, 415). He sums up this feature as follows:

> It is as if one had brought a concept to what one sees, and one

now sees the concept along with the thing. It is itself hardly
visible, and yet it spreads an ordering veil over the objects.
(*RPP*,I, 961).

This separation of concept from object, as a crucial feature of aspect-dawning, must then – according to my intepretative principles – be a central part of the notion of iconicity in aesthetics; and indeed it seems clear that Heidegger's notion of art-works as the loci of strife between world and earth centres itself on precisely this separation. As we saw earlier, this notion of strife registers the simultaneous rendering explicit of two features of Dasein's relation to the world: by being fabricated without being intended for practical use as a tool, a work of art simultaneously calls attention to the materiality of its medium and to the totality of reference-relations which are the necessary framework of human praxis and are grounded in the structures of intelligibility which permit Dasein to grasp and utilize beings in the world. The notions of earth and of world capture these two features, and – by being conceptualized as in constant strife one with another – they thereby dramatize the separation which is at the heart of aspect-dawning.

For Heidegger, of course, the strife by means of which he dramatizes this separation reveals essential structures of Being. World and earth are inseparable as well as belligerent because the work of their strife is one way in which truth happens; and in the Heideggerian context, truth is precisely *aletheia*, a disclosing denial which the experience of iconicity seems to ground and to which it gives some intelligible content. For Wittgenstein, the separation of concept from object means nothing more (and nothing less) dramatic than the following: in certain contexts – whether through the realization that a symbol can be used to represent more than one type of object, or through the striking impact made by the meaning or significance of a symbolic construct – human beings come to see that meaning is not a material property of objects in the world but rather an aspect of those objects in so far as they are *used* by human beings for the purposes of expression, communication and so on. Talk of works of art as places in which the disclosedness of beings in their Being is won is no more (and no less) than a complex, sophisticated, and poetic paraphrase of a specific experience. We may be inclined to express our experience in structurally analogous ways to those of Heidegger; but we should see the structure thereby revealed to be a means of identifying one particular shared human reaction or experience, rather than a vision of an essential structure of the world or an explanation of the experiential phenomenon itself couched in terms of independent theoretical posits. As Wittgenstein says of another example of aspect-dawning when we have a felt need to use a certain form of words:

> If someone says: 'I am talking of a visual phenomenon, in which the visual picture, that is its organization, does change, although shapes and colours remain the same' – then I may answer him: 'I know what you are talking about: I too should like to say what you say.' – So I am not saying 'Yes, the phenomenon we are both talking about is actually change of organization...' but rather 'Yes, this talk of the change of organization *etc.* is an expression of the experience which I mean too.'
>
> (*RPP*,I, 534)

This is where my attempted 'grammatical reduction' in the sphere of aesthetics must end; but it is not the last of the lessons which can be drawn from this area of Wittgenstein's thought and related to aspect perception. In fact, at this point, our investigation can widen its focus: for attention to the distinctive features of the ways in which we are inclined to express ourselves in these areas brings other, more general conclusions in its train. The reason for this is simple: the very intelligibility of expressing one's experience of aspect-dawning in terms which invoke a *separation* of concept from object presupposes that, in contexts where aspect-dawning is not at stake, the given concept is intimately involved in our encounters with the object. It would not be comprehensible, for example, that a person should be inclined to talk of a word *becoming* a mere sound in specific circumstances if, in general, he *always* regarded words as bare sounds requiring interpretation. The form of words he is inclined to employ – a form whose structure is definitive of the nature of the aspect-dawning experience – could seem apt only to someone who, in general, treats words as linguistically meaningful rather than as bare marks.

Wittgenstein signals this point in the following remark:

> When the aspect suddenly changes one experiences the second phase in an acute way (corresponding to the exclamation 'Oh,

its's a. . .!') and here of course one does *occupy* oneself with the aspect. In the temporal sense the aspect is only the kind of way in which we again and again treat the picture.

(*RPP*,I, 1022)

Just as experiencing a picture as 'living' or iconic was seen to be an extreme example of the human attitude towards pictures which Wittgenstein labelled continuous aspect perception (and defined as regarding the picture in the way we do the object depicted), so experiencing the meaning of a word exemplifies by force of contrast that same attitude as it is manifest in the domain of linguistic rather than pictorial symbols (the attitude I labelled continuous meaning perception in Chapter 2). In both cases, our investigation of aspect-dawning leads us to continuous aspect perception.

Wittgenstein sees more than a parallelism of attitudes here, however; for on his account it is the human attitude towards *language* which must be seen as underlying the experience of aspect-dawning in the case of pictures as well as that of words.

> In the triangle I can see now *this* as apex, *that* as base – now *this* as apex, *that* as base. – Clearly the words 'Now I am seeing this as the apex' cannot so far mean anything to a learner who has only just met the concepts of apex, base, and so on. – But I do not mean this as an empirical proposition. 'Now he's seeing it like *this*', 'now like *that*' would only be said of someone *capable* of making certain applications of the figure quite freely. The substratum of this experience is the mastery of a technique.
>
> (*PI*, 208e)

In Chapters 2 and 5 I examined in detail just what sort of linguistic mastery Wittgenstein has in mind here; but, in order to appreciate the underlying unity of his reflections on this issue, it is worth demonstrating that his remarks on aesthetics involve conclusions which mirror and exemplify those reached in our previous chapters. This becomes clear when Wittgenstein considers the issue of how the concept of 'seeing-as' is normally employed:

> Here it occurs to me that in conversation in aesthetic matters we use the words: 'You have to see it like *this*, this is how it is meant'; 'When you see it like *this*, you see where it goes wrong'; 'You have to hear this bar as an introduction'; 'You must hear it

in this key'; 'You must phrase it like *this*' (which can refer to hearing as well as to playing).

(*PI*, 202h)

In cases such as these, the attempt to come to an aesthetic understanding of an art-work – to grasp what the piece of music is expressing in a sense which is prior to an evaluation of its aesthetic worth (*LC*, 3–4) – is an attempt to come to perceive it *directly* in terms of what it is expressing; the aim is to regard the musical phrase *as* a conclusion rather then simply to hear it and to know that it is meant to be a conclusion. I noted earlier that our gestures and verbal behaviour in relation to a picture of a landscape – our way of treating the picture – reveal that we are taking it for granted that its basic elements are representations of the elements of the landscape (trees, houses and so on) rather than colour-patches on canvas. Now we can see the musical parallel: for the sort of phrasing of a musical piece which manifests a correct understanding of it is one which possesses those fine shades of expression that convey its organization in terms of such elements as a conclusion and introduction rather than a sequential assemblage of notes (*LW*,I, 677).

It is *this* type of mastery of a technique that Wittgenstein has in mind as being the substratum of aspect-dawning. One might view that latter experience of insight as the signal of understanding for which someone attempting to convey how an art-work should be taken is looking: rather like 'Now I can go on!' in the case of grasping a rule (*PI*, 180), the exclamation which manifests the dawning of an aspect functions as a signal of understanding whose employment is justified by the relevant person going on to prove that the meaning of the art-work has indeed become accessible to him.

In this process of gaining access to the art-work, however, we should remember that such aesthetic understanding presupposes the existence of, and familiarity with, the whole field of our language-games (*RPP*,I, 433). For example, to say that at this point in the music it is as if a conclusion is being drawn presupposes the speaker's familiarity with conclusions, confirmations, answers. Indeed, Wittgenstein deepens this interrelation by describing the musical theme and the language as being in reciprocal action (*RPP*,I, 436), a description he glosses as follows:

'there *is* a paradigm outside the theme: namely the rhythm of our language, of our thinking and feeling. And the theme is also in its turn a *new* bit of our language, it is incorporated in it; we learn a new *gesture*' (*RPP*,I, 435).

If the achievement of aesthetic understanding results in the musical theme achieving the status of a *new* bit of language, the implication would seem to be that the kind of technique mastery of which aesthetic understanding is a paradigm should be treated as an element in the everyday understanding of language. In addition, the references to rhythm imply an awareness of underlying patterns or contours which give form and unity to the agglomeration of our language-games, thereby providing us with a means of smooth, unhesitating orientation within that domain as well as a sense of the directions and forms in which that domain can be comprehensibly extended through the creation of new linguistic suburbs. In other words, the distinction between seeing something and simply knowing what something is meant to be (*PI*, 203b) – the very distinction captured by Wittgenstein's contrast between continuous aspect perception and interpretation as I defined it in earlier chapters – is also intended to reveal something about linguistic understanding in general. The task Wittgenstein's discussion of aspect-dawning in aesthetics sets us is precisely the one prosecuted in Chapter 2, and refined in Chapter 5.

This suggested reading of Wittgenstein's discussion is confirmed by certain other facets of the material I have been evaluating in this chapter. For example, it would permit me to give a further grammatical translation of the metaphysical attribute of irreducibility which both Heidegger and Steiner claim to discover in iconic art-works. In a discussion of one example of the distinction between seeing-as and interpretation, Wittgenstein asks why we are inclined to say that we *see* the friendly glance of someone's eye, and why philosophers should want to deny this by saying that in reality we merely interpret certain shapes and colours.

> Does [the philosopher] want to say it's more correct to use a different word here instead of 'seeing'? I believe he only wants to draw attention to a division between concepts. For how does the word 'see' associate perceptions? I mean: it may associate them as perceptions *with the eye*; for we do *not* feel seeing *in* the eye. But really the one who insists on the *correctness* of our normal way of

talking seems to be saying: everything is contained in the visual impression; that the *subjective eye* equally has shape, colour, movement, expression and glance (external direction). That one does not detect the glance, so to speak, *somewhere else*. But that doesn't mean 'elsewhere than in the eye'; it means 'elsewhere than in the visual picture'. But how would it be for it to be otherwise? Perhaps so that I said: 'In this eye I see such and such shapes, colours, movements – that means it's looking friendly at present', i.e. as if I were drawing a conclusion. – So one might say: the place of the *perceived* glance is the *subjective* eye, the visual picture of the eye itself.

(*RPP*,I, 1102)

By analogy, one might argue as follows. A person's tendency to regard a given art-work as unique and irreplaceable without loss of impact and significance results from his awareness that the artwork's impact is directly perceived rather than a product of interpretative inference, and a consequent feeling that if his subjective impression contains all this significance then the object (e.g. a painting) of which it *was* a subjective impression must be essential to that impact. The place of the perceived meaning becomes the object of which the visual impression is an impression; and the inclination to attribute irreducibility to that object is a distorted reflection of the key grammatical distinction between seeing-as and interpretation.

Furthermore, the twofold conclusion which my reading of Wittgenstein licenses seems to suggest a direct parallel in grammatical form to the two central elements in Heidegger's metaphysical exposition of iconicity. As I noted earlier, Heidegger's concept of strife between world and earth dramatizes the separation between concept and object that is at the heart of aspect-dawning; and by emphasizing the createdness of an art-work, that strife is held to reveal an element of createdness in all humanly produced things which is hidden in everyday existence.

> To be sure, 'that' it is made is a property also of all equipment that is available and in use. But this 'that' does not become prominent in the equipment; it disappears in usefulness. The more handy a piece of equipment is, the more inconspicuous it remains that, for example, this particular hammer is, and the

more exclusively does the equipment keep itself in its equipmentality.

(*BW*, 182)

What emerges, what separates itself from earth in the concept of world, is, then, the equipmental totality that is standardly submerged within equipment in everyday encounters with it. In effect, Heidegger is offering a dramatized version of one of my earlier characterizations of continuous aspect perception, viz. as a label for the way concepts *inform* our direct experience of things in everyday life. It is, of course, central to *Being and Time* that the world of equipmentality is grounded upon structures of intelligibility which are constituted by discourse (the essence of language) and crucial to Dasein's openness to the Being of all the beings it encounters. When this set of connections is added to Heidegger's emphasis (in the lectures on art) on the primacy of poetry over other art-forms as well as on the dependence of all art-forms upon the structures of intelligibility which discourse constitutes, then it becomes clear that iconicity leads inevitably to issues of linguistic understanding and the way concepts inform experience, i.e. to precisely the interrelations and issues dealt with in Chapter 5. We can therefore conclude that Wittgenstein's remarks on aesthetics and his views on aspect perception are not only closely connected but also direct us to conclusions of precisely the scope and form outlined in the previous chapter.

CONCLUSION

The need to make sense of Wittgenstein's treatment of aspect perception in *Philosophical Investigations* has taken us on a extremely complex interpretative journey: for achieving even a provisional clarity in this area turns out to require not only a wide-ranging examination of Wittgenstein's philosophy of psychology, but also a comparative study of two philosophical traditions which differ significantly from his own. It therefore seems essential that I should try to restate the theme of Wittgenstein's investigation upon which I have placed most emphasis in this book. Put simply, I have argued that the concept of continuous aspect perception should be seen as an attempt to characterize the physiognomy of human behaviour; and it is worth recalling how this conclusion was reached.

I began, as any study of this matter must begin, with the duck-rabbit. In Chapter 1, I argued that the experience of aspect-dawning in relation to pictures and drawings was merely an extreme manifestation of the typical human relationship or attitude towards pictures in general: as many of our practices of employing those pictures also reveals, this attitude is one in which their status as the particular pictures they are is taken for granted. We would not, for example, hang a portrait on the wall in order to remind ourselves of a friend unless the question of whether the picture is one of that particular person (or indeed, whether it is a portrait at all) were not even an *issue* for us. The many and varied roles which pictures play in our lives show that, unlike the aspect-blind, we do not have to interpret arrangements of colours and shapes in order to infer what those colours and shapes might be deemed to represent; we unhesitatingly treat the picture as a picture.

CONCLUSION

In Chapter 2, I argued that we typically stand in an analogous relation to words. We experience their meaning; but once again this unusual experience is merely an extreme manifestation of continuous meaning perception, an attitude which Wittgenstein encapsulates in the idea that words have a familiar physiognomy for us. We unhesitatingly treat words as the particular words they are, as if they carried the tie-ups and associations which go to make up their specific linguistic identity on their faces; we do not regard them as sounds or ink-marks which require interpretation in order to reveal their intended meaning. This sense of familiarity with a word's identity reflects the degree to which we assimilate words; it indicates an unhesitating mastery of the linguistic techniques of which they are bearers. This assimilation is what grounds our ability to move about unhesitatingly within the complex and variegated domain of language; and it also underpins our capacity to grasp secondary uses of words – a capacity with at least two fundamental consequences. First, it permits the use of language as an expressive medium; and secondly, it grounds the possibility of grasping (certain modes of teaching) certain language-games. The range and form of our mastery of language thus corresponds to the nature of our relationship with pictures: in both domains, our behaviour reveals an unhesitating grasp of the identity of the things we encounter.

In Chapter 3, I argued that our behaviour in relation to others has a similar form or character. We do not infer from bodily movements that the creature before us may be thoughtful or angry; we regard him as a human being, as an individual whose body is the field of expression of his heart and mind – and so as a creature whose possession of a heart and mind is not in doubt. The aspect-blind would stumble as clumsily and as hesitantly around in relation to another individual as they do in relation to language; the fine shades of meaning they are incapable of seeing in the faces of words are just as much beyond them when it is a human face and form which is giving them expression. And, in treating other people as we would robots, their own behaviour in relation to those others would be reduced to precisely the same status – inflexible, lacking in fluidity and smoothness, devoid of those fine shades which constitute the individual character of a person, the specific physiognomy of his words and deeds.

In all three cases, then, we found that human behaviour in

CONCLUSION

relation to a particular kind of thing ordinarily makes manifest the high degree to which we have absorbed its specific nature: pictures, words, and people each constitute worlds which we are capable of assimilating, and of which we can be natives. The question that immediately arose was whether such attitudes and relations with things were restricted to the worlds of pictures, words, and people. Was it only in relation to these three kinds of thing that human behaviour exhibited such an unhesitating capacity to weave the world's furniture into the fluid stream of people's purposes and projects?

This was the point at which Heidegger's analyses became indispensable reference points. The exegetical account of his concepts of seeing-as and readiness-to-hand laid out in Chapter 4 formed the necessary background for my argument (in Chapter 5) that the facets of human behaviour which I had earlier delineated were instantiations of the form or physiognomy of human behaviour *in general*. This argument fell into two stages. First, I attempted to justify the Heideggerian intuition that the smoothness and mastery, the fluidity and absence of hesitation, which the concept of continuous aspect perception picked out in our relation to pictures, words, and people, could be seen to characterize our relation to all the things we encounter in the world. Second, I tried to show that Heidegger had none the less misrepresented these features of human behaviour by treating them as revelatory of metaphysical truths about objects in their relation to Dasein.

The second step is crucial, because Heidegger's notion of readiness-to-hand characterizes these features of human behaviour in terms which imply that the objects woven into our practical activity have a peculiar essence. In fact, the readiness-to-hand of objects reflects the seamless, unhesitating way in which those objects are taken up in our practical activity, i.e. it reflects the particular grace and smoothness of the human behaviour involved, features which should be seen as defining characteristics of human practical activity *per se*. The assimilation of language mentioned in Chapter 2 thus turns out to be the manifestation in linguistic behaviour of the very physiognomy Heidegger identifies in non-linguistic behaviour in general; and it is this physiognomy which the notion of continuous aspect perception was meant to pick out in our linguistic and non-linguistic behaviour in relation to pictures, words, and people. To be at home with language, with pictures and with people is but an aspect of being at home in the world.

This is why the most fundamental of my many characterizations of the aspect-blind person is the one which compares his general behaviour with that of a robot. His disability does not rob him completely of the capacity to grasp any given concept or set of concepts, but his grasp of any of them will be hesitant and clumsy; and it is this clumsiness, this inflexibility and stumbling in his behaviour in relation to the corresponding objects, that marks him out as aspect-blind. We could intelligibly apply psychological concepts to him, although only to a limited degree (since he cannot use language as an expressive medium, and his behaviour in general lacks some of the logical multiplicity evident in that of other people). However, even if we can regard him as being to that extent possessed of a heart and mind akin to our own, the absence of the behavioural fluidity and seamlessness I have been attempting to characterize throughout this book ensures that he will strike us as being internally related to robots rather than to human beings. His body, we might say, will not seem to be the field of expression of a *soul*: we will see him under the aspect of an automaton.

The example of the aspect-blind person can therefore remind us of an aspect of what we mean by the word 'human' in the phrase 'human being'. The behaviour of a human being is not simply that to which a certain range of psychological concepts can be applied, for this condition may hold when the behaviour concerned does not have the physiognomy we have identified; the behaviour must not just be seen against the background of the environment in which it is located – it must interlock with that environment in the ways Heidegger was so concerned to point out. In Wittgensteinian terminology, of course, this entails that our conclusion is a grammatical remark: it is merely a reminder of what we *mean* when we characterize human practical activity as human at all, and so in a sense conveys no new information because it is not an empirical claim.

This does not, however, mean that there is nothing to be gained from an investigation whose terminus is grammatical in nature; for, in effect, Wittgenstein's remarks are designed to bring about the dawning of an aspect in his reader. The feature of human behaviour with which I have been concerned is one that we typically take for granted in our dealings with others, dealings in which those others play a part but where the focus of our concern is elsewhere – perhaps on the goals of our joint practical activity. The circumstances of a philosophical investigation interrupt that practical activity, and in this case focus our attention upon human behaviour itself in such a way that it becomes our explicit preoccupation; and just as Heidegger saw the readiness-to-hand of tools most explicitly revealed when the ordinary processes of engaging with those tools were suspended, so here an aspect of what is specifically human about human behaviour is lit up and brought to the foreground of our concern. We are reminded of what it means to be (called) human; and the fact that we know this and take it for granted in our everyday lives means that such reminders assume more rather than less importance – for that which informs our everyday experience, that which is closest to us, is often the most difficult of things to acknowledge and appreciate.

We watch a world-class tennis player, whose capacity to control the ball is dependent upon his control of his racquet, and we say that his racquet seems to be an extension of his arm – that it is as if he and the racquet are one. Such turns of phrase embody a recognition of just the quality of seamlessness in the relation of human practical activity to its implements that I have been attempting to emphasize in this book. We say of a craftsman that he is at home in his workshop: and what grounds such a remark is the smooth and unhesitating way in which he reaches for and employs his tools and raw materials in order to produce the objects that will satisfy our needs. Such people seem to be masters of themselves – at one with their bodies – in a truly exceptional way, as if they are beyond the ordinary run of humanity; but the notion of continuous aspect perception developed in this study is designed precisely to emphasize that the activities of such people constitute the *fulfilment* of a human possibility rather than the manifestation of something superhuman. The dancer and the gymnast do not transcend the human, but rather bring one aspect of our shared humanity to a provisional and transient perfection.

Of course, it is not the case that all human beings manifest such qualities of grace and bodily self-possession in each facet of their everyday existence; after all, if this were true, why should we pay to watch exhibitions given by such performers? On the other hand, it is often forgotten that those same qualities are manifest in human practical activities which do not have the status of an art-form: the secretary in relation to her typewriter and the bus-driver in relation to his vehicle can and do exhibit an unhesitating mastery of precisely the kind shown by the gymnast and the sportsman. And more generally, our tendency to ignore the variety of domains of human practical activity in which such achievements are possible helps to obscure the fact that it *makes sense* to evaluate any and all human behaviour (whether positively or negatively) in terms of the dimension of grace and mastery which is brought to an extreme of beauty in the performances of the gymnast and the craftsman. The dancer instantiates a human possibility, a way in which one's status as an embodied being can be acknowledged and shown to contain within itself depths of grace and beauty. To regard human beings as if they were aspect-blind would be to ignore that possibility, to exclude in advance any means of considering that in this crucial sense athletes and craftsmen do not *overcome* human limitations but rather stand as paradigms of their species and its inherent possibilities.

This investigation also suggests that certain conclusions about the nature of the philosophical enterprise itself might follow from locating that enterprise against the interpretative framework I have just been sketching in. As is well known, for Wittgenstein the goal of any given philosophical investigation is the attainment of an *Ubersicht* – a surview of a given segment of grammar such that one neither hesitates nor stumbles when requested to modulate from one form of expression to another, and such that one is not brought into confusion by the potentially misleading similarities and differences between one grammatical structure and another. On this conception of philosophy, then, its goal is the acquisition of a form of linguistic mastery of precisely the sort outlined in Chapter 2 – a mastery evident in an absence of stumbling and hesitation, in one's not making certain sorts of mistake, in one's knowing one's way around the city of language. What we can see now, however, is that this mastery (from which the aspect-blind are excluded) constitutes an achievement in the domain of linguistic behaviour which is precisely analogous to that achieved by athletes and craftsmen in their own non-linguistic practical activities. In this sense, the goal of philosophy is the realization in linguistic behaviour of a grace and seamless self-mastery which constitutes the fulfilment of a distinctively human possibility.

CONCLUSION

Of course, if it makes sense to think of philosophy in terms of such kinds of achievement, then it must also be possible for philosophers to fail to achieve such mastery of their language and their humanity – to exhibit a debilitating *blindness* to such aspects of the human. As we saw in Chapter 4, the interpretative model of perception which leads inexorably to a conception of human beings as aliens or automata is one which forms the unexamined foundation of mainstream analytical philosophy, and so infects our (philosophical) culture's conception of what it is to be human. Such a conception of our shared humanity is not only confused, but demeaning and offensive; indeed, as Wittgenstein remarked about Freudian theorizing, its very popularity may be a function of the repellent nature of its conclusions. One can only hope that this presentation of Wittgenstein's antidote to such a crippled and crippling vision – a presentation in which I have tried to show how the insights of metaphysicians can be given expression without inviting philosophical confusion – will make us less likely to fall prey to that vision's dubious attractions.

BIBLIOGRAPHY

Cavell, S., *The Claim Of Reason*, Oxford: Oxford University Press, 1979.
   Themes out of School, San Francisco: North Point Press, 1984.
Davidson, D., *Inquiries into Truth and Interpretation*, Oxford: Oxford University Press, 1983.
   'A nice derangement of epitaphs', in E. LePore (ed.), *Truth and Interpretation: Perspectives on the Philosophy of Donald Davidson*, Oxford: Basil Blackwell, 1986.
Hacking, I., 'A parody of conversation', in E. LePore (ed.), *Truth and Interpretation: Perspectives on the Philosophy of Donald Davidson*, Oxford: Basil Blackwell, 1986.
Heidegger, M., *Being and Time*, trans. J. Macquarrie and E. Robinson, Oxford: Basil Blackwell, 1962.
   Poetry, Language, Thought, trans. A. Hofstadter, New York: Harper & Row, 1971.
   Basic Writings, ed. D. F. Krell, London: Routledge & Kegan Paul, 1977.
Sartre, J.-P., *Nausea*, trans. R. Baldick, Harmondsworth: Penguin Books, 1965.
Steiner, G., *George Steiner: A Reader*, Harmondsworth: Penguin Books, 1984.
Von Wright, G. H., *Wittgenstein*, Oxford: Basil Blackwell, 1982.
Wittgenstein, L., *Philosophical Investigations*, trans. G. E. M. Anscombe, Oxford: Basil Blackwell, 1953.
   Zettel, trans. G. E. M. Anscombe, Oxford: Basil Blackwell, 1967.
   Lectures and Conversations on Aesthetics, Psychology and Religious Belief, ed. C. Barrett, Oxford: Basil Blackwell, 1970.
   Culture and Value, trans. P. Winch, Oxford: Basil Blackwell, 1980.
   Remarks on the Philosophy of Psychology, vol. I, trans. G. E. M. Anscombe, vol. II, trans. C. G. Luckhardt and M. A. E. Aue, Oxford: Basil Blackwell, 1980.
   Last Writings on the Philosophy of Psychology, vol. I, trans. C. G. Luckhardt and M. A. E. Aue, Oxford: Basil Blackwell, 1982.
   Last Writings on the Philosophy of Psychology, vol. II, Oxford: Basil Blackwell, forthcoming.

INDEX

aesthetic understanding 26, 67–8, 124, 152–4, 187, 191–3
aesthetics 156–95
aletheia 164, 175–7, 189–90
aspect concepts 28–9, 61,. 71–8, 111, 121, 123, 127, 128–37
aspect-blindness 31–4, 35, 49–51, 73, 78, 83–8, 106, 124, 146, 148, 149, 150, 196
aspect-dawning 6–15, 22, 29–30, 35, 38–9, 47, 49, 72, 121, 123, 128, 134–7, 151, 152–5, 179–85, 188–92, 196–7, 199
Ausserung 11–12, 16, 32, 39, 47, 128

Beethoven, Ludwig van 156, 157, 177
behaviourism 61–71
Being 108, 143, 153–4, 164–5, 166, 167, 170, 171, 174, 176–7, 180–1, 186, 189, 195
Being-in-the-world 107–22, 125, 132, 171
Being-with 115–6, 118
Bennet, Elizabeth 157, 158

Cavell, Stanley 53, 78–88, 117
confessions 70
continuous aspect perception 17–21, 22–8, 30–4, 40, 61–2, 72–8, 85, 88–90, 106, 121, 123, 126, 128, 132–3, 137–55, 190–5, 196–202
continuous meaning perception 40–52, 191, 197

Darcy, Fitzwilliam 158
Dasein 107–22, 125, 143, 163, 167, 170, 171, 174, 177, 186, 189, 195, 198

Davidson, Donald 1, 3, 91–106, 108, 117, 119–20, 122, 125, 139
Descartes 54
Desdemona 84
discourse 118–9, 121, 176–7, 195
Doctor Faustus 67

earth 158, 164, 165, 167–9, 170–95
equipment 110–14, 122, 141–3, 151, 163, 164, 165, 166–7, 169–70, 171–3, 175, 189, 194–5
everyday 107–8, 120, 122, 151, 178, 195, 200
experience of meaning 35–40, 68, 183–4, 188

Freud, Sigmund 202

gestures 156, 177, 182–95
grammar 60–71, 120, 122, 123–55, 157–8, 159–60, 183, 186–90, 201–2

Hacking, Ian 103
Heidegger, Martin 1, 3, 4, 85, 88, 89, 107–22, 125–8, 132, 136, 137–55, 156–95, 198–202
hope 66
Hopkins, Gerard Manley 157
Husserl, Edmund 103

Iago 64, 157
icons 156–7, 160–5, 173–7, 179–95
imponderable evidence 82–5
intention 36–8, 65–6
interpretation 22–8, 31–4, 49–51, 79–81, 91–106, 108, 116–17, 119–20, 125–6, 129, 138–9, 146, 148, 150, 190, 193–4, 197–9, 202

INDEX

Jastrow, Joseph 19

Kant, Immanuel 29, 126, 172
Kierkegaard, Søren 89

language 33–52, 64–9, 91–106, 118–9, 121, 126–8, 140, 148, 152–5, 175, 176–7, 184–5
linguistic understanding 35–8, 76–7, 100–22, 125, 148, 171, 191–3, 195, 197–9, 201–2
lying 64, 74

Marlowe, Christopher 67
meaning-blindness 35–40, 146
music 26, 156, 177, 182–3, 192

Nausea 152–5

Othello 64
Othello 84–5

Peirce, Charles Sanders 160
phenomenology 108, 120, 177, 178
physiognomy: of behaviour 86, 89, 149, 196–202; of faces 76–7, 79–80; of words 40–46, 76–7, 149, 183, 197
physiology 7, 47
picture-objects 16–21
practical activity 111, 120, 139–43, 171, 173, 189, 198–202

praxis *see* practical activity
presence-at-hand 85, 109, 113, 115–6, 119, 121, 126, 132, 138–9
private language 53, 55–60
private ostensive definitions 54–60
psychological concepts 45, 49–51, 53–90, 97–9, 104–5, 114–16, 144–51, 196–202

Quine, Willard Van Orman 96

radical interpretation 91–106, 120
readiness-to-hand 18, 23–4, 40, 45, 73, 76, 85, 88, 107–22, 126, 138–41, 148–50, 198
real presence 160–3, 164, 174, 182
regarding-as 23–8, 134, 179, 181–2
relativism 144–7
religion 182, 184

Sartre, Jean-Paul 152–5
Schubert, Franz 43, 51
Steiner, George 158–63, 164, 165, 173–5, 179, 181, 182–6, 193

truth *see* aletheia

van Gogh, Vincent 163, 173, 175, 178–80, 187
visual impression 8–9, 33, 130, 194

world 158, 164, 165, 166–7, 169–95